"... Your Jesus was here."

THE GOSPELS record Jesus age twelve in the temple. Then about age thirty at the river Jordan. That leaves approximately seventeen years unaccounted for.

During those so-called lost years, the child "increased in wisdom and stature," as Luke wrote. But was it in the carpenter shop at Nazareth?

According to ancient Tibetan manuscripts, Jesus secretly withdrew from the home of Mary and Joseph at age thirteen. Young "Issa" joined a merchant caravan. Destination: India and the Himalayas.

At Juggernaut, "the white priests of Brahma made him a joyous welcome. They taught him to read and understand the Vedas, to cure by aid of prayer, to teach, to explain the holy scriptures to the people, and to drive out evil spirits from the bodies of men."

- Buddhist scholars documented "The Life of Saint Issa" two thousand years ago.
- Nicolas Notovitch discovered the long-lost document in 1887 at the Himis monastery in Ladakh.
- Swami Abhedananda published a Bengali translation of the Himis manuscript in 1929.
- Nicholas Roerich quoted the same verses in a 1929 travel diary of his Asian expedition.
- And in 1939, a beaming lama at Himis presented a set of parchments to Elisabeth Caspari with the words:

"These books say your Jesus was here!"

Now you can read the controversial stories of these travelers together with the original Buddhist scriptures on the most important events that shaped the life and work of the Saviour Jesus Christ.

An historical breakthrough that will shake the foundations of modern Christendom!

Issa and the Skull of the Giant 1933

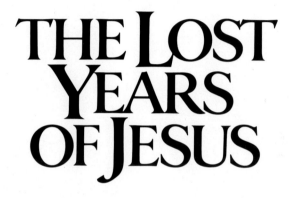

THE LOST
YEARS
OF JESUS

Elizabeth Clare Prophet

THE LOST YEARS OF JESUS

Elizabeth Clare Prophet

*on the discoveries of
Notovitch, Abhedananda,
Roerich, and Caspari*

SUMMIT UNIVERSITY  PRESS®

To the disciples of the Master
following in his footsteps

Contents

Leh is a remarkable site. Here the legends connected the paths of Buddha and Christ. Buddha went through Leh northwards. Issa communed here with the people on his way from Tibet. Secretly and cautiously the legends are guarded. It is difficult to sound them because lamas, above all people, know how to keep silent. Only by means of a common language— and not merely that of tongue but also of inner understanding—can one approach their significant mysteries.

Nicholas Roerich

Chapter One

THE LOST YEARS OF JESUS

*Analysis of eyewitness accounts
of travelers who have made the trek to Himis*

And there are also many
other things which Jesus did,
the which, if they should be
written every one, I suppose
that even the world itself
could not contain the books
that should be written . . .
                                    John

The Case for Issa

IMAGINE you are a detective. An unusual case comes across your desk. You open a yellowed folder. It isn't exactly a case of a mistaken identity or a missing person. It is a missing background—some lost years. And the particulars are spare.

Date of birth unknown. Exact year of birth also unknown; sometime between 8 and 4 B.C.

Place of birth disputed. Thought to be Bethlehem.[1]

Father, Joseph, a carpenter. Came from a noble and illustrious line beginning with Abraham and continuing through Isaac and Jacob to David the King—then through Solomon to Jacob, the father of Joseph, husband of Mary.

Human lineage thus established through paternal descent, though father's paternity vehemently denied by some in favor of doctrine of virgin birth. One account records him "being, as was supposed, the son of Joseph" but traces his royal origin through genealogy of Mary, his mother.[2]

Adventurous early life. Fled with parents to Egypt after father had a dream. Returned to Nazareth, or thereabouts, an unspecified number of years later.

By this time you realize what you might be getting into. But it doesn't add up. Why a file on Jesus? You read on.

At about age thirty, began a mission. Was baptized by a cousin, John. Traveled extensively with a band of twelve disciples for about three years. Preached, healed the sick, raised the dead. Was framed by Jewish high priest Caiaphas and Sanhedrin. Sentenced by Roman procurator Pontius Pilate against his better judgment. Crucified by four Roman soldiers. Taken down from cross and laid in tomb by Joseph of Arimathea and Nicodemus.

Orthodox position: Rose from the dead on the third day.[3] Taught disciples forty days. Then disappeared from their sight in "a cloud." Ascended into heaven and sat on the right hand of God.

Contradicted by second-century tradition that he spent many years on earth after resurrection.[4] Church Father Irenaeus asserts he lived at least ten to twenty years after crucifixion:

> On completing His thirtieth year He suffered, being in fact still a young man, and who had by no means attained to advanced age. Now, that the first stage of early life embraces thirty years, and that this extends onwards to the fortieth year, every one will admit; but from the fortieth and fiftieth year a man begins to decline towards old age, which our Lord possessed while He still fulfilled the office of a Teacher, even as the Gospel and all the elders testify; those who were conversant in Asia with John, the disciple of the Lord, [affirming] that John conveyed to them that information. [*Against Heresies*, c. 180][5]

View supported by third-century Gnostic text Pistis Sophia:

> It came to pass, when Jesus had risen from the dead, that he passed eleven years discoursing with his disciples and instructing them.... [6]

Impact of his life and teachings incalculable. Sought to effect change by purifying men's hearts. Called the greatest revolutionary.

Story told in various forms in New Testament and apocryphal writings. Followers, now 1.4 billion, called Christians.[7] Largest of all faiths.

Christian nations now culturally, economically, and politically dominant. All human history divided by his birth—B.C., A.D. Suggests his coming is the pivot of history.

You take a deep breath and exhale slowly. This is no small case. An investigation into the past of one of the most influential persons in history. You look up from your desk, past the typewriter to a calendar on the wall. It is an old, old case. You return to the file. It is full of unanswered questions.

No record of his existence made during his life. If made, did not survive. Nothing he may have written survived either.

No record of what he looked like: height, weight, color of hair or eyes. No distinguishing marks.[8]

Few details about his childhood. Little information about his family and home life. May have moved to Memphis, Egypt, shortly after his birth and lived there with his family three years.[9] Legends from the Isles say his great-uncle Joseph of Arimathea took him to Glastonbury as a youth. May have studied there.[10]

Most puzzling of all: aside from Glastonbury traditions and apocryphal writings,[11] no record of any kind about where he was or what he was doing from age twelve to thirty—a period called "the lost years of Jesus." Generally thought to have been in Palestine, in or about Nazareth, during that time, occupied as a carpenter. Facts to support this hypothesis: none.

You leave your desk, walk to the window and look out. You're thinking, "How do cases like this find me? No witnesses. Maybe no solid clues. Chance of cooperation and pay negligible."

It's night. The city is asleep. You're tempted to close the file and send it back. But you're intrigued: *Where was Jesus during the lost years?* You walk to your desk, pick up the file, and go out into the dark looking for a lead.

Of course, no such file exists. No Bogart-like detective is prowling a major metropolitan city searching for clues. And if there were, it is questionable how successful he could be. As our informative but imaginary file suggests, we simply do not know a great deal about Jesus, even though his life has been the focus of the most detailed, painstaking, exhaustive historical inquiry ever attempted.

The search for the historical Jesus began at the end of the eighteenth century when scholars and theologians began to examine critically the principal sources for Jesus' life—the Gospels. The intellectual ferment of the Enlightenment, combined with the development of historiography and the historical sense (that is, the recognition that it was both possible and desirable to find out what actually happened at a particular point in time), spurred "the quest of the historical Jesus"—a quest which has dominated the critical theology of the nineteenth and most of the twentieth centuries. [12]

Scholars discussed whether Jesus was a man or a myth or some of each; whether he came to establish a new religion or if he was an eschatological figure—a herald announcing the end of the world. They debated whether there was a rational explanation for the miracles, whether Jesus was necessary to the development of Christianity, whether the synoptic Gospels were historically more relevant than the Gospel of John, and even if there was anything to be gained by further study. The scholarship was so intense and the writings so profuse that entire libraries on the subject of the historical Jesus could be assembled. [13]

Scholars are now virtually in agreement that Jesus did in fact exist, but because of a scarcity of historical information no biography of his life, in the modern sense of the word, can be drawn.

The earliest writings about Jesus fall into two categories: Christian and non-Christian. The non-Christian records, written by Josephus, Pliny the Younger, Tacitus, and Suetonius about sixty to ninety years after the crucifixion, are so brief that they do little more than help establish his historicity. [14]

The Gospels, probably written between A.D. 60 and 100, are the principal source of information about Jesus. Although of immense historical value, scholars contend they were never intended to be biographies—a judgment that must be reconsidered in light of the fact that we do not necessarily have the writings of the Evangelists and the apostles in their original, unedited form.

With the exception of a few papyrus fragments

from the second century, the earliest known manuscripts of the Gospels are from the fourth century. Furthermore, the texts of the Gospels were in a fluid state—that is, subject to change by copyists for theological or other reasons—until they were standardized in about the middle of the fourth century. As a result, we have no way of telling whether we have received the Gospels intact or to what degree they have been edited, interpolated, subjected to scribal errors, or otherwise altered to meet the needs of orthodoxy as the Church struggled to curb so-called heresies, such as Gnosticism.[15]

The discoveries of a Gnostic library at Nag Hammadi, Egypt, by Muḥammad 'Alī al-Sammān, an Arab peasant, in 1945 and a fragment of a "Secret Gospel" of Mark in the Judean desert at Mar Saba by Morton Smith in 1958 strongly suggest that early Christians possessed a larger, markedly more diverse body of writings and traditions on the life and teachings of Jesus than appears in what has been handed down to us as the New Testament.[16]

While contemporary profiles of the famous abound in purely personal detail—we can learn how many cigars Winston Churchill smoked daily and what Mahatma Gandhi ate at any number of meals—the Gospels do not say what Jesus looked like, provide only the vaguest of geographic and chronological data, and even leave a question about his exact occupation.[17]

Scholars believe that Jesus was a carpenter. Joseph was a carpenter, and at that time it was customary for a boy to carry on his father's occupation. The language of carpenters, fishermen, and other common people is embedded in Jesus' words as recorded in the Gospels.[18] But there is no definitive

proof that Jesus was a carpenter. In fact, Origen
objected to the entire notion on the grounds that
"Jesus himself is not described as a carpenter anywhere in the Gospels accepted by the churches." [19]

Apocryphal writings say that while Jesus was
growing up in Egypt and Palestine, he performed
many healings and other miracles. In one instance,
he commanded a serpent that had bitten a youth,
Simon the Canaanite, to "suck out all the poison
which thou hast infused into that boy." The serpent
obeyed, whereupon Jesus cursed the serpent and it
"immediately burst asunder and died." Jesus then
touched Simon and restored his health. In other
passages, Jesus healed the foot of a boy, carried
water in his cloak, made a short wooden beam
longer to help Joseph with his carpentry, and fash-
ioned twelve sparrows out of clay, bringing them to
life with a clap of his hands. [20]

These accounts provide somewhat of a record
of the early Christian traditions concerning Jesus'
childhood, whereas only four of the eighty-nine
chapters of the Gospels, two each in Matthew and
Luke, describe Jesus' life prior to his ministry.
Known as the infancy narratives, they dwell on
Jesus' genealogy, conception and birth, and a
number of familiar events, such as the annuncia-
tion, the coming of the wise men from the East,
the manger visit of the shepherds, the circumcision,
the presentation in the Temple at Jerusalem, the
flight into Egypt where the family remained until
the death of Herod in 4 B.C., and the return to
Nazareth. [21]

After these extraordinary events, Jesus' life is
cloaked in obscurity until the start of his mission.
In fact, only two other things are recorded in the

Gospel of Luke—his physical and spiritual growth and his visit at the age of twelve to the Temple in Jerusalem on the occasion of Passover.

In a short but powerful vignette, Luke records that on their way back to Nazareth after attending the Passover feast, Joseph and Mary suddenly realized that Jesus was missing from their company, returned to the city and "found him in the temple, sitting in the midst of the doctors, both hearing them and asking them questions. And all that heard him were astonished at his understanding and answers." When reproached by Mary, Jesus replied, "Wist ye not that I must be about my Father's business?"[22]

Jesus then departed for Nazareth with his parents, "subject unto them."[23] Once again the veil descends, obscuring all of Jesus' activities for the next seventeen or so years, until he is baptized by John in the Jordan River at about the age of thirty.

The Gospel of Luke has only one transitional verse: "And Jesus increased in wisdom and stature, and in favour with God and man."[24] When all is said and done, as Christian scholar Kenneth S. Latourette points out, "The authentic records of his life and teachings are so brief that they could easily be printed in a single issue of one of our larger daily papers, and in these a substantial proportion of the space [would be] devoted to the last few days of his life."[25]

Why didn't anyone make a more complete record of Jesus' life? Scholars have given considerable thought to that question. Dr. John C. Trever, director of the Dead Sea Scrolls Project of the School of Theology at Claremont, California, believes the dearth of information is an irony of history, the natural sociological result of a people who were not oriented academically or historically, but religiously.[26]

Because of our education and culture, we naturally tend to see things in a historical mode. We want to know "what happened." But as noted in the *Dictionary of the History of Ideas,* "the earliest Christians seemed to have little place for mundane history; in a sense they were too otherworldly, too intent on the spiritual life."[27]

Like many other scholars, Dr. Trever theorizes that early Christians, expecting Jesus' imminent return and with it the end of history, probably thought it was not necessary to write anything down. New Testament scholar James M. Robinson, author of *A New Quest of the Historical Jesus,* believes that the first generation of Jesus' followers certainly knew what Jesus looked like, as well as a lot of other personal information, but did not record it because they were interested in his teaching, not his personal traits.

Throughout this quest, scholars have focused on Jesus' ministry and ignored the lost years. This has not been due to a lack of interest, but a lack of evidence. "If we had a bit of information [about the lost years], we'd all pounce upon it," says Professor Robinson. "But we're sort of helpless." To use a scholarly cliché, it is a case of "no texts, no history."[28]

The traditional position taken by Christian theologians and scholars is that Jesus was in Nazareth or nearby during the lost years and that nothing was written about that period of his life because he did nothing noteworthy to report.

In 1894, Nicolas Notovitch, a Russian journalist, published a book, *La Vie inconnue de*

*Jésus-Christ—*in English, *The Unknown Life of Jesus Christ—*which challenged that point of view. Notovitch claimed that while traveling in Ladakh (Little Tibet) late in 1887, he found a copy of an ancient Buddhist manuscript which explicitly said where Jesus was during the lost years—India.

Notovitch is something of an enigma. According to *The National Union Catalog,* he wrote eleven books. Yet there is almost no biographical information available about him. Apparently we know even less about him than we know about Jesus! Although we have been able to verify his birth in the Crimea in 1858,[29] we have not been able to locate a record of his death. He may have been a war correspondent as well as a journalist—and was certainly mistaken for a physician while traveling in the East.[30]

Notovitch affirmed his belief in the Russian Orthodox religion but was probably a convert since a brief entry in the *Encyclopaedia Judaica* notes that his brother Osip Notovitch was born Jewish but converted to the Greek Orthodox church as a youth.*

Writing mostly in French, Nicolas dealt with Russian affairs of state and international relations in many of his works, which include *The Pacification of Europe and Nicholas II, Russia and the English Alliance: An Historical and Political Study,* and *The Czar, His Army and Navy,* to name a few.

The Unknown Life of Jesus Christ was his first and, as far as we know, his only book on a religious subject. It contains a transcript of the text he

---

*Osip (1849–1914) was also a journalist. In 1876, he acquired *Novosti,* a small daily which he developed into an important political journal. In 1905, the paper was confiscated after he published a revolutionary appeal for a trade union. Osip subsequently fled Russia and died abroad.[31]

claimed to have discovered but is primarily a travelogue recap of the find. And this, if we are to believe his account, came about because of a series of coincidences.

In brief, Notovitch's story goes like this. Following the Russo-Turkish War of 1877–78, our adventurer began a series of travels in the East. He was interested in the people and the archaeology of India. Wandering randomly, he reached India by way of Afghanistan. On October 14, 1887, he left Lahore for Rawalpindi, worked his way to Kashmir and then to Ladakh. From there, he planned to return to Russia by way of Karakorum and Chinese Turkestan.

Along the way, he visited a Buddhist *gompa,* or monastery, at Mulbekh. A gompa, literally "a solitary place," is just that—a place of refuge from the world of temptation. Some gompas derive their solitude by being located a reasonable distance from a village. Others, like the one at Mulbekh, are built on top of a mountain or on the face of a cliff.[32]

Mulbekh is the gateway to the world of Tibetan Buddhism. Notovitch was received by a lama who told him that in the archives at Lhasa, capital of Tibet and at that time the home of the Dalai Lama, there were several thousand ancient scrolls discussing the life of the prophet Issa, the Eastern name for Jesus. While there was no such document at Mulbekh, the lama said that some of the principal monasteries had copies.

Notovitch was determined to find the records of the life of Issa, even if it meant going to Lhasa. Leaving Mulbekh, he visited several convents where the monks had heard of the documents but said they did not possess copies. He soon reached the great convent Himis, located about twenty-five miles from Leh, the capital of Ladakh.

Himis, named by its founder *"Sangye chi ku sung thug chi ten"* ("the support of the meaning of Buddha's precepts"),[33] is the largest and most celebrated monastery in Ladakh; it is also the scene of a well-known religious festival held annually in honor of Saint Padma Sambhava. It depicts Buddha's victory over the forces of evil, the driving away of evil spirits, and the ultimate triumph of good over evil.

The convent is tucked away in a hidden valley in the Himalayas, 11,000 feet above sea level. Some who have visited it say it brings to mind visions of Shangri-La. Because of its position, it is one of the few gompas that has escaped destruction by the invading armies of Asiatic conquerors. As a result, according to L. Austine Waddell, "more interesting and curious objects, books, dresses, masks, etc., are found at Himis than in any other monastery in Ladak."[34]

While visiting Himis in 1974–75, Tibetologists David L. Snellgrove and Tadeusz Skorupski were told that "other monasteries, availing themselves of its concealed position, had often in the past brought their treasures there for safe keeping, and there is certainly a considerable collection locked away in a safe room, known as the 'Dark Treasury'. . . which is said to be opened only when one treasurer hands on to a successor."[35]

At Himis, Notovitch witnessed one of the numerous mystery plays performed by the lamas. Afterward, he asked the chief lama if he had ever heard of Issa. The lama said that the Buddhists greatly respected Issa but that no one knew much about him other than the chief lamas who had read the records of his life.

In the course of their conversation, the lama mentioned that among the many scrolls at Himis "are to be found descriptions of the life and acts of the Buddha Issa, who preached the holy doctrine in India and among the children of Israel." According to the lama, the documents, brought from India to Nepal and then to Tibet, were originally written in Pali, the religious language of the Buddhists. The copy at Himis had been translated into Tibetan.

Notovitch asked, "Would you be committing a sin to recite these copies to a stranger?" While the lama was willing to make them available—"that which belongs to God belongs also to man"—he was not sure where they were. He told Notovitch that if he ever returned to the convent, he would be glad to show them to him.

Not wanting to compromise his chance of seeing the records by appearing too interested, yet determined to find them before he was forced to return to Russia, Notovitch left Himis and began looking for a pretext that would allow him to return to the monastery. Several days later, he sent the lama gifts of an alarm clock, a watch, and a thermometer with a message stating his desire to visit Himis again.

Notovitch said he planned to go to Kashmir prior to returning to Himis but "Fate ordained otherwise." Near the gompa of Pintak, Notovitch fell from his horse, fractured his leg, and used his injury as an excuse to return to Himis, which was only a half-day's journey away.

While the Russian was convalescing, the chief

lama finally assented to his "earnest entreaties," produced "two large bound volumes with leaves yellowed by time," and read aloud the sections dealing with Issa. Notovitch's interpreter translated the text, which the Russian journalist carefully wrote in his notebook.

The biography of Issa, according to Notovitch, was composed of isolated verses which were untitled and scattered out of sequence throughout the text. The Russian author grouped the verses and put them in order, and then published the document several years later along with his account of its discovery.

The text is called *The Life of Saint Issa: Best of the Sons of Men,* evidently a title of Notovitch's own making. It is not a long work—244 verses arranged into 14 chapters, the longest of which has 27 verses.

Some of it will sound familiar to anyone acquainted with the Old and New Testaments: the Egyptian captivity, the deliverance of the Israelites by Mossa (Moses), the backsliding of the Israelites followed by foreign invasions, subjugation by Rome, and finally the incarnation of a divine child to poor but pious parents. God speaks by the mouth of the infant and people come from all over to hear him.

The narrative quickly jumps to Issa's thirteenth year, the first of the "lost years," and the time, according to the story, "when an Israelite should take a wife." His parents' house, humble though it was, became a meeting place for the rich and noble who desired to have as a son-in-law the young Issa, "already famous for his edifying discourses in the name of the Almighty."

Issa had set his sights on other goals. According

to the manuscript Notovitch published, he secretly left his father's house, departed Jerusalem and, with a caravan of merchants, traveled east in order to perfect himself in the "Divine Word" and to study the laws of the great Buddhas.

They say Issa was fourteen when he crossed the Sind, a region in present-day southeast Pakistan in the lower Indus River valley, and established himself among the "Aryas"—no doubt a reference to the Aryans who migrated into the Indus valley beginning in the second millennium B.C. His fame spread and he was asked by the Jains to stay with them. Instead, he went to Juggernaut where he was joyously received by the Brahmin priests who taught him to read and understand the Vedas and to teach, heal, and perform exorcisms.

Issa spent six years studying and teaching at Juggernaut, Rajagriha, Benares, and other holy cities. He became embroiled in a conflict with the Brahmins and the Kshatriyas (the priestly and warrior castes) by teaching the holy scriptures to the lower castes—the Vaisyas (farmers and merchants) and the Sudras (the peasants and laborers). The Brahmins said that the Vaisyas were authorized to hear the Vedas read only during festivals and the Sudras not at all. They were not even allowed to look at them.

Rather than abide by their injunction, Issa preached against the Brahmins and Kshatriyas to the Vaisyas and Sudras. Aware of his denunciations, the priests and warriors plotted to put Issa to death.

Warned by the Sudras, Issa left Juggernaut by night and went to the foothills of the Himalayas in southern Nepal, birthplace five centuries earlier of the great Buddha Sakyamuni (a title of Gautama), born prince of the Sakya clan—literally, the sage (muni) of the Sakya tribe.

After six years of study, Issa "had become a perfect expositor of the sacred writings." He then left the Himalayas and journeyed west, preaching against idolatry along the way, finally returning to Palestine at the age of twenty-nine.

The Life of Saint Issa can be divided into three sections. The first part, chapter 1 through the middle of chapter 4, deals with the conditions that led to his incarnation, his birth and very early life. The second part, the remainder of chapter 4 through chapter 8, details the lost years—ages thirteen to twenty-nine, when Issa was studying in India and the Himalayas. And the final part, chapters 9 through 14, covers the unfoldment of events during his mission in Palestine.

The account of what took place after Issa returned to Palestine, while similar to that recorded in the Gospels, has major differences. John the Baptist does not appear in *The Life of Saint Issa.* The resurrection is omitted, if not completely denied. And, in a perplexing reversal (or perhaps an alteration of the story as it was transmitted orally across the miles, translated, and copied), Pilate—who is clearly the antagonist—tries through a series of intrigues to trap Issa and finally condemns him, while the Jewish priests and elders find no fault in him.

Pilate fears Issa's popularity and the possibility that he might be chosen king. After Issa has preached for three years, Pilate orders a spy to accuse him. Issa is arrested and Roman soldiers torture him in a vain effort to extract a treasonable confession.

Hearing of his sufferings, the chief priests and elders implore Pilate to release Issa on the occasion of a great feast. When Pilate flatly rejects their plea, they ask him to let Issa appear before the tribunal of the elders so that he can be acquitted or condemned prior to the feast. Pilate consents.

Issa is tried with two thieves. During the trial, Pilate interrogates Issa and produces false witnesses against him. Issa forgives the witnesses and rebukes Pilate who, becoming enraged, acquits the two thieves and condemns Issa to death. The judges tell Pilate, "We will not take upon our heads the great sin of condemning an innocent man and acquitting thieves," and proceed to wash their hands in a sacred vessel saying, "We are innocent of the death of this just man."

Pilate then orders Issa and the two thieves to be nailed to crosses. At sunset, Issa loses consciousness and his soul leaves his body "to become absorbed in the Divinity."

Wary of the people, Pilate gives Issa's body to his parents, who bury it near the place of execution. Crowds come to pray at Issa's tomb. Three days later, Pilate, fearing an insurrection, sends his soldiers to remove Issa's body and bury it elsewhere.

The following day, the people find Issa's tomb open and empty, which causes the immediate spread of a rumor "that the supreme Judge had sent his angels to carry away the mortal remains of the saint in whom dwelt on earth a part of the Divine Spirit." The text ends with the persecution of Issa's followers, the disciples going forth to preach, and the conversion of the pagans, their kings and warriors.

This story was allegedly written down three to four years after the crucifixion based on accounts brought to India by merchants who had witnessed the event.[36]

The Unknown Life of Jesus Christ was an

immediate success. At least eight editions were published in France in 1894, and three separate English translations appeared in the United States. Another English translation was published in London the following year. It was also translated into German, Spanish, Swedish, and Italian.[37]

The book was controversial to say the least. On May 19, 1894, a reviewer for the *New York Times* said that the particulars of Notovitch's story were "not improbable."[38] Having conceded that, he asserted, "But if skeptics should believe that this Tibetan or Indian relation of the life of Christ is trustworthy, they would be very credulous."

The reviewer held that Notovitch's find was no more important than "the assurances of theosophists that Christ was well acquainted with Buddhist theology" and warned that an English scientific commission preparing to verify the authenticity of the original documents "will have wasted its time and its scientific knowledge," whether or not it found them to be authentic.

Noting the appearance of another English translation of the book, the *Times* (June 4, 1894) again conceded that the documents might be genuine but questioned whether Buddhist records were of greater value than Christian ones. "It is to be remembered that we may have here authentic documents, without having authentic records. Christians know that the doctrines of Sakya Muni have created a barren civilization. If infidels believe that the Buddhist records are more worthy of belief than the Christian, they are very credulous. Notovitch's discovery is, nevertheless, worthy of the attention that it is attracting and of the discussions whereof it is the subject."[39]

Other critics—who not only denied the authenticity of the documents but also questioned whether Notovitch had gone to Ladakh at all—were not so charitable. In the pages of the *North American Review,* May 1894, Edward Everett Hale, a prominent Unitarian minister and author, even questioned the existence of the "somewhat mythical convent" of Himis, "which we do not find on our own calendar of Buddhist ecclesiastical establishments near Leh, the capital of Ladak."[40]

Hale charged that Notovitch, having previously written a biography of Alexander III, was probably the author of *The Life of Saint Issa* as well. Among other things, Hale found it hard to believe that in the course of his travels a lama should "mention the fact—which oddly enough had never been mentioned to other travellers—that at Lassa there are ancient memoirs of the life of Jesus Christ."

Nor was Hale willing to accept the Russian's version of how the chief lama at Himis came to show him the documents. Recounting the event, Hale wrote, "He was obliged to seek the hospitality of the convent of Himis again, and while the broken parts were knitting together he skilfully led conversation round to the old manuscripts."

Notwithstanding the fact that Hale's "skilfully led conversation" is a departure from Notovitch's "earnest entreaties," he asserted, "it was as if a Buddhist delegate to the Parliament of Religions had been wounded in watching a Princeton foot-ball match, and Dr. McCosh [president of the College of New Jersey, renamed Princeton University] had received him to his hospitality. What more natural than that Dr. McCosh should give his guest a New Testament?"

In October 1894, F. Max Müller, professor of modern European languages and comparative philology at Oxford University, entered the lists. Müller, editor of the Rig Veda and *The Sacred Books of the East,* was a scholar of renown and a noted Orientalist. He published "The Alleged Sojourn of Christ in India," a critique of *The Unknown Life of Jesus Christ,* in the *Nineteenth Century,* a scholarly review.[41] Müller was convinced that *The Life of Saint Issa* was a fraud, possibly carried out by the lamas at Himis, but most likely perpetrated by the Russian journalist. In fact, he was far from certain the Russian had even gone to Himis.

The Oxford professor claimed that after making on-the-spot inquiries, Moravian missionaries and English officers reported that no Russian by the name of Notovitch had passed through Leh and no one had been laid up at Himis with a broken leg. He speculated that "M. Notovitch may have travelled in disguise." But then he argued that, assuming "M. Notovitch is a gentleman and not a liar" and did go to Himis, he was far too easy prey for Buddhist monks "who enjoy mystifying inquisitive travellers"—not that he would have been the first traveler to be given the manuscripts he was seeking "for a consideration."

Müller admits a certain amount of plausibility in parts of Notovitch's tale. Pali was the language of Buddhism and Buddhism did reach Tibet through Nepal. But there were two parts of Notovitch's story that Müller found "impossible, or next to impossible." The first, that the Jews who came to India from Palestine in about A.D. 35 should have met the very people who had known Issa when he was a student at Benares.

According to the Oxford savant, the Russian traveler should have been

a little more skeptical when he was told that the Jewish merchants who arrived in India immediately after the Crucifixion knew not only what had happened to Christ in Palestine, but also what had happened to Jesus, or Issa, while he spent fifteen years of his life among the Brahmans and Buddhists in India, learning Sanskrit and Pali, and studying the Vedas and the Tripi*t*aka. With all their cleverness the Buddhist monks would have found it hard to answer the question, how these Jewish merchants met the very people who had known Issa as a casual student of Sanskrit and Pali in India—for India is a large term—and still more, how those who had known Issa as a simple student in India saw at once that he was the same person who had been put to death under Pontius Pilate.

The other factor which Müller thought discredited *The Life of Saint Issa* was the fact that it was not listed in either the *Kanjur* or the *Tanjur*—the standard catalogues of translated Buddhist sacred texts and commentaries.

Finally, Müller took issue with comments the Russian author had made in his preface. Notovitch said that he never doubted the authenticity of the chronicle and determined to publish it upon his return to Europe. But before he did so, he claimed he addressed himself to several well-known ecclesiastics, including a Monsignor Platon of Kiev, who reportedly tried to dissuade him from publishing them. He also claimed to have showed them to an unnamed cardinal on good terms with the pope, world-famous French historian and critic Ernest Renan, and a Cardinal Rotelli in Paris.[42]

The unnamed cardinal allegedly told Notovitch he would only make a lot of enemies by publishing his manuscript and said, "If it be a question of money which interests you, I might ask that a reward should be made to you for your notes, which should indemnify you for the expenses you have incurred and the time you have lost."

Cardinal Rotelli reportedly opposed the publication of Notovitch's work on the grounds that it would aid the enemies of the "evangelical doctrine."

According to Notovitch, Renan, author of a popular but extraordinarily controversial *Life of Jesus,* asked him to entrust him with the manuscript so that he could make a report to the Academy. Notovitch said he declined to do so because, flattering as that might be,

> I foresaw that if I accepted this combination, I should only have the honor of having discovered the chronicle, while the illustrious author of the *Vie de Jésus* would gain all the kudos through commenting upon it and making it public.
>
> Therefore, as I believed myself sufficiently prepared to publish the translation of the chronicle and to accompany it by my notes, I declined the very kindly meant offer thus made to me. Not however to hurt in any way the susceptibility of the great master, whom I deeply respected, I determined to await his demise, which sad occurrence I foresaw—judging from his enfeebled condition—could not be far off.

These explanations served only to erode what little credibility Notovitch might have had with Müller. The Oxford professor wrote: "When a Cardinal at Rome dissuades him from publishing his book, and also kindly offers to assist him, he hints that this was simply a bribe, and that the Cardinal wished to suppress the book. Why should he?" This did not make sense to Müller. "If the story of Issa were historically true, it would remove many difficulties. It would show once for all that Jesus was a real and historical character."

Moreover, Müller found Notovitch's strategy of waiting for Renan's death—to insure the better part of the glory for his discovery—to be uncharitable, to say the least. In the final analysis, however, Müller said that he preferred to suppose the Russian was duped because "it is pleasanter to believe that Buddhist monks can at times be wags, than that M. Notovitch is a rogue."

Müller ends the article with a P.S. containing a letter from an unnamed English lady dated Leh, Ladakh, June 29 [1894]: "Did you hear of a Russian who could not gain admittance to the monastery in any way, but at last broke his leg outside, and was taken in? His object was to copy a Buddhist Life of Christ which is there. He says he got it, and has published it since in French. There is not a single word of truth in the whole story! There has been no Russian there. No one has been taken into the Seminary for the past fifty years with a broken leg! There is no Life of Christ there at all!"[43]

Notovitch described Müller's critique as an "attempt to demolish me" but did not shrink from the controversy. Instead, he vigorously defended himself against his detractors. In a note "To the

Publishers" of one of his English editions, reproduced in this volume, he acknowledged that "a skillfully devised criticism" had prejudiced the public against the book and he briefly answered the major criticisms.

First he tried to explain why the lama at Himis, when later asked to verify the existence of the manuscripts, refused to do so. Orientals, he claimed, tend to see Westerners as robbers and would interpret inquiries about a manuscript tantamount to an admission that they wished to carry it off. His own success in the matter was the result of his use of "Eastern diplomacy"—an indirect approach which veiled his real interests and allayed their fears.

In response to the allegations that he had never been to Himis, Notovitch provided the names of various people who could verify his presence in the region, including Dr. Karl Marx (yes, that is his real name), a European physician employed by the British government who treated Notovitch in Ladakh.

To those who claimed he authored *The Life of Saint Issa,* he protested, "My imagination is not so fertile."

Since Max Müller had a reputation in the scientific world, Notovitch spent even more time addressing his arguments. The Russian journalist acknowledged that the manuscripts he claimed to have found were not listed in either the *Tanjur* or *Kanjur* and if they were, "my discovery would be neither a curious nor a rare one." Any Orientalist could then have gone to Tibet and, aided by the catalogues, found the relevant passages.

In his defense, Notovitch offered two reasons why the manuscripts were not in these catalogues. First, the catalogues were incomplete. Notovitch said there were more than one hundred thousand scrolls at the monastery at Lhasa, while "according to Mr. Max Müller's own statement, these tables contain a list of about two thousand volumes only." (Notovitch's rebuttal did not perfectly restate Müller's argument on this point, but he was essentially correct— the *Tanjur* and *Kanjur* list only a small portion of Buddhist literature.) Notovitch also pointed out that the verses he published in his book were not likely to be found in any catalogue since they were "scattered through more than one book without any title."

In answer to Müller's charge that it would be difficult for Jewish merchants to find just the people who had known Issa as a student in India, Notovitch replied that they were not Jewish but Indian merchants who happened to witness the crucifixion prior to returning home from Palestine.

Although he did not mention it, Notovitch could have pointed out that there was yet another reason why the connection between the merchants returning from Palestine and those who had known Jesus in India was not so difficult or unlikely: India has a very efficient human grapevine. If Jesus had made as much of a stir in India as the text suggests, it is not improbable that people throughout the whole of India might have known of him. Furthermore, there is no reason to assume that Jesus, in his fifteen or so years in India, would have made any less of an impact than he did in his final three or so years in Palestine. After all, based solely on those three years his name and fame have been passed to the nations of the world by the planetary grapevine.

During the course of his defense, Notovitch said that the verses communicated to him by the lama at Himis "may have been actually spoken by

St. Thomas—historical sketches traced by his own hand or under his direction." He offered no proof for that statement nor gave any indication of how it could be reconciled with his assertion that the texts were derived from the eyewitness reports of Indian merchants. He simply observed that Saint Thomas, Saint Bartholomew, and Saint Matthias professed to have preached the gospel in Tibet, India, and China and asked rhetorically if they had written nothing.

Not much of a certainty is known about Saint Thomas. But according to universal tradition, Christianity was first introduced into India by Thomas in A.D. 52. The Syrian Christians of Malabar, India, claim that Saint Thomas was their founder. And in his study *The Indian Christians of St. Thomas: An Account of the Ancient Syrian Church of Malabar,* Leslie Brown points out that "there was a considerable Jewish colony in north-western India in the first century, which might have attracted the attention of the first Christian missionaries."[44]

Whether or not Saint Thomas actually wrote anything, as noted in *The Catholic Encyclopedia,* "his name is the starting-point of a considerable apocryphal literature, and there are also certain historical data which suggest that some of this apocryphal material may contain germs of truth."[45]

The *Acta Thomae*—the Acts of Thomas—an early manuscript (pre-A.D. 220) bearing signs of Gnostic origin, is the principal document concerning him. The story contained therein is, according to *The Catholic Encyclopedia,* "utterly extravagant" in many of its particulars.[46]

In brief, the Acts of Thomas tells how the apostles, when they were in Jerusalem, divided the world by lot prior to going forth to preach the gospel. India fell to Thomas, who declared he could not go: "How can I, being an Hebrew man, go among the Indians to proclaim the truth?"

Jesus appeared to Thomas and said, "Fear not, Thomas; go away to India and proclaim the word, for my grace shall be with thee." Thomas still refused to go. So it happened that Abbanes, a merchant, had been sent by the Indian king Gundaphoros to buy a carpenter and bring him back to India. Jesus saw Abbanes in the market, approached him, and, according to the story, in order to achieve his ordained purpose for his beloved disciple, sold Thomas into slavery to serve Gundaphoros. Thomas then sailed with Abbanes to India where the king gave him money to build a palace. Instead, he spent the money on the poor and preached in Christ's name.

Hearing of this, Gundaphoros had Thomas imprisoned. Later the king discovered that the disciple had actually built him a palace in the heavens, whereupon he was converted and freed Thomas.[47] Thereafter, Thomas traveled throughout India, preaching and meeting with strange adventures, and was eventually condemned to death and pierced with spears by four soldiers.[48]

Despite what may seem to be the fanciful nature of the tale, *The Catholic Encyclopedia* notes:

Now it is certainly a remarkable fact that about the year A.D. 46 a king was reigning over that part of Asia south of the Himalayas now represented by Afghanistan, Baluchistan, the Punjab, and Sind, who bore the name Gondophernes or Guduphara. This we know both from the discovery of coins, some of the

Parthian type with Greek legends, others of the Indian type with legends in an Indian dialect in Kharoshthi characters. Despite sundry minor variations the identity of the name with the Gundafor of the "Acta Thomae" is unmistakable and is hardly disputed. Further we have the evidence of the Takht-i-Bahi inscription, which is dated, and which the best specialists accept as establishing that the King Guduphara probably began to reign about A.D. 20 and was still reigning in 46.[49]

But whether Saint Thomas went to India to preach the gospel and helped write the text Notovitch claimed to have discovered, or the story was written in Pali from the account of Indian eyewitnesses, or the text appeared in either the *Tanjur* or *Kanjur,* or even whether Notovitch broke his leg is really beside the point. The issue, as Notovitch declared in his note "To the Publishers," is this: "Did those passages exist in the monastery of Himis, and have I faithfully reproduced their substance?"

The *New York Times,* April 19, 1896, took note of Notovitch's "bold and vigorous defense," which, "while it did not convince his critics, more or less silenced them."[50] Ladakh, it noted, was far away and not easy to get to.

It was not the purpose of that *Times* article to praise Notovitch, but to bury him. It mentioned the story of one J. Archibald Douglas who accepted the Russian journalist's challenge, went to Himis, and then published an account of his journey in the *Nineteenth Century,* which in the words of the *Times* was "a complete refutation of every assertion made by the Russian traveler, except the assertion that he did make a journey into Little Tibet."

While a professor at Government College in Agra, India, Douglas had become acquainted with the controversy and had read Müller's review article before having had the opportunity to read Notovitch's *Unknown Life of Jesus Christ.* That, incidentally, is just about all we know about Mr. Douglas.

As every detective knows, most criminals have a discernible method of operation, a repetitive pattern of behavior which tends to indicate their future course of action. It seems this mystery has a repetitive pattern of behavior of its own—and an ironic one at that: key figures in the drama leave no biographical traces. After a long and thorough search, all we know about Douglas is that he wrote an article for the *Nineteenth Century,* corresponded with Max Müller, and claimed to have gone to Himis. Period.

To continue, Douglas thought that in declaring the work to be a literary forgery, Müller had treated Notovitch harshly on inconclusive evidence. Impressed by the Russian's staunch self-defense, Douglas went to Himis in 1895, "fully prepared to find that M. Notovitch's narrative was correct, and to congratulate him on his marvellous discovery."

In his review article, "The Chief Lama of Himis on the Alleged 'Unknown Life of Christ,'"[51] written in June of 1895, published in April of 1896, Douglas claimed that he was received by the chief lama and, through the services of an able interpreter, read to him sections of Notovitch's book. Then he asked the chief lama a series of questions based on those excerpts.

Douglas affirmed that he had "the fullest confidence in the veracity and honesty of this old and respected Chief Lama," that the lama understood the passages from Notovitch's book, which were

translated slowly, and that the questions and answers
were discussed during two lengthy interviews before
a final document was prepared for signing.

Douglas then published the text of his questions and answers. According to the professor's
story, his host at Himis said that he had been chief
lama at the monastery for fifteen years—a span that
would have encompassed Notovitch's visit. The
lama said that during that time no European with a
broken leg had sought refuge at Himis, although
he distinctly remembered that several European
gentlemen had visited the monastery. Furthermore,
he had not shown a book on the life of Saint Issa to
any "sahib."

"There is no such book in the monastery, and
during my term of office no sahib has been allowed to copy or translate any of the manuscripts
in the monastery," Douglas documented the lama
as saying.

When asked if he was aware of any book in the
Buddhist monasteries of Tibet which had a bearing
on the life of Issa, he replied:

> I have been for forty-two years a Lama, and
> am well acquainted with all the well-known
> Buddhist books and manuscripts, and I have
> never heard of one which mentions the name
> of Issa, and it is my firm and honest belief that
> none such exists. I have inquired of our prin-
> cipal Lamas in other monasteries of Tibet, and
> they are not acquainted with any books or
> manuscripts which mention the name of Issa.

The lama, if we can believe Douglas' story,
also assured him that he never received presents of
a watch, an alarm clock, or thermometer from anyone (he did not know what a thermometer was and

was sure he did not possess one), did not speak English or Urdu as Notovitch claimed, knew of no Buddhist writings in Pali (the only writings at Himis had been translated from Sanskrit and Hindi into Tibetan), and said that the Buddhists "know nothing even of his [Issa's] name; none of the Lamas has ever heard it, save through missionaries and European sources."

According to the article, on June 3, 1895, the chief lama of Himis signed a document containing these questions and answers and affixed his official seal in the presence of Douglas and his translator, Shahmwell Joldan, the former postmaster of Ladakh.

At that point Douglas asserted that he had met the criteria of criticism that Notovitch had established for his work: "Did those passages exist in the monastery of Himis, and have I faithfully reproduced their substance?"

Wrote Douglas:

> I have visited Himis, and have endeavoured by patient and impartial inquiry to find out the truth respecting M. Notovitch's remarkable story, with the result that, while I have not found one single fact to support his statements, all the weight of evidence goes to disprove them beyond all shadow of doubt. It is certain that no such passages as M. Notovitch pretends to have translated exist in the monastery of Himis, and therefore it is impossible that he could have 'faithfully reproduced' the same.

While Douglas concluded that Notovitch's *Life of Saint Issa* was a "literary forgery," he satisfied himself that Notovitch had indeed visited Leh and

possibly Himis. The chief lama told Douglas that no
Russian had been to Himis in 1887 and 1888, but in
the course of his investigation the professor discovered that the lama could not distinguish between a
Russian, a European, and an American. Douglas reported that the lama, on being shown a photograph
of Notovitch, confessed that "he might have mistaken him for an 'English sahib.'"

Through "careful inquiries," Douglas determined that a Russian by the name of Notovitch had
been treated by a "Dr. Karl Marks," the medical officer at Leh Hospital, "when suffering not from a broken leg, but from the less romantic but hardly less
painful complaint—toothache." Douglas even conceded that Notovitch could have broken his leg after
departing from Leh, but maintained that "the whole
story of the broken leg, in so far as it relates to Himis
Monastery, is neither more nor less than a fiction."

In a postscript to Douglas' article, Müller said
that from the start he had been convinced that Notovitch's *Unknown Life of Jesus Christ* was pure
fiction. But when writing his own article, he said he
felt he had to give the Russian "the benefit of a
doubt and to suggest that he might possibly have
been hoaxed by Buddhist priests from whom he professed to have gathered his information about Issa,
i.e., Jesus."[52]

Müller said that at the time he had not thought
the priests at Himis would be offended by his remarks. But after reading Douglas' article he felt
bound "to apologise to the excellent Lamas of that
monastery for having thought them capable of such
frivolity" and declared that Douglas had effected
not only a refutation, but an "annihilation" of Notovitch's tale.

The credibility of *The Unknown Life of Jesus Christ* was seriously damaged and the book became harder to find. Notovitch went back to writing less controversial works like *The Pacification of Europe and Nicholas II* and *Russia and the English Alliance.* The story could have ended right there.

But it didn't. In fact the plot, as every lover of a good mystery knows it must, began to thicken.

Naturally, to some it seemed like an open-and-shut case of literary forgery: the Russian in the drawing room with a fountain pen. Douglas had caught him "red-handed"—he had taken a deposition from the old and venerable and highly respected lama in the presence of the former postmaster of Ladakh, who had served as his interpreter.

In the midst of the proceedings, while Douglas was reading him excerpts of Notovitch's book, the lama was reported to have spontaneously cried out, *"Sun, sun, sun, manna mi dug!"*—that is, "Lies, lies, lies, nothing but lies!" At another time, according to Douglas, the lama asked if anyone could be prosecuted for writing such blatantly false accounts.

On the basis of these and other allegations, it might have been hard to conclude anything other than that Notovitch was guilty as charged. But any detective worth his London Fog knows that things are seldom what they seem. In fact, it would be precisely at that point that the sleuth in him would start to ask: Is *The Life of Saint Issa* really a literary forgery? Did Notovitch artfully conceive and execute a hoax? If so, what was his motive?[53] Fame? Fortune? Did he have accomplices? Was he an agent of the Czar as Hale suggested?[54] If he was, did that have any bearing on the case? And if Notovitch did pass a forgery, did he really think he could get away with it?

Ladakh is a high, cold, remote, barren land. It was an independent kingdom on and off for about one thousand years. In 1834, it was subdued by the rulers of Jammu and in 1947 became a district of India's Jammu and Kashmir State, bordering Pakistan, Tibet, and Chinese Turkestan.

Himalayan peaks rise from its lofty plateaus. It is an exotic place, a refuge of Tibetan Buddhist culture—no doubt a romantic setting for a story. But it was by no means inaccessible. Notovitch must have known that someone would go to Himis, probably sooner than later, and check out his story as he urged them to do. With the chance of detection so likely, as Müller himself pointed out, would the Russian have taken such a chance? Even Müller found that hard to believe.[55]

Still, that is the way it looked. In reality, however, there was conflicting testimony: the word of a Russian journalist and the contradictory word of a British(?) professor. The fact that Douglas failed to see a copy of a manuscript was no more decisive proof that it did not exist than Notovitch's claim that it did. Nevertheless, it seemed as if either Notovitch or Douglas were telling the truth—not both. And if the weight of publicly expressed opinion was a litmus of honesty, Douglas tested true.

Appearances can be deceiving, of course. Were there other possibilities? Could the lama have deceived Notovitch, as Müller first suggested? Did Notovitch faithfully record what was read to him as translated by his interpreter, group the verses, and publish it, as he claimed? Or, could it be that the chief lama at Himis was not entirely candid with Professor Douglas?

Assuming for a moment that the core of

Notovitch's account is accurate (that is, allowing for any possible dramatization of the story, that the manuscript did indeed exist and he reproduced it) and that Douglas, as everyone has assumed, wrote an accurate account, how can we explain the discrepancy? Perhaps the answer lies in the realm of "Eastern diplomacy."

Notovitch asserted that when a Westerner asks about a particular treasure, the lamas believe it is because he intends to carry it off. That being the case, the Russian said he was circumspect in his approach to the documents and was convinced that his discretion was instrumental in gaining him access to them. From his article, it appears that Professor Douglas was forthright and direct. If Notovitch's assessment is correct, that could have led to a flat denial.

We will never know precisely what happened between Douglas and the lama at Himis, or between Notovitch and the lama—if such a visit actually took place. However, after spending most of the 1974–75 winter in Ladakh, Tibetologists Snellgrove and Skorupski made an observation about Himis that lends credence to the "Eastern diplomacy" theory. In *The Cultural Heritage of Ladakh* they wrote:

> Hemis is not an easy monastery to get to know. It seems to attract far more visitors than any monastery in Ladakh, and very few of them have any idea of what they are looking at. This tends to produce on the part of the monks a supercilious attitude and even outright contempt, and *they seem convinced that all foreigners steal if they can. There have in fact been quite serious losses of property in recent years,* which were still being investigated by the

Superintendent of Police while we were there, and as usual foreigners are not in fact responsible.[56] [emphasis added]

Whatever happened, the whole affair began to develop the flavor of an offbeat drama with curious characters: a professor of undetermined nationality, a Russian writer, a Ladakhi lama, a famous philologist, and a supporting cast of scholars, newsmen, Moravian missionaries, English officers, a physician with a suspicious name, some travelers, and a missing document *maybe*—the existence of which had not yet been established. Notovitch did not bring back a copy of it, or even photographs of its pages, as proof of its existence. And Douglas was told that no such document existed at all.

Was it a case of no document or a reluctant lama? A fabrication by Notovitch? Naïveté on the part of Douglas? Something else? Due to a lack of evidence, it was impossible to tell. In fact, at that point there was so little conclusive evidence that even a great detective might have been stymied. So what thickened the plot? Elementary, my dear Watson: more evidence.

It came in the form of eyewitness reports from visitors to Himis—the first of which had more than a touch of irony. It was made by Swami Abhedananda—a close acquaintance if not an outright friend of Max Müller—who claimed not only to have seen the document but to have verified, in a manner of speaking, Notovitch's story.

Abhedananda was the ideal kind of person to make an on-the-spot assessment of the situation at Himis. Born Kaliprasad Chandra, October 2, 1866, in Calcutta, India, he became proficient in English and Sanskrit at an early age.[57] When he was eighteen, he entered Calcutta Oriental Seminary where his father, Professor Rasiklal Chandra, held the chair in English for twenty-five years.

A precocious scholar versed in the literature of both East and West, Kaliprasad was a voracious reader with a penchant for philosophy who in his youth digested works as diverse as the *Bhagavad Gita* and John Stuart Mill's *System of Logic*. He examined all schools of thought, attended numerous lectures by yogis, pundits, and exponents of Christianity, Brahmoism, and Hinduism, and in 1884 became a disciple of the Indian saint Ramakrishna.

Beginning in 1886, he walked the length and width of Hindustan, barefoot and without money. For ten years he endured privations, contemplated the Absolute, made pilgrimages to the sacred places at Puri, Rishikesh, and Kedarnath, among others, and lived at the sources of the Jumna and Ganges rivers in the Himalayas.

In 1896, he donned Western garb and sailed to London where he began his career as a preacher and exponent of Vedanta (a Hindu philosophy based on the Vedas) and met distinguished scholars such as the noted German Sanskritist Paul Deussen and the redoubtable Max Müller.

It is difficult to tell just how deep a bond developed between the two men. Abhedananda was in London only a year before he left to spread Vedanta in the United States. Nevertheless, they met a number of times—conversing in English (Müller could only read Sanskrit, not speak it)—and seemed to have enjoyed each other's company.

If nothing else, their relationship was based on a mutual respect and common interests, not the least of which was Ramakrishna, for whom Müller had a deep and abiding regard. Abhedananda spoke at length to him about his master; and what Müller learned about the Indian saint from his disciple aided considerably in the preparation of his book *Ramakrishna: His Life and Sayings.* On Müller's passing in 1900, Abhedananda—representing the Hindu and Sanskrit scholars of India—paid tribute to him at a public meeting organized by the philosophy and philology departments at Columbia University.

No doubt it would have been something of a shock for the Oxford professor to have heard his friend corroborate Notovitch's tale. Would he have accepted it graciously? Denied it? Demanded further proof? We will never know. Müller passed away twenty-two years before Abhedananda determined for himself that Notovitch's account was true.

It is even difficult to say if the two men ever discussed *The Unknown Life of Jesus Christ.* Although Abhedananda was in London shortly after the book's publication, he may not have read it until he went to America.[58]

There are conflicting reports about Abhedananda's attitude toward the book, but he was not necessarily a true believer—at least at first. In *The Jesus Mystery* (1980), Richard and Janet Bock's account of their search for evidence to corroborate the Issa legend,* Mrs. Bock reports that Abhedananda

---

*The Bocks became interested in the lost years after reading *The Aquarian Gospel of Jesus the Christ* by Levi and Notovitch's *Unknown Life of Jesus Christ.* In the course of their frequent journeys to India, they spent four months shooting a film retracing Jesus' footsteps through the subcontinent as outlined in *The Life of Saint Issa.* Their film, *The Lost Years,* completed in 1978, has acquainted many in America and Europe with the story of Jesus' pilgrimage to the East prior to his Palestinian mission.

was skeptical and went to Himis to "expose" Notovitch—a conclusion she based on an interview with
Abhedananda's disciple Swami Prajnananda.

Yet several passages from the work of one of
Abhedananda's biographers, Sister Shivani (Mrs.
Mary LePage), suggest that "expose" is too strong a
word. While working at Princeton University Press
sometime between 1912 and 1916, Sister Shivani
recalled a remark "I had once heard the Swami
make from the platform to the effect that the years
preceding Christ's ministry had been said to have
been spent in India with the Yogis of Tibet."[59]

Her interest thus reawakened, she wrote to both
a Dr. Miller, who held the chair in Church History at
Princeton, and Swami Abhedananda. Dr. Miller, in
reply, said he knew of no such historical record. But,
reported Sister Shivani, "the Swami wrote telling me
to read the Russian writer Notovitch's *The Unknown
Life of Christ.*"[60]

It took her several years to locate a copy. Nevertheless, if Abhedananda had been sufficiently skeptical of Notovitch's book to want to expose it, it is
puzzling that he would have told his disciple to read
it without informing her of his misgivings.

Two of his biographies, *An Apostle of Monism:
An Authentic Account of the Activities of Swami
Abhedananda in America* by Sister Shivani and
Swami Abhedananda: A Spiritual Biography by Dr.
Moni Bagchi, state that Abhedananda was eager to
"verify and confirm" (they used identical words)
Notovitch's claim.[61]

Keen though his interest may have been, it was
years before Abhedananda got the chance to sub-
stantiate it. He was busy spreading Vedanta in
America. From 1897 to 1921, he traveled extensively
throughout the United States, Canada, and Mexico,

lecturing on various aspects of Vedanta in almost every major American city.

As in London, he became acquainted with the American glitterati and intelligentsia: he was received at the White House by President William McKinley, met Thomas A. Edison and, at the home of William James, discussed at length the problem of "the unity of the ultimate Reality" with his host and professors Josiah Royce, Nathaniel Shaler, and Lewis Janes, chairman of the Cambridge Philosophical Conferences.[62]

Finally, in July of 1921, Abhedananda sailed for India from the port of San Francisco. In 1922, at the age of 56, the peripatetic pilgrim took his staff in hand and set off for Himis. "It had been my cherished dream all along to cross the Himalayas on foot," he is recorded to have said.[63] In his diary he wrote:

> In 1922. . . I went to Tibet from Kashmere, crossing the Himalayas on foot, to study the manners, customs and the Buddhistic philosophy and Lamaism which prevail among the Tibetan Lamas. I went along Yarkand Road, the highway to Europe and stopped at "Leh," the capital of Ladak, in Western Tibet. My destination was "Hemis Monastery" about twenty-five miles north of the City of Leh.[64]

Abhedananda recorded the events of his journey in *Kashmir O Tibbate* (in English, *In Kashmir and Tibet*). Here he writes that after a tour of the monastery he asked the lamas about the veracity of Notovitch's tale. It was then that he "learned from them that the account was indeed true."[65]

In Kashmir and Tibet is a curious book. It was

composed in stages, partly by Abhedananda himself and partly by an assistant who worked from his diary and original notes. According to Dr. Bagchi, after the journey Abhedananda returned to Calcutta and gave his notes to Brahmachari Bhairav Chaitanya, an attendant who accompanied him to Tibet. He asked Chaitanya to prepare an outline of his journey, which he apparently intended to develop into a travelogue.[66]

With the help of some standard references on Kashmir and Tibet, Chaitanya did so. But in the years that followed, Abhedananda was too busy to revise and expand the notes.

In 1927, the rough account appeared in serial form in *Visvavani,* the monthly organ of the Ramakrishna Vedanta Math (monastery), evoking considerable interest. Then, with the aid of his own notes and ancillary source materials, Abhedananda reportedly revised the entire work. In 1929, it appeared in book form and was entitled *Parivrajaka Swami Abhedananda,* later renamed *Kashmir O Tibbate.*

In 1954, fifteen years after Abhedananda's passing, it was edited by his disciple Swami Prajnananda and published in a revised second edition. It would appear that the book was not entirely revised by Abhedananda, inasmuch as in the section describing his verification of the document, Abhedananda is referred to in the third person as "Swamiji."

Despite the peculiar manner in which *In Kashmir and Tibet* was written, there is little doubt as to its message concerning the matter of Notovitch and his alleged find. The text unambiguously recounts the essentials of the Russian author's tale, including his convalescence at Himis with a broken leg,

Abhedananda's inquiry about Notovitch, and the lama's confirmation:

"The lama who was showing Swamiji around took a manuscript [about Issa] off the shelf and showed it to Swamiji. He said that it was a copy and the original was in a monastery at Marbour near Lhasa. The original was written in Pali, but this was a translation into Tibetan"[67]—all consistent with Notovitch's claim.

At Abhedananda's request, a lama helped him translate the text into English,[68] which was later translated into Bengali and published (along with excerpts of the English version of *The Life of Saint Issa* from Notovitch's *Unknown Life of Jesus Christ*) in *In Kashmir and Tibet.* Whatever skepticism Abhedananda may have had at the onset, after having gone to Himis, interrogated the lamas, and examined the document in question, he felt sufficiently sure of its authenticity to reprint selections from the Notovitch account in his own book.

With the exception of an excerpt from *The Unknown Life of Jesus Christ, In Kashmir and Tibet* was written in Bengali. To the best of our knowledge, the book has never been translated into English. In order to give our readers access to the basic documents needed to understand this issue, we have had the relevant portions of *Kashmir O Tibatte* translated into English for the first time—through the kindness and devotion of Prasan Kumar De, Per Sinclair, and Jayasri Majumdar.

Like Abhedananda, biographers Bagchi and Shivani had complete faith in the Notovitch story. Both stated, again using nearly identical words, that "those who have read this work and considered soberly its strange intriguing research, and which no scholar has been able to refute, may realize it was no idle quest" that led Abhedananda to undertake the trek to Himis.[69]

A third biographer, Ashutosh Ghosh, concurred. In *Swami Abhedananda: The Patriot-Saint* he wrote, "He reached the 'Himis Monastery' on the 4th October, and discovered a manuscript of the unknown life of Jesus Christ which was previously recorded by a Russian traveller, Nicholas Notovich, and with the help of a senior Lama he got a translated copy of the important portions of the life of Jesus and had it incorporated in Bengali in his book 'Kashmir O Tibbate.'"[70]

The chemistry between Abhedananda and the lamas at Himis was entirely different than that between Notovitch or Douglas and the lamas. Abhedananda was not a culturally distant journalist or professor. He was a disciple of Ramakrishna, a scholar, a preacher, a world traveler, and a one-time ascetic who lived for three months in a Himalayan cave at the source of the Ganges. He was too much a kinsman and too perceptive to be taken in by any "waggish monks," as Müller put it.

There are a few discrepancies, however, between Notovitch's and Abhedananda's version of the text, probably due to the fact that both have gone through numerous translations. The Pali original was first translated into Tibetan. It is not known in what language Notovitch first wrote down the verses as they were being translated to him—perhaps his native Russian or French. But we do know they were eventually published in French and later translated into English. The verses Abhedananda published had a similar odyssey: Tibetan, English, Bengali, and then back to English.

Abhedananda added a few details that are absent from the Russian's account, including a footnote which described how "Jesus halted at a wayside pond near Kabul to wash his hands and feet, and rested there for a while. That pond still exists. It is known as 'Issa-pond.' To mark the event, every year a fair is held at this place. This is mentioned in an Arabic book, *Tariq-A-Ajhan*."[71] Whether this indicates the existence of a different version or a more complete rendering of the same text it is hard to say.

Like Douglas, Abhedananda went to Himis for the express purpose of verifying Notovitch's story. Unlike Douglas, he claimed not only to have seen but to have written down verses translated by a lama from the same book that was read to Notovitch. Although this does much to authenticate Notovitch's story—especially the existence of the document and his faithful reproduction of its verses—it still falls short of conclusive proof. Abhedananda did not bring back either photos or a copy of the text. And he was entirely dependent on the lama for its translation from Tibetan.

More evidence was needed, and more evidence was forthcoming—this time from the able pen of Nicholas Roerich, a remarkable man who wrote extensively about Saint Issa's travels in the East. Between 1924 and 1928 he led an expedition through Central Asia—Sikkim, Punjab, Kashmir, Ladakh, Karakoram, Khotan, Kashgar, Karashahr, Urumchi, Irtysh, the Altai Mountains, the Oyrot region, Mongolia, Central Gobi, Kansu, Tsaidam, and Tibet. In the course of his journey he recorded the living history of Issa's sojourn in the East embodied in traditions cherished by peoples of various nations and religions across the vast expanse of Asia and discovered one or more manuscripts on the subject. His writings on Saint Issa are included in chapter 4 of this volume.

Born in St. Petersburg, Russia, on October 10, 1874, Roerich studied at the University of St. Petersburg and the Academy of Fine Arts. In 1898 he was appointed to a professorship at the Imperial Archaeological Institute and by 1920 he was already an internationally acclaimed artist.

Typically described in biographical notes as "a Russian-born painter, poet, archeologist, philosopher, and mystic,"[72] Roerich was also a diplomat, writer, critic, educator, set and costume designer, and explorer.

"Perhaps no traveler from the West has been better equipped, in knowledge, spirit and psychology to travel in the East," wrote Dr. Garabed Paelian in his study *Nicholas Roerich*. "Few, certainly, have gone there with higher motives, ideas of synthesis, service and the desire to find truth and beauty."[73]

Nicholas, his wife, Helena, and son George were the "main force" of his Central Asian expedition, which consisted of nine Europeans, thirty-six natives, and 102 camels, yaks, horses, and mules. They were accompanied during their journey through Sikkim by Roerich's other son, Sviatoslav, and a well-known scholar of Tibetan literature, Lama Lobzang Mingyur Dorje.

The expedition had many purposes. The principal objective was to create a pictorial record of the lands and peoples of Central Asia. During the trek, Nicholas Roerich painted 500 pictures, some of which have been reproduced in this book. The team had other goals as well—to study the position of

ancient monuments and the condition of contemporary religions, to trace the migrations of nations,
survey the possibilities for future archaeological
explorations, and obtain a far-reaching collection of
ethnographic and linguistic material on the culture
of inner Asia.

Because of his unique skills, George Roerich
made untold contributions throughout the journey.
He was a noted archaeologist and Orientalist trained
at Harvard and the School of Oriental Languages in
Paris, among other places, and by Lama Lobzang
Mingyur Dorje.

George had studied Persian, Sanskrit, Chinese,
and Tibetan. "This extensive knowledge of languages provides him with the key to the mysteries of
the 'closed land,'" wrote Louis Marin, former president of the Society of Ethnography, Paris, in the
preface to George Roerich's account of the expedition, *Trails to Inmost Asia,* published in 1931.

"Because of his knowledge of the languages
and customs of the countries," Marin continued,
"George Roerich visited Buddhist monasteries, usually completely forbidden to strangers; he discovered a complete collection of the sacred books of the
Bön-po religion, three hundred volumes, which constitute an inestimable treasure for the history of
religions and oriental research."[74]

In order to insure the success of the expedition,
George spent a year (1924) in Sikkim, in the Eastern
Himalayas, honing his language skills. "It was imperative to acquire a good speaking knowledge of
the Tibetan language before starting on a journey
which would require constant relations with natives," George wrote in *Trails to Inmost Asia.*[75]
Evidently the time was well spent because Nicholas

later wrote, "How wonderful that George knows all necessary Tibetan dialects."[76]

There was probably another though less official reason for the journey. Long before Leonard Nimoy led millions of Americans in search of all kinds of intriguing mysteries, Nicholas Roerich was searching for the factual realities veiled by the folk legends of the Orient. According to Garabed Paelian, Roerich believed, as did Pliny, that "one is led to truth through the interpretation of a myth."[77]

"In every city, in every encampment of Asia," said Roerich, "I tried to unveil what memories were cherished in the folk-memory. Through these guarded and preserved tales, you may recognize the reality of the past. In every spark of folklore there is a drop of the great Truth adorned or distorted."[78]

While traveling in Asia, he collected legends of a race of underground dwellers,[79] legends and factual evidence of the early migrations of Europeans (including the Goths and Druids) to and from Asia, stories of Solomon and his flying carpet, the coming of Maitreya, the legend of Shamballa and, of course, the legend of Saint Issa.

Professor Roerich's experiences on the expedition provided him with a wealth of material which subsequently appeared in numerous books. Three, in particular, concentrate on the expedition: *Himalaya* (1926), *Heart of Asia* (1929), and his travel diary *Altai-Himalaya* (1929) which, "more than almost any other book that has been written," observed a reviewer for *American Magazine of Art* (December 1929), "manifests the supreme dominance of beauty in the mind of a true artist, and indicates at one and the same time the simple greatness, the unique character of the author."[80]

Altai-Himalaya is an unusual work in that it is a series of observations by the author—notes "penned on horseback and in the tent"[81]—rather than a book with a formal organization or line of attack. In it Roerich wrote extensively about Issa's sojourn in the East because, among other reasons, he came across it so often, beginning in Kashmir at the very start of his journey.

"In Srinagar we first encountered the curious legend about Christ's visit to this place. Afterwards we saw how widely spread in India, in Ladak and in Central Asia, was the legend of the visit of Christ to these parts during his long absence, quoted in the gospel," he recorded in *Heart of Asia.*[82]

As the legend cropped up again and again—in Kashmir, Ladakh, Mongolia, Sinkiang, and other places—Professor Roerich "learned how widespread are the legends about Issa" and that the "lamas know the significance of these legends."[83] He heard several variations of the legend but in *Heart of Asia* noted that "all versions agree on one point, that during the time of His absence, Christ was in India and Asia."[84]

Professor Roerich found more than legends. He referred repeatedly to "writings" and "manuscripts." For example, while in Ladakh he noted, "The *writings* of the lamas recall how Christ extolled woman—the Mother of the World. And lamas point out how Christ regarded the so-called miracles."[85] (emphasis added)

An entry in *Himalaya,* which precedes a long quote from an ancient manuscript, reads: "Let us hearken to the way in which, in the mountains of Tibet, they speak of Christ. In the documents which have the antiquity of about 1500 years one may read: 'Issa secretly left his parents and together with the merchants of Jerusalem turned towards Ind to become perfected in the Divine Word. And for the study of the laws of the Great Buddha.'"[86] The story that follows is in many places nearly the same as Notovitch's *Life of Saint Issa.*

One long passage from *Altai-Himalaya,* recorded while Roerich was in Leh, is particularly noteworthy and poses some difficult questions.

Three items of information reached us in one day about the legends of Jesus. A Hindu said to us: "I have heard from one Ladaki official that *according to the words of the former Abbot of Hemis, there was a tree and a small pool in Leh beside which Jesus taught.*" (This is some new version about a tree and a pool, unheard before.)

The missionary says: "A nonsensical invention composed by a Pole who sat in Hemis several months." (One may ask why invented, when it coincides with other versions and proofs.). . .

A good and sensitive Hindu spoke meaningfully about the manuscript of the life of Issa. "Why does one always place Issa in Egypt during the time of his absence from Palestine? His young years of course were passed in study. The traces of his learning have naturally impressed themselves upon his later sermons. To what sources do these sermons lead? What is there in them of Egyptian? And why does one not see traces of Buddhism—of India? It is difficult to understand why the wandering of Issa by caravan path into India and into the region now occupied by Tibet should be so vehemently denied.". . .

. . . There are always those who love scornfully to deny when something difficult enters their consciousness; but then, knowledge is transformed into seminaristic scholasticism and slander is cultivated as a fine art. *In what possible way could a recent forgery penetrate into the consciousness of the whole East? And where is the scientist who could write a long treatise in Pali and Tibetan? We do not know such an one.*[87] [emphasis added]

Naturally, while in Ladakh Roerich visited Himis. But he found it to be a disappointing place where "one feels the strange atmosphere of darkness and dejection," where "black ravens fly above" and "the lamas are half-literate."

As a prelude to his comments on Himis, in *Himalaya* he noted:

Regarding the manuscripts of Christ— first there was a complete denial. Of course denial first comes from the circle of missionaries. Then slowly, little by little, are creeping fragmentary reticent details, difficult to obtain. Finally it appears—that about the manuscripts, the old people in Ladak have heard and know.

Then referring specifically to Himis, he continued:

And such documents as manuscripts about Christ and the Book of Chambhalla lie in the "darkest" place. And the figure of the lama—the compiler of the book—stands like an idol in some sort of fantastic headgear. And how many other relics have perished in dusty

corners?* For the tantrik-lamas have no interest in them. It was necessary to see this other
side of Buddhism.[88]

In sum, Roerich's writings do about everything
that can be done to establish the existence and authenticity of one or more documents that describe
Jesus' sojourn in the East, short of actually retrieving
one. He discovered the legend throughout Asia, preserved among peoples of varying lands and religions. He made numerous references to "writings"
and "manuscripts"—some of which he saw, others
of which people talked about—that said Issa had
traveled to the East. His reference to the Himis
manuscript lying in the "darkest place" is reminis-
cent of the stronghold of the "Dark Treasury" described by Tibetologists Snellgrove and Skorupski.
And he even recorded a story in which the head
abbot of Himis speaks of the legend.

Although there is no question that Roerich was
familiar with Notovitch's work, his sources of the
legend were his own. "Many remember the lines
from the book of Notovitch," he wrote while in Leh,
"but it is still more wonderful to discover, on this
site, in several variants, the same version of the legend of Issa. The local people know nothing of any
published book but they know the legend and with
deep reverence they speak of Issa."[89]

Moreover, while there is a resemblance between the texts that Roerich and Notovitch found
(sixty verses spread over ten chapters of Notovitch's
Life of Saint Issa are parallel to the text Roerich
included in *Himalaya*), Roerich published material

---

*We now see why it is entirely possible that the lama at Himis told
Notovitch he was not sure just where in the monastery the manuscripts about Issa were to be found (see p. 15).

about Saint Issa from manuscripts that were not reproduced by Notovitch.

Roerich recorded the pattern of the initial denial of the legend, followed by the emergence of
salient details, and then the open and frank discussion of the legends and/or manuscripts. He noted
that in Leh

> Issa communed. . . with the people on his way
> from Tibet. Secretly and cautiously the leg-
> ends are guarded. It is difficult to sound them
> because lamas, above all people, know how to
> keep silent. Only by means of a common lan-
> guage—and not merely that of tongue but also
> of inner understanding—can one approach
> their significant mysteries. One becomes con-
> vinced that every educated Gelong knows
> much. Even by his eyes one cannot guess when
> he agrees or inwardly laughs at you, knowing
> more than yourself. How many stories these
> silent ones can tell of the passing "savants"
> who have found themselves in the most ridicu-
> lous positions! But now has come the time of
> the illumination of Asia.[90]

Without question, Professor Roerich believed
the texts were authentic. When the historical reli-
ability was less certain, as in the case of some
material he published about Issa in *Himalaya,* he
made a point of it.[91]

Because of George Roerich's ability to speak
the various Tibetan dialects, the Roerichs had no
problem communicating in Ladakh, nor would they
have been dependent upon a lama at Himis for a
translation. Not to mention the fact that George was
more than capable of making an expert assessment
of such documents.

Finally, the eminent scholar of Tibetan literature Lama Lobzang Mingyur Dorje accompanied
the Roerichs for part of the journey. It is not clear
from the writings of either Nicholas or George if he
was with them at Himis—or wherever they found the
manuscripts—where he could also have offered an
expert opinion and warned them if the documents
were a fake or of questionable origin. And in the
unlikely circumstance that Professor Roerich had
published spurious manuscripts, no doubt the lama
would have spoken up and spared his friend further
embarrassment.

Did Nicholas Roerich discover the same document that Notovitch and Abhedananda claimed to
have found? We do not know. Roerich himself does
not specify. George Roerich, concentrating on scientific data, does not discuss the documents. If what
Notovitch allegedly found existed, it is possible that
Nicholas Roerich saw a copy of it. Or it is possible
that he found variant texts. Or both.

After the publication of the three books in
which he wrote at length about Issa's sojourn in the
East *(Himalaya, Altai-Himalaya, Heart of Asia)*,
Nicholas Roerich continued to refer to Issa here
and there in later works. But—and this is a turn of
events that would stop any detective in his tracks—
even though he wrote *more* extensively on the subject than Notovitch, Roerich was not fiercely
attacked in the press as the Russian journalist had
been when he first reported finding documentation
that Jesus had been to the East. In fact, to the best of
our knowledge, Roerich was not criticized at all by
reputable scientists, linguists, theologians, or even
newsmen.

When Roerich reported the discovery, the *Literary Digest* (September 1, 1928) treated it as an aside:

Professor Roerich has already sent back 250 of his Tibetan paintings to the museum in New York. . . . Two years ago, when the first consignment of these Himalayan pictures arrived, his admirers brought out a monograph about them, telling incidentally of documents he had found in old Buddhist monasteries in Tibet, which, he believed, furnished proof that Jesus had spent ten years studying in that part of Asia prior to His preaching in Palestine.[92]

And later when Penelope Chetwode—author of *Kulu: The End of the Habitable World* (1972)—dealt with the subject, she treated Roerich's "discovery" of a document about Issa as a rediscovery that was a bit old hat. She wrote:

In Tibet he claimed to have discovered an ancient Buddhist chronicle which stated that Christ had spent the 'hidden years' partly there and partly in India. This, in fact, was nothing new as there has always been a strong tradition that these were spent in Kashmir where a collection of Our Lord's sayings from this mysterious period of his life is still preserved: one of them was quoted by Akbar on his Victory Gate at Fatehpur Sikri: 'Said Jesus, on whom be peace! The world is a bridge, pass over it but build no house there. He who hopeth for an hour, may hope for eternity; the world is but an hour, spend it in devotion; the rest is worth nothing.'[93]

To be sure, the Roerichs met with their share of controversy. The British government suspected them of being spies, Henry Wallace (secretary of agriculture 1933–40, vice-president of the United

States 1941–45), who was once an ardent friend and supporter, became an enemy, and they had major legal battles. But the accusations never centered on the validity of Roerich's discovery of the legends or the writings which held that Jesus was in India and Tibet.

Even though Roerich was an eminent scientist, neither the academic nor the theological worlds stopped to reassess the theory that Jesus had gone to India. However, when Notovitch's *Unknown Life of Jesus Christ* was republished in 1926, the noted theologian Edgar J. Goodspeed wrote a critique of it in his book *Strange New Gospels.*

Goodspeed's book was published in 1931, time enough for him to have heard about both the Abhedananda and Roerich visits to Himis. Yet in his article, he mentions only that when *The Unknown Life of Jesus Christ* was first published, "the book called forth a vigorous controversy, attracting the attention of no less an authority than Professor F. Max Müller of Oxford. It was discussed at length in the pages of *The Nineteenth Century,* and then forgotten." Goodspeed noted Douglas' "annihilation" of Notovitch and also added some comments of his own by way of proving *The Life of Saint Issa* had to be a forgery.[94]

But there was no mention of the writings or adventures of Professor Roerich, who—if Abhedananda was somewhat of a remote figure to the author—was frequently the subject of articles in the *New York Times* and other major papers.

Then the story took an unexpected twist. Like a ghostly galleon sailing into the mists, the documents in question apparently disappeared. In an interview with Richard Bock, Abhedananda's disciple Swami

Prajnananda disclosed: "I heard from his own lips that he [Abhedananda] saw the scrolls [at Himis] and he translated from them. Years afterwards he inquired but they said the scrolls were no longer there. I also requested to see the scrolls, but there is nothing. There are no scrolls. They have been removed, by whom we do not know." Swami Prajnananda also said that the Pali original had been removed from the Marbour monastery in Lhasa, Tibet. [95]

The Bocks do not say what year Abhedananda made his inquiry. But just before he died on September 8, 1939, the ghostly galleon slipped out of the mist to make another brief appearance. This time in the presence of perhaps the sole surviving Westerner allegedly to see (and thus provide another glimmer of corroboration) the document in question—Elisabeth G. Caspari.

In the summer of 1939, Madame Caspari, a Swiss musician and professor of music pedagogy, and her husband, Charles, were on a pilgrimage to Mount Kailas organized and directed by a religious leader of considerable renown, Mrs. Clarence Gasque. Kailas—located in Tibet near the headwaters of the Brahmaputra, Indus, and Sutlej rivers—is famous in Sanskrit literature as Shiva's paradise and was a popular pilgrimage retreat.

The pilgrims took the same route as Notovitch, across the Zoji Pass, through Mulbekh and Lama-yuru, to Himis on their way to Mount Kailas. They planned to reach Himis in time to see the three-day festival held each year in commemoration of Saint Padma Sambhava.

In many ways their journey was not unusual. There is only one road that leads from Srinigar to Leh and, when traveling to Himis from that part of

India, that is the road that must be taken. Nor was it
unusual to arrive around the time of the annual
Himis festival, which is a major attraction. But there
was something unique about their journey that was
related to a spell of bad luck Notovitch said he
experienced.

The Russian journalist claimed that he took numerous photographs in Ladakh and throughout his
journey but lost them due to the carelessness of one
of his servants who had inadvertently opened the
box of exposed plates and destroyed them. Max
Müller made much of this "unfortunate" loss which
at the time could have proven Notovitch had
actually gone to Himis. Later, of course, Douglas
established that the Russian author did visit Leh and
possibly Himis, but as for the photographs—it would
take something of a miracle to get those back.

Well, now and then miracles do happen. Was it
Providence? Fate? or some other unseen force that,
in a manner of speaking, retrieved the lost photos
after the fact? Whatever it was, the Casparis took
pictures documenting the entire journey and recap-
tured the same scenes that Notovitch had witnessed—even pictures of the festival at Himis.

Mrs. Gasque was known internationally and
she and her party were most cordially received
everywhere they went throughout the pilgrimage. In
one case, an Indian maharajah literally rolled out a
red carpet to greet them. And at Himis, although the
travelers arrived just after the mystery play was
over, the lamas performed it a second time in honor
of their coming!

But that was not all. A few days after the
performance, when seated alone on the roof of the
monastery, Mrs. Gasque and Madame Caspari were

approached by the librarian of the convent and two other monks. They were carrying three manuscripts in ornate coverings, one of which the librarian ceremoniously unwrapped. He then presented Mrs. Gasque the parchment leaves and with great reverence said, "These books say your Jesus was here."

The manuscripts? Three books presented by the convent's librarian with the explanation that they said Jesus had been there?

While we have no reason not to take the monks at their word, unfortunately we do not know what the books said. They were written in Tibetan and neither of the two women asked for a translation. However, Madame Caspari did take a picture of the lama proudly displaying the book.

As an eyewitness, Madame Caspari's background differs considerably from that of Douglas, Abhedananda, and Roerich—all of whom were quite familiar with Notovitch's work when they made the journey to Himis. Although Madame Caspari had once heard it mentioned that Jesus had gone to India, it had long since passed from her mind. She was not aware of Notovitch's alleged discovery or of the publication of *The Unknown Life of Jesus Christ* in 1894, nor of the controversy that followed, or even of the subsequent writings on the subject by Swami Abhedananda or Professor Roerich. She did not come seeking the manuscripts in order to verify their authenticity or for any other reason. Plainly, the lamas took the documents from their safekeeping and brought them to the ladies on their own initiative.

Madame Caspari, now eighty-five years old, recently shared her recollection of her journey to the

Himalayas with us and has graciously given us permission to publish the pictures she and her husband took along the way—including the photo of the monk at Himis displaying the books which he claimed said "your Jesus was here."

Tibet was overrun by the Chinese Communists in 1950. Since the Chinese suppression of an uprising in 1959, virtually all the monasteries have been destroyed or converted to secular uses, while the lamas have been forced out of religious service.[96] If the Pali original of the text was still in Lhasa in 1959, it was probably confiscated or destroyed.

Ladakh is the last remaining refuge of Tibetan Buddhist culture. Because of its unique geographical position and some able diplomacy by at least one of the head abbots, the Himis monastery avoided destruction by various invading armies and became a repository for the books, paintings, statuary, costumes, and valued property of the other convents.

In 1947, Ladakh was closed to outside travelers by the Indian government because of military tensions with China and Pakistan. But it was reopened in 1974 and once again it is possible, for anyone who has the interest, to go to Himis "to see for himself" whether the documents actually exist—*if* they are still there.

A story like this is full of intriguing footnotes. U.S. Supreme Court Justice William O. Douglas traveled to Himis in 1951. Describing his experiences in *Beyond the High Himalayas,* Douglas noted:

Hemis, the first monastery in all of Ladakh, is still an ideal physical setting for a retreat; and over the centuries it has become rich not only in lands and other wealth, but in legends as well.

One of these apocryphal tales concerns Jesus. There are those who to this day believe that Jesus visited the place, that he came here when he was fourteen and left when he was twenty-eight, heading west, to be heard of no more. The legend fills in the details, saying that Jesus traveled to Hemis under the name of Issa.[97]

In 1975, Dr. Robert S. Ravicz, professor of anthropology at California State University, Northridge, made his first journey to Leh. Dr. Ravicz is a cultural anthropologist with a long-standing interest in South Asia and Latin America. On this and other visits to India and Ladakh, he lived for extended periods in monasteries and religious communities and observed the way of life of indigenous peoples—from their Buddhist practices, weaving and agricultural methods to their family life. He met with the Dalai Lama on three occasions and was familiar with the problems and aspirations of the people of Tibet.

On this particular journey he was conducting research on Tibetan refugees and, in the course of his investigation, visited Himis. While there, he was told by a friend, an eminent Ladakhi physician, that it was said there were documents at the monastery which stated that Jesus had been to Himis. This was news to Dr. Ravicz, who had never before heard, nor even suspected, that Jesus had traveled to the East.

Is it possible to do research at Himis? Yes, according to Dr. Ravicz, if one were dedicated. In his opinion, it would take at least several months for anyone to win the confidence of the lamas sufficiently to gain access to whatever manuscripts they might have. And then, in order to be able to read them, he would have to have a working knowledge of classical Tibetan.

Although Dr. Ravicz does not claim firsthand evidence of the books at Himis on the life of Jesus, he does bear witness to the oral tradition as told to him by a reputable citizen.[98]

Another footnote comes from Edward F. Noack of Sacramento, California, a world traveler whose greatest love is journeying to the forbidden lands of the East. Since 1958 he and his wife, Helen, have made eighteen expeditions to such places as Tibet, Nepal, Sikkim, Bhutan, Ladakh, Afghanistan, Baltistan, China, and Turkestan and have visited Leh four times.

Noack, age eighty-nine, is a fellow of the Royal Geographical Society of London and the California Academy of Sciences. His forthcoming book, *Amidst Ice and Nomads in High Asia,* is a record of his travels in the northwest frontier of Pakistan, Nagar, Hunza, the Wakhan corridor, and the rugged Pamir Mountains. Recently Noack told us that during his stay at Himis in the late seventies a lama at the monastery informed him that a manuscript describing Jesus' pilgrimage to Ladakh was locked in the storeroom.*[99]

And so, just before press time, the final testimony in this chapter of the case for Issa arrives on our desk from three independent, contemporary sources: a Supreme Court justice, a cultural anthropologist, and a seasoned traveler. None of them

_____

*Ravicz and Noack, both prolific photographers, have graciously allowed us to print some of their choice photographs—including the shot of the monk at Himis who told Noack of the Issa manuscript.

went to Himis on the trail of the story. But they were all told that Jesus had been there.

Three more clues at the end of a long search, the warmest pieces of evidence in our hands—evidence that has been unraveling for nearly a century...

Once again, imagine you are a detective. This time, it is not a yellowed folder, but a book that comes across your desk—this book.

Did Jesus go to India during the lost years? Are the manuscripts and reports of the lamas at Himis and the accounts of Notovitch, Abhedananda, Roerich, and Caspari accurate and authentic? Are there other explanations for these writings? Did Jesus spend the lost years in Palestine? Or Egypt? Or elsewhere?

In order to provide a few clues for your investigation and to assist you in drawing your own conclusions, we present to you herewith the work of Nicolas Notovitch, *The Unknown Life of Jesus Christ,* including *The Life of Saint Issa,* with the author's maps of his travels; the English translation of the key portions of Swami Abhedananda's *In Kashmir and Tibet,* together with his version of the text;* the reports and writings about Saint Issa collected in Nicholas Roerich's books *Himalaya, Altai-Himalaya,* and *Heart of Asia,* and sixteen of his paintings—some of which were painted while he was on his first Asian expedition; and finally the able testimony of Elisabeth Caspari on her chance discovery of the texts with supporting photographs that she and her husband took on their pilgrimage.

---

*In the writings of Nicolas Notovitch and Swami Abhedananda we have reproduced in this book, archaic spellings and punctuation have been updated where necessary to assist the reader.

THE ART OF NICHOLAS ROERICH

PORTRAIT OF NICHOLAS ROERICH   *1937*

THE MOUNTAIN SCHITROVAYA

PINK MOUNTAINS, HIMALAYAS

1933

MIDNIGHT

1925

THE WATCH ON THE HIMALAYAS

THE WALLED STRONGHOLD

1925

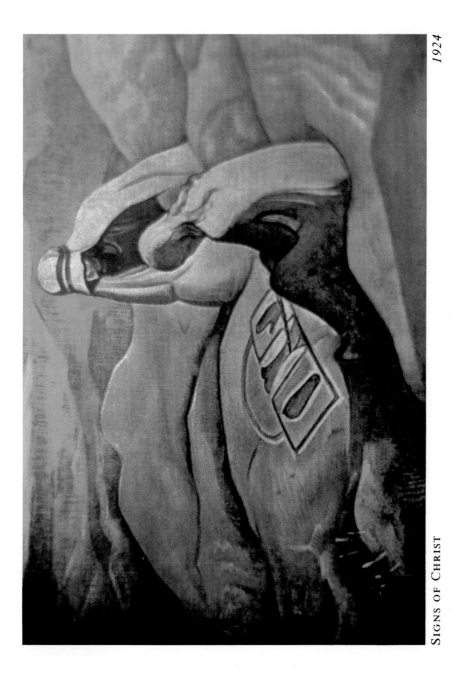

Signs of Christ

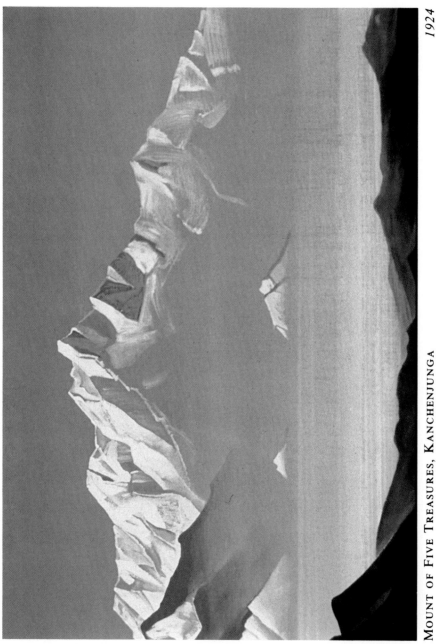

Mount of Five Treasures, Kanchenjunga

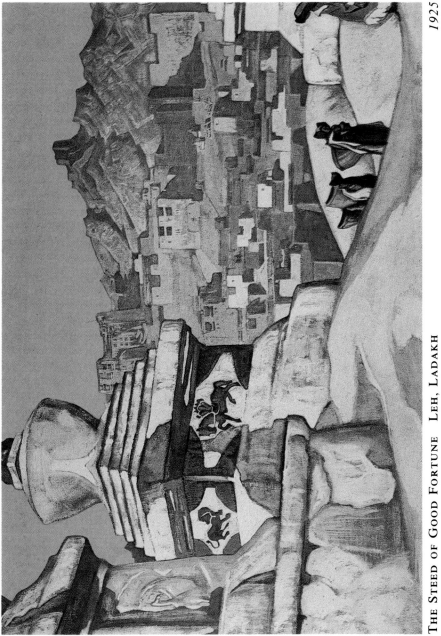

THE STEED OF GOOD FORTUNE   LEH, LADAKH

1925

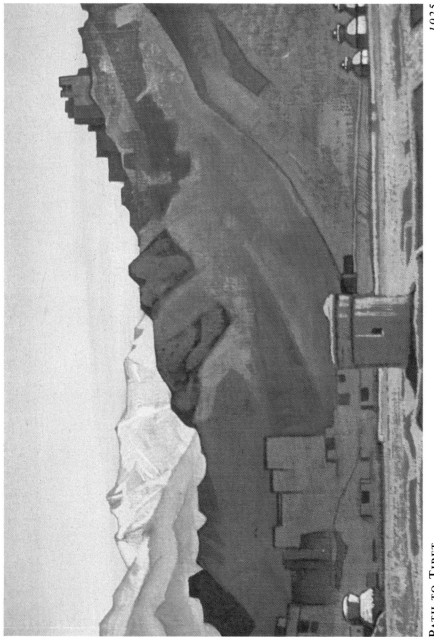

PATH TO TIBET   1925

TSAM IN MONGOLIA

TIBET

1933

REMEMBER

1924

1933

STAR OF THE HERO

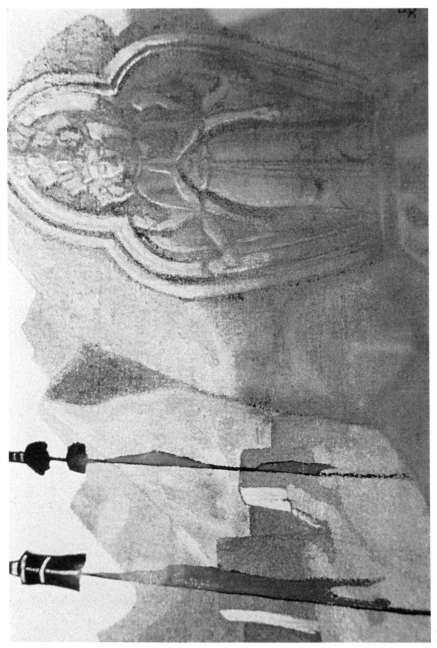

MAITREYA

Chapter Two

THE UNKNOWN LIFE OF JESUS CHRIST

Nicolas Notovitch's original work, including The Life of Saint Issa

NICOLAS NOTOVITCH

Translator's Note

IN translating the travels of Mr. Nicolas Notovitch in Thibet, *The Life of Saint Issa,* with the résumé and explanatory notes,* I desire to say that I in no way adopt or identify myself with the theological speculations, theories, or controversial points contained in this volume.

I accept in good faith the assurance conveyed to me by Mr. Notovitch that the "records" of Saint Issa were discovered by him at the convent Himis, but I guard myself from expressing any opinion as to the authenticity or veracity of the document now presented to the English reader.

I venture, however, to supplement the brief reference made by Mr. Notovitch to the curious resemblance which exists between the Catholic and Thibetan religions.

By reference to the *Biographie Universelle,* published at Paris in 1814, I find that Hippolyte Desideri, a Jesuit priest, visited Thibet in 1715 and Lassa (Lhasa) in 1716 and that he translated into Latin the *Kangiar* or *Sahorin,* a work which among the Thibetans has the same authority, so his biographer says, as the Holy Scriptures among the Christians. The biographer states that Desideri applied himself principally to studying the

*[not included in this volume—ED.]

similarities which seemed to him existent in the Christian and Thibetan religions.

The earliest known visitor to Thibet was Father Odoric of Pordenone, who is supposed to have reached Lassa about the year 1328. He was followed three centuries later by the Jesuit Antonio Andrada and in 1661 by Fathers Grueber and D'Orville.*

The first Englishman known to have entered Thibet was George Bogle, who, as ambassador of Warren Hastings, went in 1774 to the lama of Shigatse. Mr. Bogle remained in Thibet for some length of time but published no account of his expedition.

From a letter, however, of Mr. Stewart to Sir John Pringle† relative to his embassy, it seems clear that Mr. Bogle had himself been struck by the similarities which Desideri investigated, as will be seen from the following passages extracted from the *Encyclopaedia Britannica,* vol. 20, 1810, which I fancy do not appear in the more recent encyclopedias:

"It is an old notion that the religion of Thibet is a corrupted Christianity, and even Father Desideri, the Jesuit who visited the country about the beginning of this century (the eighteenth), thinks he can resolve all their mysteries into our own, and insists with a truly mystical penetration that they (the Thibetans) have certainly a good notion of the Trinity. . . . The truth is that the religion of Thibet, from *whatever* source it sprung, is pure and simple; in its source, conveying very exalted notions of the

---

*Encyclopaedia Britannica, 9th ed., s.v. "Tibet."
†Mr. Stewart to Sir John Pringle, *Royal Society of London Philosophical Transactions,* vol. 67.

Deity, with no contemptible system of morality, but in its progress greatly altered and corrupted by worldly men."

Du Halde translated the letters of Hippolyte Desideri from Italian into French,* and in one dated from Lassa, April 10, 1716, the priest writes: "As to their religion, they call God 'Konchok,' and seem to have a notion of the Trinity, for sometimes they name Him 'Konchokchik,' or the One God; at other times, 'Konchoksum,' or the Trine God. They use a kind of beads, on which they repeat Om, Ha, Hum. Om, they say, implies intelligence, or the arm—*id est,* power; Ha, the word; and Hum, the heart, or love; and that these three words signify God."

Grueber the Jesuit and Horace de la Penna, head of a Capuchin mission, pointed out the resemblance existing between the religion of the country and their own.† Their conjectures were founded upon: (1) the dress of the lamas, which is not unlike that of the apostles in ancient paintings; (2) their subordination, which has some likeness to the ecclesiastical hierarchy; (3) the resemblance between certain of their ceremonies and those of the Roman ritual; (4) their notion of an incarnation; and (5) their maxims of morality.

Gerbillon mentions some of their ceremonies, as: (1) use of holy water, (2) singing services, prayers for the dead, and adds: "Their dress is like that in which the Apostles are painted; they wear

*Charles Le Gobien, ed., *Lettres edifiantes et curieuses* [Edifying and curious letters], 2 vols. (n.p.: 1707–1709), bk. 15, p. 183.
†An account of these proceedings was published at Rome in 1742, entitled *"Relazione del principio e stato presenti del vasto Regno del Tibet ed altri due Regni consinanti."*

the mitre like bishops; and, further, their Great Lama, among them, is nearly the same as the Sovereign Pontiff among the Romanists."*

Grueber goes much farther: he affirms that although no European or Christian was ever there before,[†] yet their religion agrees with the Romish in all essential points. Thus they celebrate the Sacrifice of the Mass with bread and wine, give Extreme Unction, bless married couples, say prayers over the sick, make processions, honor the relics of idols (he should have said saints), have monasteries and nunneries, sing in the service of the choir like the Romish monks, observe divers fasts during the year, undergo most severe penances—among which whippings—consecrate bishops, and send out missionaries, who live in extreme poverty and travel barefoot through the deserts as far as China. "These things," adds Grueber, "I was an eyewitness of."[‡]

Even this wonderful combination of similarities is not all. Friar Horace de la Penna—who is not, however, so much to be trusted—says:

"In the main the religion of Thibet is the counterpart of the Romish. They believe in one God and a Trinity, in paradise, hell, and purgatory; make suffrages, alms, prayers, and sacrifices for the dead; have a number of convents filled with monks and friars,[§] who, besides the three vows of poverty, obedience, and charity, make several

---

*Jean Baptiste Du Halde, *History of China,* 2:263. Gerbillon travelled in 1688–98. *Dictionnaire de Géographie Universelle,* s.v. "Tibet."

[†]This seems an error of Grueber's, which was corrected by Thévenot, his collector.

[‡]Jean de Thévenot, "Grueber's Letters," in *Voyages de M. de Thévenot en Europe, Asie & Afrique* [The Voyages of M. de Thévenot in Europe, Asia & Africa], 5 vols. (Paris: Angot, 1689), 4:18 +.

[§]Desideri says they have the monastic life and the tonsure.

others. They have confessors, who are chosen by their Superiors, and receive their licences from a Lama or from a bishop, without which they cannot hear confessions* or impose penances. They use holy-water, crosses, and beads."†

Monsieur Huc, who travelled in Thibet in 1844–46, refers to the affinities between the Lamanesque worship and Catholicism:

"The cross, the mitre, the dalmatica; the cope, which the Grand Lamas wear on their journeys; the service with double choirs; the psalmody, the exorcisms; the censer, suspended from five chains; the benedictions, the chaplet, ecclesiastical celibacy, spiritual retirement, the worship of the saints; the fasts, the processions, the litanies, the holy-water—all these are analogies between the Buddhists and ourselves.

"Now, can it be said that these analogies are of Christian origin? We think so. We have indeed found, neither in the traditions nor in the monuments of the country, any positive proof of their adoption; still it is perfectly legitimate to put forward conjectures which possess all the characteristics of the most emphatic probability."‡

Reference to Pinkerton's *Travels,* vol. 7, under head "A Description of Thibet," will show that "several missionaries have imagined *that in the ancient books of the Lamas* some traces remain of the Christian religion, *which, as they think, was preached there in the time of the Apostles.*"§

---

*Andrada says they use a sort of confession among themselves.
†*Nouvelle bibliotheque* 14 (Jan.–Mar. 1743): 55 + .
‡ Everiste Regis Huc, *Travels in Tartary, Thibet, and China, 1844–1846,* trans. William Hazlitt (London: n.d.).
§St. Bartholomew. It is thought this apostle travelled as far as India to propagate the Gospel; for Eusebius relates that a famous philosopher

However that may be, and without entering on the debatable ground of affinities of rites, ceremonies, and observances which may have been pagan in their origin or Romanistic in inception, it may be urged for Mr. Notovitch, as a reason for admitting the genuineness of his discovery, that the two churches might in fact have had one common origin and that if in the time of the apostles—as contended by the missionaries—the Gospel was preached to the Thibetans, nothing is more natural than that the companions of Christ, who must have learned from him how and where the wonderful gap in his life was passed, should have desired to visit and did visit the scene of their Master's early labors. The limit of a translator's note prevents my entering into such discussion, and I leave the speculation to others.

I have translated *The Life of Saint Issa* literally but have taken more license with the personal part of Mr. Notovitch's narrative.

Violet Crispe

Hotel des Alps,
Lac de Genève, Territet,
February 1, 1895

---

and Christian named Pantaenus found there, among those who yet retained the knowledge of Christ, the Gospel of St. Matthew written out, as the tradition states, by St. Bartholomew, one of the twelve apostles. There is mention made of a Gospel of St. Bartholomew in the preface to Origen's *Homilies,* but it is generally looked upon as spurious and is placed by Pope Gelasius among the Apocryphal books.

To the Publishers

Sirs,

I am pleased to hear that you have decided on publishing a translation in English of my work, *The Unknown Life of Jesus Christ,* which appeared in French for the first time in the beginning of last year.

This translation is not a literal transcript of the French edition. Through unavoidable exigencies connected with its publication, my book was first brought out with an amount of haste which has been much to its detriment. I had only five days allowed me to draw up the preface, introduction, and résumé, and barely a few hours to correct the proofs.

This must account for a certain paucity of proof in support of some of my assertions, some gaps in the narrative, and many printers' errors which my adversaries have loudly proclaimed without perceiving that in their overrighteous zeal to lop off suckers and to draw attention to any blemishes in the bark, they only demonstrate their own powerlessness to attack the trunk itself of the tree I have planted, which defies the hardest blows to lay it low.

Indeed, they have rendered me a service for which I now tender my grateful thanks, as they have facilitated a rehandling of the subject which I should myself have deemed indispensable. I am always glad to avail myself of any information and am not so infatuated with the Oriental knowledge which I possess, not to be aware that I have still a great deal to learn.

The English public will, therefore, be the first to profit by those well-grounded criticisms which I have accepted and the corrections which I should have made spontaneously.

I thus offer to the English reader a book purged from all offense and free from any of the inexactness of detail with which I have been reproached so bitterly and with somewhat puerile persistence, as in the case of a certain Chinese emperor whose dynasty I had erroneously stated and whom I have relegated to his proper chronological rank.

It has been my aim and desire that the English public, whose intelligence is so keen but whose susceptibilities are always on the alert against any new thing, especially if it happen to be a religious novelty, should be able to judge of the work on its intrinsic merits and not from the grammatical or typographical errors on which my detractors have relied up to this moment to weaken the full import of my document. I hope, above all, that after having read the work it will be conceded that I have written it in perfect good faith.

I am well aware that a skillfully devised criticism has prejudiced the public beforehand against the book. And although generously defended by known and unknown friends, *The Unknown Life of Jesus Christ* has been so rancorously attacked by zealots who seemed to imagine that I desired to inaugurate a theological controversy (whereas my sole aim was to contribute another stone to the edifice of modern science) that it makes its first appearance in England enveloped in an atmosphere of mistrust.

Everything has been urged that could invalidate the authenticity of my documents. But the attack has been principally directed against the author, impugning his honor as a writer, doubtless in the hope that such insults would have the effect of disturbing his calm attitude and causing him to utter sentiments which would militate against the book itself.

I could treat injurious accusations with contempt: insults are not reasons, even when advanced in the tone of affected moderation which characterizes Mr. Max Müller's attempt to demolish me. But I shall, nevertheless, take up those which relate to my sojourn in Thibet, at Leh, at Ladak, and at the Buddhist monastery of Himis. I will first briefly resume the objections which have been advanced relative to the means of verifying the authenticity of my document.

It was objected: Why does the lama of Himis refuse to answer in the affirmative the questions which have been put to him as to the manuscripts? Because Orientals are in the habit of looking upon Europeans as robbers who introduce themselves in their midst to despoil them in the name of civilization.

That I succeeded in having these narratives communicated to me was because I made use of the Eastern diplomacy which I had learnt in my travels. I knew how to approach from afar the question which interested me, whilst everybody now asks point-blank questions.

The lama says to himself, "If these manuscripts are asked for, it is to carry them off," so he naturally holds aloof and refuses any explanation. This prudence is easy to understand when one remarks the procedure of those Europeans who, in contact with Orientals, only make use of civilization to plunder them and commit the most barefaced robberies.

A lady writes to Europe that I "have never been seen out there" and that no one has ever heard my name. Upon which the pack of janitors of the temple declare that I never set foot in Thibet; in other words, that I am an impostor.

A Moravian missionary, the worthy Mr. Shaw, repeats this little joke, which I must call childish; and then the seekers after Truth add his testimony to the rest and renew the insulting accusation. It is true that since then Mr. Shaw has loyally withdrawn it.

It costs me not a little to defend myself on this point, but I must not let the error go unrefuted and gain ground. If the English lady in question and her friends never came across me, I can cite Lieutenant Younghusband, whom I met at Matayan on October 28, 1887, and who was the first to cross China and ascend the Mustagh Pass at an elevation of 21,500 feet (English), also many others.

I still possess a photograph of the sympathetic governor of Ladak, Surajbal, with an inscription written in his own hand and which I reproduce in this volume.

I was even attended in my illness at Ladak by a European physician in the service of the English government, Dr. Karl Marx, whose letter of November 4, 1887, you have seen. Why not write directly to him to ascertain whether or not I was actually in Thibet, as they seem to desire so earnestly to prove the contrary? It is true that it takes some little time to write out and get a reply from Thibet; but still letters are sent there, and answers come back.

It has also been alleged that the manuscript of *The Unknown Life of Jesus Christ* never existed at all in the convent of Himis and that I simply evolved the whole from my imagination. This is indeed an honor I do not deserve, for my imagination is not so fertile.

If even I had been capable of inventing a romance of this magnitude, common sense alone would point out that I should have heightened the value of such an invention by attributing my discovery to some mysterious or supernatural intervention and should have abstained from stating precisely the locality, the date, and the circumstances of the discovery. In any case, I should hardly have limited my own share in the matter to that of simply transcribing certain old manuscripts.

I have also been held up to ridicule as a butt of the facetious lamas, as was the case it appears with Willfor and M. Jacolliot; that, not being sufficiently on my guard against certain Indian forgers who live by taking advantage of European credulity, I accepted as ready money—even as gold ingots— what was only some ingenious false coinage.

It is Mr. Max Müller who lays the greatest stress on this accusation. Now, as Mr. Max Müller enjoys a reputation in the scientific world, I owe it to myself and the public to refute him at a little greater length than the rest of my critics.

Mr. Max Müller's principal argument seems to consist in saying that the narrative of *The Unknown Life of Jesus Christ* as I have transcribed it in this book is neither to be found in the catalogued tables of the Tanjur, nor in those of the Kanjur.

I would here observe that if it were so, my discovery would be neither a curious nor a rare one, as these catalogues have long since been open to the investigations of European scholars and that the first Orientalist who chose to do so could easily have done what I did—go to Thibet, provided with his guidebook, and extract from the rolls of parchment the passages indicated by the catalogue.

According to Mr. Max Müller's own statement, these tables contain a list of about two thousand volumes only. Truly these be very incomplete catalogues indeed, the monastery of Lassa alone containing more than a hundred thousand, and I sincerely pity my adversary if he thinks this germ furnishes him with a key to the whole cycle of Eastern science.

The truth, indeed, is that the verses of which I give a translation in my book are probably not to be found in any kind of catalogue, either of the Tanjur or the Kanjur. They are to be found scattered through more than one book without any title; consequently, they could not be found in catalogues of Chinese and Thibetan works. They figure as mementos of a remarkable fact which took place in the first century of the Christian era and which the scribes amongst the lamas jotted down, according to the best of their recollection, with more or less of clearness or confusion.

If I have had the patience to join these verses,

the one to the other, arranging them in consecutive order to form sense and deducing from them what forms my translation, shall this work of patient labor be called into question?

Does not tradition inform us that the *Iliad*, as we have possessed it for 2,500 years, was constituted in this manner by order of Pisistratus from scattered chants commemorating the Trojan war and piously preserved in the memory of Greek creeds?

Mr. Max Müller further reproaches me with not having mentioned by name the cardinal of the Roman Church who honored me by curious confidences on the subject of *The Unknown Life of Jesus Christ* and whose frank utterances might be held to confirm my discovery. But I invoke the imperious laws of propriety, and everyone must own that in the circumstances I mention, it would not be seemly to disclose the cardinal's name.

I may, however, add to what I have already said in my introduction, as to having learnt from him that *The Unknown Life of Jesus Christ* is no novelty to the Roman Church, this: that the Vatican Library possesses sixty-three complete or incomplete manuscripts in various Oriental languages referring to this matter, which have been brought to Rome by missionaries from India, China, Egypt, and Arabia.

This question brings me to explain, once for all, my aim in handing over to the Western public a document of such importance, which, I confess, anyone has a right to criticize freely.

Was it to invalidate the authority of the Gospels and the whole New Testament? Not in the least degree. In the French journal *La Paix,* I concisely affirmed my belief in the orthodox Russian religion, and I hold to that affirmation. Invalidation could not exist without antinomy in doctrine and contradiction as to facts. But the doctrine contained in these Thibetan verses is the same as that of the Gospels, and the facts only differ in outward seeming.

Indeed, we should remark that the first who drew up these verses in the Pali tongue scrupulously reproduced the narratives of the indigenous merchants (not Jewish, as Mr. Max Müller will have it) on their return from Palestine, whither they had gone for their business and had happened to be at the time of the drama of Calvary.

There should be nothing astonishing in these witnesses seeing things from a different point of view to that of the Romans, who were ultimately to adopt the religion of their victim. It was only natural that they should, preferably, adopt the version which was current amongst the Jewish people.

What should be authenticated is whether these were impartial witnesses and whether the scribes faithfully and intelligently transmitted their sayings. But this is a question of exegesis, which it does not behoove me to settle.

I would rather restrict myself, and would advise my detractors to restrict themselves, to this simpler question: Did those passages exist in the monastery of Himis, and have I faithfully reproduced their substance? That is the only ground on which I recognize any honest right to provoke me to enter the lists.

I offered to return to Thibet in the company of recognized Orientalists to verify the authenticity of these passages on the spot. No one responded to this proposal. The greater number contented themselves with attacking me, and those who did make an attempt to find these passages set about it in the wrong way.

I learn, however, that an American mission is in course of formation, irrespective of any participation on my part, and is preparing to take this journey with a view of undertaking a serious enquiry for itself. I do not fear its investigations; on the contrary, I acclaim them with all my heart. This enquiry will demonstrate that, far from innovating, I have merely given a tangible form to a tradition that from all time has been afloat in the Christian world.

The New Testament is absolutely silent concerning that period of the Saviour's life which extends from his thirteenth to his thirtieth year. What had become of him during that lapse of time? What had he done? Show me any passage that will even approximately establish as a fact that he never did go either to Thibet or to India and I lay down my arms. But the most obstinate sectarians would have much difficulty in showing me such a passage.

Moreover, would it be strange if the founder of the Christian religion inspired himself with these Brahmanical or Buddhist doctrines with a view of transforming them, of purifying them from their dross and bringing them within reach of Western intelligences? Moses did not act differently. When he wrote Genesis and promulgated the law of justice, he referred himself to books and laws which were anterior to his own. He acknowledges this on several occasions. This is the ABC of exegesis.

Is it not invariably the case that all religions,

even the most barbarous and absurd, have ever preserved some fragments of truth and have possessed some opening by which integral Truth should one day enter—thus showing that their roots issued from a common stock and that after being subdivided into many branches, they would later on be gathered into one sheaf under a sole guardianship? Far from rejecting these shreds of truth without examination, Christianity hastened to adopt them by bestowing on them their true sense and adapting them to the mystic needs of nations.

If it were not so, would St. John the Evangelist have made so many efforts to appropriate the *Logos* of Plato and to transform it into that Eternal and Incarnate Word whose incomparable majesty has relegated to oblivion the highest conceptions of the Greek philosopher?

If it were not so, why should the Fathers of the Greek and Latin churches, St. John Chrysostom, St. Augustine (to quote only the most famous amongst them), have taken so much trouble to disengage from the medley and trash of mythologies those profound interpretations and moral teachings which they admit of—regenerating the fable, if I may be allowed this neologism, by restoring the myths to their true inner meaning?

I leave to experts the task of disengaging from Brahmanism and Buddhism the truths enshrouded in the parables of Sakyamuni and the Vedas.

To return to my book. I maintain that if it undeniably establishes an agreement between the teachings of the Gospels and those of the sacred books of India and Thibet, it will have rendered signal service to the whole of humanity.

Is it a new thing in the Christian world—a book

that aims at completing the New Testament and throwing light on hitherto obscure points? The works known as apocryphas were so numerous in the sixteenth century that the Latin Council of Trent was forced to curtail an immense number of them so as to avoid controversies that would have been hurtful to the interests of the public and to reduce the Book of Revelation to the minimum accessible to commonplace minds.

Had not the Nicene Council, with the Emperor Constantine's consent, already proscribed many manuscripts in the hands of the faithful, which were regarded by them with a veneration almost equal to that which they professed for the four canonical Gospels? The Nicene Council, in common with that of Trent, also reduced to a minimum the sum of transcendental truths.

Is it not on record that Stilicho, a general of Honorius, caused the Sibylline Books to be publicly burnt in the year 401? Can it be denied that these were full to overflowing of moral, historical, and prophetic truths of the highest order? That would be giving the lie to the whole of Roman history, whose most important events were determined by the decisions of the Sibylline Books.

In the times of which we speak, there was every motive for establishing or supporting a badly consolidated or already tottering religion, and the spiritual and temporal authorities believed that this could not be done better than by organizing a vigorous watch and an implacable censorship over eternal truths.

But enlightened minds were so little desirous of rejecting in a mass all documents that did not tally with official measurement that they themselves rescued a certain number from oblivion. In the last three hundred years those editions of the Bible which admit as appendices the Book of the Pastor of St. Hermas, the Epistle of St. Clement, that of St. Barnabas, the Prayer of Manasses, and the two complementary Books of the Maccabees are by no means rare.

The Four Gospels form the basis of Christian teaching. But there were twelve apostles. St. Bartholomew, St. Thomas, St. Matthias profess to have preached the glad tidings to the peoples of the Indies, of Thibet, and of China.

Have these friends of Jesus, these familiar witnesses of his preaching and his martyrdom, written nothing? Did they leave to others exclusively the office of transcribing on papyrus the sublime teachings of the Master? But these others wrote in Greek, and the Greek tongue was not heard or understood beyond the Euphrates. How could they have preached in Greek to men who only understood Pali, Sanskrit, or the multiplied Hindustani and Chinese dialects?

St. Thomas notably had the repute of being the most lettered disciple amongst his colleagues, who were mostly workingmen. In default of marble or brass, would not St. Thomas have engraved on imperishable tablets those things which he had seen, those lessons which he had learnt from the crucified Lord?

The verses which were communicated to me by the Buddhist lama of the monastery of Himis, which I put in their order of sequence so as to give them consecutive sense and render them conformable to the rules of literary composition, may have been actually spoken by St. Thomas—historical sketches traced by his own hand or under his direction.

May not this resurrection of books which have been buried under the dust of secular ages be the starting point of a new science which should be fertile in unforeseen and unimaginable results?

These are the questions which are raised by my book. Criticism would do itself honor by examining them seriously. The subject is well worth the trouble. It contains all the problems which agitate humanity. I am convinced that researches would not be fruitless. I gave the first blow with the pickaxe and revealed the hidden treasure, but I have reasons for believing that the mine is inexhaustible.

It is no longer today as it was in those past centuries when one class of men alone were depositaries of integral Truth and dispensed to the masses their share of indivisible property, each one according to his needs. Today the world is eager for knowledge, and everyone has a right to turn a page of the book of science and to know the truth concerning the Man-God who belongs to us all.

I believe in the authenticity of the Buddhist narrative because I see nothing that can contradict or invalidate it from a historical or theological point of view. Let it be studied and discussed. Let it even be proved to me that I am wrong. But that is no reason for insulting me. Insults only prove one thing—the impotence of their authors.

I have put into practice the words of the Prophet Daniel, that the time will come when "many shall run to and fro, and knowledge shall be increased." I have studied, I have sought, I have learnt, I have discovered. I hand over my knowledge and my discovery to those readers who, like myself, are desirous of learning and knowing.

I hand them over, through your agency, to the English public in entire confidence, and I defer beforehand to its verdict in the full conviction that it will be an equitable one.

Yours very truly,

N. NOTOVITCH

Preface

SINCE the Turkish War (1877–78) I have made a series of travels in the East. After having visited even the least remarkable localities in the peninsula of the Balkans, I started across the Caucasus in Central Asia and Persia and finally in 1887 left for India, which wonderful country had attracted me since my childhood.

My object in this journey was to become acquainted with the peoples of India, to study their manners and customs, and at the same time to investigate the grand and mysterious archaeology and majestically colossal nature of this marvelous country.

Wandering without any fixed plan from one place to another, I reached as far as mountainous Afghanistan, whence I regained India by the picturesque passes of Bolan and Guernai. I then reascended the Indus as far as Rawalpindi, travelled over the Punjab, the country of the five great streams, visited the Golden Temple of Amritsar, the tomb of the King of Punjab Ranjit Singh near Lahore, and directed my steps towards Kashmir, "the valley of eternal happiness."

There I recommenced my peregrinations as curiosity led me until I arrived in Ladak, whence

I had the intention of returning to Russia by way of Karakorum and Chinese Turkestan.

One day, in the course of a visit I made to a Buddhist convent on my route, I learned from the chief lama that there existed in the archives of Lassa very ancient records treating on the life of Jesus Christ and the nations of the West and that certain great monasteries possessed copies and translations of the same.

As it seemed then very improbable I should ever revisit that country, I determined to postpone my return to Europe to a later date and, *coûte que coûte,** to find these copies either in the great convents already mentioned or by going to Lassa. The journey to Lassa is far from being as dangerous and difficult as we are led to believe; it presented only such perils as I was well accustomed to and which would not have deterred me from attempting it.

During my stay in Leh, capital of Ladak, I visited the great convent Himis, situated in the environs of the town, whose library I was informed by its chief lama contained certain copies of the manuscripts in question. Not to awaken the suspicions of the authorities as to the object of my visit to the convent and to avoid any obstacles that might be raised to my further journeying in Thibet—I being a Russian—I made known my intention of returning to India and at once left the capital of Ladak.

An unfortunate fall from my horse, through which I fractured my leg, furnished me with a quite unexpected excuse for returning to the monastery, where first aid was given me. I profited by my

*[cost what it may—ED.]

short stay among the lamas to obtain the consent of their superior that the manuscripts relative to the life of Jesus Christ should be brought to me. Thus, aided by my interpreter, who translated from the Thibetan language, I was enabled to carefully write down in my notebook what the lama read to me.

Not doubting for one moment the authenticity of this chronicle, written with great precision by the Brahmanic and more especially Buddhistic historians of India and Nepal, I determined on my return to Europe to publish a translation of it. With this intent I addressed myself to several well-known ecclesiastics, begging them to revise my notes and to tell me what they thought of them.

Mgr. Platon, the celebrated metropolitan of Kiev, formed the opinion that this discovery was of great importance. Nevertheless he dissuaded me from publishing the memoirs, on the pretext that their appearance could only be prejudicial to me. In what way the venerable prelate refused to explain more fully. As our conversation took place in Russia, where the Censor would have assuredly put his veto on a work of the kind, I resolved to wait.

A year later, finding myself in Rome, I showed my manuscript to a cardinal who is *au mieux** with the Holy Father. He answered me textually as follows: "What would be the good of publishing this? No one will attach much importance to it, and you will make yourself a crowd of enemies. However, you are still very young! If it be a question of money which interests you, I might ask that a reward should be made to you for your notes, which should indemnify you for the expenses

*[on the best of terms—ED.]

you have incurred and the time you have lost."
Naturally I refused.

In Paris I spoke of my projects to Cardinal
Rotelli, whose acquaintance I had previously made
in Constantinople. He also opposed the publication
of my work, for the ostensible reason that it would
be premature. "The Church," he added, "suffers
already too much from the new wave of atheistical
thought. You will only give fresh pasture to the
detractors and calumniators of the evangelical
doctrine. I tell you this in the interest of all the
Christian churches."

Then I went to see M. Jules Simon. He found
my communication interesting and recommended
me to ask M. Renan's advice as to the best means
of publishing the memoirs.

The next day I was seated in the study of the
great philosopher. Our interview ended in this way:
M. Renan proposed that I should entrust him with
the memoirs in question, with the view of his making a report on them to the Academy.

This proposition was, as may be imagined, very
alluring and flattering to my *amour propre*.* Nevertheless I carried away my work on the pretext of further revising it. I foresaw that if I accepted this
combination, I should only have the honor of having
discovered the chronicle, while the illustrious author
of the *Vie de Jésus* would gain all the kudos through
commenting upon it and making it public.

Therefore, as I believed myself sufficiently
prepared to publish the translation of the chronicle
and to accompany it by my notes, I declined the very
kindly meant offer thus made to me. Not, however,
to hurt in any way the susceptibility of the

*[self-esteem—ED.]

great master, whom I deeply respected, I determined to await his demise, which sad occurrence I foresaw—judging from his enfeebled condition—could not be far off.

This prognostication having come true, I hastened to put the notes I now publish in order, reserving to myself the right of affirming the authenticity of these chronicles and developing in my commentaries the arguments which should convince us of the sincerity and good faith of the Buddhist compilers.

I suggest in conclusion that before criticizing my communication, any learned society can, at relatively small outlay, equip a scientific expedition having for its mission the investigation of these manuscripts on the spot and thus verifying their historic value.

NICOLAS NOTOVITCH

P.S. During my journey I took a considerable number of very curious photographs, but when on arrival at Bombay I examined the negatives, I found they had all become obliterated. This misfortune was due to the imprudence of my Negro, Philippe, to whom I had entrusted the box containing the plates. During the journey, finding it heavy, he had carefully removed the contents, thus rendering by exposure to the light all my labor useless.

I have therefore in illustrating my book had recourse to the extreme kindness of my friend M. d'Auvergne, who, having made a journey to the Himalayas, graciously offered me a selection from his photographs.

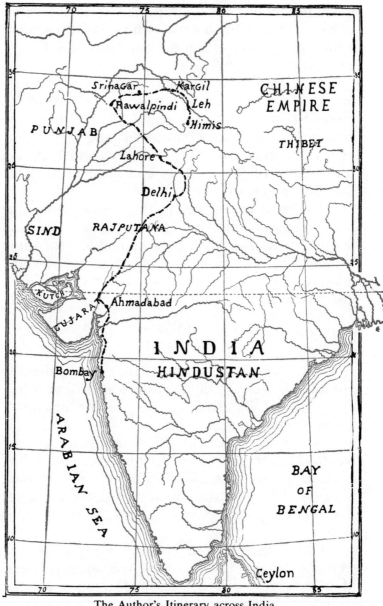

The Author's Itinerary across India

Journey to Thibet

DURING my sojourn in India I had frequent opportunity of conversing with the Buddhists, and the
accounts they gave me about Thibet excited my
curiosity to such an extent that I resolved to make a
journey into that comparatively unknown country.
With this object, I chose a route crossing the
province of Kashmir, a place I had long intended
to visit.

On October 14, 1887, I took my seat in a train
crowded with soldiers and started from Lahore for
Rawalpindi, where I arrived next day towards
noon. After resting a little and inspecting the town,
which, from its permanent garrison, has the aspect
of a war camp, I purchased such things as seemed
necessary for a campaign in districts not yet
reached by the railway.

Assisted by my servant "Philippe," a Negro of
Pondicherry whom I had taken into my service on
the warm recommendation of the French consul at
Bombay, I packed up my baggage, hired a *tonga*
(a two-wheeled conveyance drawn by ponies), and
having installed myself on the seat behind, set out
along the picturesque road which leads to Kashmir.

Our tonga made rapid progress over the
ground, though at one time we had to steer with

considerable dexterity through a large convoy of
soldiers, who, with their baggage carried on the
backs of camels, formed part of a detachment
returning from encampment to the town. We soon
passed the valley of the Punjab and, climbing a
path with endless windings, entered the zigzags of
the Himalayas.

Here the steeps became more and more
abrupt, the delightful panorama of the region we
had just traversed rolling behind us and becoming
engulfed at our feet. The sun had illumined the
mountaintops with its last rays when our tonga
gaily left the zigzags we had traced on the crest of
the wooded height, at whose foot nestles Murree,
a sanatorium always crowded in summer with the
families of English functionaries who go there to
seek freshness and shade.

Usually the tonga is available from Murree to
Srinagar; but at the approach of winter, when all
Europeans desert Kashmir, the service is suspended. I undertook my journey precisely at the
wane of the season, much to the astonishment of
the English I met upon the road returning to India,
who tried in vain to guess the object of my doing so.

The roadway being at the time of my departure still in course of construction, I hired saddle
horses—not without difficulty—and evening had set
in by the time we began our descent from Murree,
which stands at an altitude of 5,000 feet.

Our journey, along a dark road seamed with
ruts by the recent rains, was not a particularly
merry one, our horses having to feel rather than see
their way. As night fell, a storm of rain surprised us
while, owing to the thick oaks bordering our path,
we were plunged into such impenetrable darkness

that, for fear of losing sight of each other, we were obliged to shout out every now and again. In this profound obscurity we realized heavy masses of rock almost above our heads, while to the left, hidden by the trees, roared a torrent whose waters must have formed a cascade.

The icy rain had chilled us to the bone, and we had been tramping in the mud for nearly two hours when a faint light in the distance revived our energies.

Lights in the mountains, however, are but treacherous beacons. They appear to be burning quite close, when in reality they are far away and disappear only to shine forth anew as the road twists and turns—now to the right, now to the left, now above, now below—seeming to take pleasure in deluding the weary traveller, from whom the darkness hides the fact that his longed-for goal is really motionless and its distance becoming lessened every second.

I had given up all hope of ever reaching the light we had descried when it suddenly reappeared, and this time so near to us that our horses stopped of their own accord.

Here I must sincerely thank the English for the forethought they have displayed in building on all the roads small bungalows—one-storied inns destined to shelter travellers. It is true one must not expect much comfort in these semi-hotels, but that is a matter of small importance to the weary traveller, who is more than grateful to find a dry, clean room at his disposal.

Doubtless the Hindus in charge of the particular bungalow we had come across had not expected to see visitors at such an advanced hour of the night and at such a season of the year, for they had left the place and carried off the keys, necessitating our breaking open the door. Once inside, I flung myself on a bed hastily prepared by my Negro—boasting a pillow and a rug half saturated with water—and was almost instantaneously asleep.

At the break of day, after having taken tea and a small portion of our tinned meats, we continued our journey, bathed by the burning rays of the sun. From time to time we passed villages, at first in a splendid defile and then along a road which winds through the very heart of the mountains. We descended at last as far as the river Jhelum, whose waters flow smoothly amid the rocks by which their course is impeded and between two ravines whose summits seem almost to touch the azure vault of the Himalayan sky, here presenting an aspect remarkably cloudless and serene.

Towards midday we reached the hamlet of Tongue, situated on a bank of the river. It presents a unique row of cabins, having the appearance of cases open in front. Here eatables are sold and all kinds of goods. The place swarms with Hindus, bearing on their foreheads the diversely colored insignia of their castes. Handsome Kashmirians are also to be seen, wearing long white shirts and spotless turbans.

I hired here at a high price the Hindu cabriolet of a Kashmirian. This vehicle is constructed in such a fashion that to sit in it, one is obliged to cross one's legs *à la Turque,* the seat being so small that it is only just possible for two persons to squeeze into it. Although the absence of any kind of back renders locomotion somewhat dangerous, I nevertheless preferred this sort of circular table mounted on wheels to a horse, anxious as I was to reach my journey's end as quickly as possible.

I had not driven more than half a kilometer when I began seriously to regret the animal I had abandoned, so tired did I feel from my constrained position and the difficulty I experienced in maintaining my equilibrium.

Unfortunately, it was already late, evening had set in, and by the time I reached the village of Hori my legs were horribly cramped. I was worn out with fatigue, bruised by the incessant jolting, and utterly incapable of enjoying the picturesque scenery stretching before my eyes along the Jhelum, from whose banks rise on one side steep rocks and on the other wooded hills.

At Hori I met a caravan of pilgrims returning from Mecca. Believing me to be a doctor and hearing of my haste to reach Ladak, they begged me to join their party, which I promised to do after reaching Srinagar, for which place I started on horseback next day at dawn.

I passed the night in a bungalow, seated on a bed with a light in my hand, not daring to close my eyes for fear of being attacked by a scorpion or centipede. The place simply swarmed with them, and though I felt ashamed of the loathing they awakened in me, still I could not overcome the feeling. Where, indeed, is the line to be drawn between courage and cowardice in a man? I should certainly never boast of especial bravery, neither would I confess to want of courage; yet the repulsion with which these obnoxious little creatures inspired me banished sleep from my eyelids, in spite of my extreme fatigue.

At daybreak our horses were making their way

at a gentle trot along a level valley enclosed by high hills and, bathed as I was by the sun's hot rays, I very nearly fell asleep in my saddle. A sudden sense of freshness awakening me, I perceived we were beginning to ascend a mountain path through a vast forest which at times opened out, allowing us to admire at leisure the magnificent course of an impetuous torrent, and at others hid from our gaze the mountains, the sky, and the entire landscape, leaving us *en revanche** the songs of a crowd of birds with spotted plumage.

We emerged from the forest towards midday, descending as far as a little hamlet by the riverside where we lunched before continuing our journey. Here I visited the bazaar and tried to buy a glass of warm milk from a Hindu, whom I found squatting before a large pail of the boiling beverage. My surprise may be imagined when this individual proposed I should carry off the pail with its contents, affirming that I had contaminated the same.

"I only want a glass of the milk, not the pail," I protested. But the Hindu remained obdurate.

"According to our laws," he insisted, "if anyone not belonging to our caste looks fixedly and for a length of time on any object or eatable belonging to us, it is our duty to wash the object and to throw the food into the street. Thou, O sahib! hast polluted my milk. No one shall further drink of it; for not only hast thou fixed it with thine eyes, but thou hast pointed at it with thy finger."

This was quite accurate. In the first instance I had carefully examined the milk to find out if it were genuine, and I had, moreover, pointed to the pail from which I wished the man to fill me a glass.

*[in return; in compensation—ED.]

Full of respect for foreign laws and customs, I paid without demur the rupee demanded—the price of all the milk the merchant had emptied into the gutter—though I had only benefited by one glass of it. From this incident I learned a lesson—never to fix my eyes upon Hindu food again.

There is no religious belief more entangled with ceremonies, laws, and commentaries than Brahmanism. Whilst each of the three principal religions has but one Bible, one Testament, and one Koran—books from which the Jews, Christians, and Muhammadans draw their beliefs—the Brahmanical Hindus possess so great a number of commentaries in folio that the most learned Brahman has rarely had time to master more than a tenth part of them.

Putting on one side the four books of the Vedas; the Puranas, written in Sanskrit and containing 400,000 stanzas relating to theogonies, law, medicine, and the creation, destruction, and regeneration of the world; the vast Shastras, treating on mathematics, grammar, etc.; the Oupo-vedas, Oupanichadas, and Oupo-puranas, serving as indices to the Puranas; and a crowd of other many-volumed commentaries, there still remain the twelve exhaustive books containing the laws of Manu, grandson of Brahma, books dealing not only with the civil and penal laws but also the canonical rules, which impose on their adepts such an amazing number of ceremonies that one is lost in wonder at the unchangeable patience of the Hindus in their observance of the precepts dictated to them by their saint.

Manu was indisputably a great legislator and a great thinker, though he has written so exhaustively that it happens sometimes that he contradicts himself in the course of a page. The Brahmans do not take the trouble to remark this, however; and the poor Hindus, on whose labor their caste virtually subsists, obey them with servility, taking as gospel their mandates never to touch a man belonging to another caste and never to countenance a stranger fixing his attention on their goods.

Keeping to the strict sense of this law, the Hindu imagines his merchandise contaminated if on the part of a stranger it has been subjected to any particular scrutiny. And yet Brahmanism was, even at the commencement of its second birth, a religion purely monotheistic, recognizing but one eternal and indivisible God.

As has happened since all time and in all religions, the clergy have taken advantage of their privileged position above the ignorant crowd to hastily devise different laws and external forms of worship, thinking thus to act more surely on the masses—the result being that the principle of monotheism, so clearly instilled by the Vedas, has degenerated into a limitless series of absurd gods, goddesses, demigods, genii, angels, and devils, represented by idols, diverse in form and horrible without exception.

The people, once great, even as their religion was pure and elevating, have now degenerated into a condition bordering on idiocy, slaves as they are to the performance of those rites which the day is scarce long enough to enumerate.

One may positively assert that the Hindus merely exist to support the principal sect of Brahmans, who have taken into their hands the temporal power formerly enjoyed by the independent sovereigns of the people. In their government of

India, the English do not interfere with this side of public life, and the Brahmans take advantage of this in encouraging in the nation the hope of a different future.

But to return to our journey. The sun had sunk behind the summit of a mountain, and the shades of night had suddenly enveloped the country we were traversing. Soon the narrow valley through which the Jhelum flows seemed to have fallen asleep, while our path, winding along a contracted corniche of peaked rocks, gradually became hidden from our eyes. Mountains and trees became blended in a single somber mass, and the stars shone out brightly overhead.

We were eventually obliged to dismount and to grope our way along the side of the mountain for fear of becoming victims to the abyss yawning at our feet. At an advanced hour of the night, we crossed a bridge and climbed the peaked ascent which leads to the bungalow of Uri, perched on its height in complete isolation.

The next day we traversed a charming region, almost skirting the river, at a turn of which we saw the ruins of a Sikh fortress standing solitary and as if meditating in sadness on the glory of its past. In a little valley enclosed in the midst of the mountains we came upon another friendly bungalow, in whose close proximity lay the encampment of a cavalry regiment of the maharajah of Kashmir.

Hearing of my Russian nationality, the officers invited me to mess with them, and I had the opportunity of making the acquaintance of Colonel Brown, who was the first to compile a dictionary in the Afghan-Pushtu language.

Being anxious to reach Srinagar as soon as

possible, I continued my journey through a picturesque region which, after having for a considerable time followed the course of the river, spread out at the foot of the mountains. Before our eyes, wearied by the monotony of the preceding landscape, a well-populated valley now disclosed itself with two-storied houses surrounded by gardens and cultivated fields. A little further on commences the celebrated Vale of Kashmir, situated behind a range of high hills, which I crossed towards evening.

By the time I had reached the summit of the last elevation separating the mountainous country I had just been traversing from the valley, a superb panorama met my gaze. The picture it formed was a truly enchanting one. The Kashmirian vale, whose limits are lost in the horizon and which throughout is thickly peopled, nestles amid the high mountains of the Himalayas. At sunrise and sunset the zone of the eternal snows appears like a ring of silver, girding this rich and charming plateau, seamed in all directions by fine roadways and streams.

Gardens, hills, a lake whose numerous islets are covered with bizarre constructions, all conspire to transport the traveller into another world. For him the limits of enchantment seem reached, and he believes himself at last in the paradise of his childhood's dreams.

The shades of night were slowly falling—merging mountains, gardens, and lakes in one somber mass, pierced only by distant lights like stars—when I descended into the valley, directing my steps towards the Jhelum which has here traced for itself, to unite its waters with those of the Indus, a passage through a narrow defile in the midst of the mountains. According to legend, the valley was once a kind of inland sea, which a passage opening between two rocks had dried up, leaving only in its place the lake, a few pools, and the Jhelum, whose banks are now lined with a number of long, narrow vessels inhabited all the year round by the families of their proprietors.

From here Srinagar may be reached in one day's journey on horseback, while the journey by boat takes a day and a half. I decided upon the latter means of conveyance, and after having chosen a canoe and struck a bargain with its owner, I installed myself comfortably at the prow on a carpet, protected by a kind of awning.

The boat left the shore at midnight, bearing us rapidly towards Srinagar. At the other end of the bark a Hindu prepared tea for me, and before long I fell asleep, well satisfied at the thought that my journey was progressing the while.

I was awakened by the warm caress of the sun's rays creeping in through the tent, my first impression of the surrounding scene being an indescribably delightful one. The banks of the river were green, the distant outlines of the mountain summits snow-covered, the villages picturesque, and the surface of the water crystalline.

I imbibed with avidity the air, which was peculiarly rarefied and delicious, listening all the while to the warbling of a myriad of birds who were soaring above in the cloudless serenity of the sky. Behind me plashed the water, swished by a pole wielded with ease by a superb woman with marvelous eyes, skin browned by the sun, and mien full of stately indifference.

The dreamy enchantment of the scene had a

mesmeric effect upon me. I forgot the reason for my presence on the river, and at that moment, in the excess of my well-being, I had not even the desire to attain the end of my journey. And yet how many privations there remained for me to undergo and dangers to encounter!

The canoe glided rapidly, the landscape ever unfolding before my eyes, losing itself behind the confines of the horizon, merging itself and becoming one with the mountains we had passed. Then a fresh panorama would spread out, seeming to roll from the sides of the mountains, which every moment appeared to increase in size. Twilight set in and I was not yet tired of contemplating this splendid nature, whose vision had awakened in me the happiest memories.

As one nears Srinagar, villages embowered in verdure become more and more numerous. At the approach of our boat the scanty inhabitants hurried out to see us, men and women attired alike in long garments reaching to the ground—the former turbaned, the latter wearing caps, the children being in a state of nudity.

At the entrance of the city one sees a line of barks and houseboats, in which whole families reside. The summits of the far-off snowcapped mountains were caressed by the last rays of the setting sun when we glided between the two rows of wooden houses which border the banks of the river at Srinagar.

Business life seems to cease here at sunset. Thousands of multicolored boats *(dunga)* and palanquined barks *(bangla)* were moored along the shores, where natives of both sexes, in the primitive costumes of Adam and Eve, were engaged in the performance of evening ablutions, a sacred rite far exceeding in their eyes all human prejudices.

On October 20, I awoke in a clean little room with a bright outlook on the river, which then lay shimmering in the Kashmirian sunshine. As it is not my intention to describe here minute details of my journey, I will not attempt to enumerate the wonders of this beautiful spot with all its lakes, enchanting isles, historic palaces, mysterious pagodas, and coquettish villages: the latter lie half hidden in vast gardens, while on all sides rise the majestic summits of the gigantic Himalayas, covered as far as eye can see with their white shroud of the eternal snows. I shall merely note the preparations I made in view of my further journeying towards Thibet.

I passed in all six days at Srinagar, making long excursions in its enchanting environs, examining the numerous ruins which testify to the ancient prosperity of the region, and studying the curious customs of the country.

Kashmir, as well as the other provinces attached to it, such as Baltistan, Ladak, etc., are vassals of England. Formerly they formed part of the possessions of the "Lion of the Punjab," Ranjit Singh. At his death, the English troops occupied Lahore, the capital of the Punjab, separated Kashmir from the rest of the empire, and ceded it, under the title of hereditary right and for the sum of 160,000,000 francs, to Ghulab Singh, one of the intimates of the defunct sovereign—conferring on him, moreover, the title of maharajah. At the time of my journey, the reigning maharajah was Pertab Singh, the grandson of Ghulab, whose residence is at Jammu on the southern slope of the Himalaya.

The celebrated Happy Valley of Kashmir—
eighty-five miles long and twenty-five miles wide—
was at the height of its glory and prosperity under
the Grand Mogul, whose court loved to taste here,
in the pavilions on the islets of the lake, the plea-
sures of a rural life. Most of the maharajahs of
Hindustan came here to while away the summer
months and at the same time to take part in the
magnificent fêtes given by the Grand Mogul.

Time has now changed the aspect of the
"Happy Valley." It is a happy valley no longer:
weeds cover the limpid surface of the lake, the wild
juniper runs riot over the isles, stifling all other
vegetation, and the palaces and pavilions are but
grass-grown ruins, the ghosts of their former grandeur.

The mountains around seem invaded by the
universal gloom and yet to instill a hope that better
times may yet surround their immortal beauties.
The inhabitants, once handsome, intelligent, and
cleanly, have degenerated into a half-idiotic condition. They are both idle and dirty, and the whip
governs them now and not the sword.

The people of Kashmir have had so many
different masters and have been so often exposed
to pillage and inroads of various kinds that with
time they have grown apathetic to all things. They
spend their days near their mangals,* gossiping with
their neighbors, or occupying themselves either with
the minute work of their famous shawls or the
execution of filigree designs in gold or silver.

The Kashmirian women are melancholic, their
features marked with ineffable sadness. Misery and
filth reign everywhere, the fine men and superb

*small stoves filled with burning wood

women going about dirty and in rags. The costumes of both sexes consist, in winter as in summer, of a long, full-sleeved shirt made of thick material. This shirt is not discarded until it is completely worn out, and never by any chance is it washed, so that the snowy turbans of the men look dazzlingly white in comparison with these dirty grease-stained garments.

A great sadness fills the traveller at the contrast formed between the richness and opulence of the surrounding nature and the miserable condition of the people, clad in rags.

The capital of the country, Srinagar (the City of the Sun), or, to call it by the name it bears here after the country, Kashmir, is situated on the banks of the Jhelum, along which it extends southwards for a distance of five kilometers. Its two-storied houses, occupied by a population of 132,000 inhabitants, are built of wood and border both sides of the Indus. The town is not more than two kilometers wide and everyone lives on the river, whose banks are united by ten bridges.

Footpaths lead down from the houses to the water's edge, where all day long ablutions are performed, baths taken, and the household utensils—consisting generally of two or three copper pitchers—washed. Part of the inhabitants practice the Muhammadan religion, two-thirds are Brahmans, and there are but few Buddhists to be found among them.

The time soon drew near for me to make preparations for my next venture into the unknown. I laid in a store of tinned goods, some cases of wine, and other things indispensable for a journey across so uninhabited a country as Thibet. I had all these items packed up in boxes, hired ten carriers and a chicari, bought a horse for my own use, and fixed the day of my departure for October 27.

To enliven my journey I took with me, through the kindness of M. Peychaud, a Frenchman, the cultivator of the maharajah's vineyards, a splendid dog who had previously travelled across the Pamir with my friends Bonvalot, Capus, and Pepin, the well-known explorers.

Having chosen a route which would shorten my journey by two days, I sent on my coolies at dawn from the other side of the lake, which I crossed in a boat, joining them later on at the foot of the chain of mountains separating the valley of Srinagar from the gorge of Sind.

Never shall I forget the tortures we endured in climbing almost on all fours to a summit 3,000 feet high. The coolies were breathless, and every moment I feared lest I should see one of them roll down the steep with his burden. My heart ached at the sad spectacle offered by my poor dog Pamir, who, with protruding tongue, at last gave a low moan and sank exhausted to the ground. I forgot my own extreme fatigue in stroking and encouraging the poor beast, who, as if understanding me, struggled to his feet, only to fall again a few paces further on.

Night had come when we reached the summit of the height, where we threw ourselves greedily upon the snow in the hope of quenching our thirst. After a short halt we commenced our descent through a very thick pine forest, hastening to gain the village of Haïena at the foot of the defile before the advent of the beasts of prey.

A level, well-kept road leads from Srinagar to

Haïena, straight to the north by Ganderbal, where, after having skirted the Sind and traversed the superbly fertile country extending as far as Kangra, it turns abruptly to the east. Six miles further on it approaches the village of Haïena, whither I had directed my steps by a more direct route across the pass already mentioned, which considerably shortened for me both time and distance.

My first step in the unknown was marked by an incident, causing us all to pass a *mauvais quart d'heure.** The defile of Sind, sixty miles long, is above all famed for its inhospitable inmates, among whom are found panthers, tigers, leopards, black bears, wolves, and jackals. As if for our express discomfiture, the snow had just covered with its white carpet the heights of the chain, thus obliging these formidable and carnivorous inhabitants to descend a little lower to seek shelter in their dens.

We followed in silence a narrow path in the darkness, winding between ancient firs and birches, the sound of our footsteps alone breaking through the calm of the night. Suddenly, in close proximity to us, a terrible howling broke upon the silence of the wood. Our little band came to an abrupt standstill. "A panther!" whispered my servant, with voice trembling with fear, the other coolies remaining motionless and as if riveted to the spot.

At this juncture I remembered that during the ascent, having felt tired out, I had entrusted my revolver to one of the carriers and my Winchester rifle to another. I now felt a sharp pang of regret at having parted with either, asking in a low voice where the man was to whom I had given the rifle.

*[bad quarter hour; an uncomfortable though brief experience—ED.]

The howls had become more and more violent, awakening the echoes of the silent wood, when suddenly a dull thud was heard, like the fall of a body. Almost instantaneously we were thrilled with the noise of a struggle and the cry of a man in agony, mingled with the hoarse howling of some famished beast.

"Sahib, take the gun," I heard close to me. I feverishly seized hold of my rifle, but it was only *peine perdue,** for I could not see two steps before me. A fresh cry followed by a smothered howling gave me a slight clue to the scene of the struggle and I groped my way on, divided between my desire "to kill a panther" and to save, if possible, the life of the victim whose cry had reached our ears, and the horrible fear of being lacerated in my turn.

My followers were all paralyzed with fright, and it was only after five long minutes that I succeeded—remembering the dislike wild beasts have for fire—in inducing one of them to strike a match and set light to a heap of brushwood. We then saw about ten steps ahead of us, stretched out on the ground, one of our coolies, whose limbs had been literally torn to pieces by the claws of a superb panther who, standing motionless, yet held a portion of flesh in his jaws. At its side gaped a case of wine that had been completely broken open.

Hardly had I time to raise the rifle to my shoulder when the panther reared and, turning upon us, let go a part of its horrible meal. For one instant it seemed on the point of springing upon me, when suddenly it wheeled round and, uttering a howl enough to freeze the blood in one's veins,

*[to no avail—ED.]

sprang into the midst of the thicket and disappeared before our eyes.

My coolies, whom abject fear had kept pros-
trated all this time on the ground, now recovered
somewhat from their fright. Keeping in readiness
bundles of twigs and matches, we hurried on in the
hope of gaining Haïena, abandoning the remains
of the unfortunate Hindu for fear of becoming victims to a similar fate.

An hour later we had left the forest and
entered the plain. There I had my tent pitched
under a thickly foliaged plane tree, ordering at the
same time a large fire to be lit—the only means we
possessed of keeping at bay the wild beasts whose
terrific howlings came from all directions. My dog,
with drooping tail, had kept close to me all the time
in the forest; but once under the tent, he suddenly
regained his valor and all night long he barked
without cessation, not however once daring to
venture his nose outside.

The night for me was an awful one. I spent it
rifle in hand, listening to the concert of fearful
howls whose funereal echoes filled the defile. Several panthers approached our bivouac, attracted by
Pamir's barking, but the fire kept them off and
they made no attempts against us.

I had left Srinagar at the head of eleven coolies, four of whom were laden with so many cases
of wine and stores, four with my personal belong-
ings, one with my firearms, another with various
utensils, while the province of the last of all was
to act as scout. This individual bore the title of
"chicari," which signifies "he who accompanies the
hunter to pick up the game."

I discharged him after our night in the defile

because of his extreme cowardice and absolute ignorance of the country, and at the same time I gave six of the coolies notice to quit, retaining only four with me and replacing the others on arrival at the village of Gund by horses. Later on I took another chicari into my service, who fulfilled the role of interpreter and who had been highly recommended to me by M. Peychaud.

How beautiful is nature in the gorge of Sind and how justly well beloved by all sportsmen! Besides wild beasts, stags are to be met, hinds, wild sheep, and a great variety of birds, among which may be especially mentioned the golden, red, and snow-white pheasants, large partridges, and immense eagles.

The villages situated along the Sind are not conspicuous for their dimensions. Generally they consist of from ten to twenty cottages of miserable aspect, their inhabitants going about in rags and tatters. The cattle belong to a very small breed.

Having passed the river at Sumbal, I stopped near the village of Gund to procure horses. Whenever it happened that these useful quadrupeds were refused me, I always began playing about with my whip, which had the instantaneous result of inspiring obedience and respect, while for the rest a little money procured extreme servility and the immediate execution of my smallest orders.

The stick and the rupee are the true sovereigns of the East. Without them the Grand Mogul himself would have been of no importance.

Before long, night fell and I hastened to cross the defile which separates the villages of Gogangan and Sonamarg. The road is in a very bad condition and infested by wild beasts, who come out at night in search of prey, penetrating even into the villages. Panthers abound and, for fear of their ravages, few people dare take up their abode in this district, beautiful and fertile though it is.

At the outlet of the defile, near the village of Tchokodar or Thajiwas, I distinguished in the semi-obscurity two dark forms crossing the road. They turned out to be a couple of bears, followed by a young one.

As I was alone with my servant at the time (we having gone before the caravan), I did not feel in a particular hurry to confront them with only one rifle. My sportsman's instinct, however, had become so strongly developed by my long excursions among the mountains that I could not resist the temptation of a rencontre. To jump from my horse, aim, fire and, without even marking the result, to quickly reload my gun was the affair of a second.

At this juncture one of the two bears was on the point of bounding upon me, when a second shot caused him to turn tail and disappear. Holding my gun reloaded in my hand, I then approached with circumspection the spot I had aimed at, to find there the other bear lying on its flank with the little cub gambolling beside it. Another shot laid the young one low, whereupon my servant hastened to skin both animals, their fur being superb and as black as jet.

This encounter lost us two hours and night had completely fallen by the time I pitched my tent near Tchokodar, which place I left at dawn to gain Baltal by following the course of the river Sind. At this spot abruptly terminates the exquisite landscape of the "golden prairie" with a village which bears the same name (*Sona* 'gold' and *marg* 'prairie').The height of Zoji La* now supervenes, an abrupt acclivity of 11,500 feet, beyond which the whole country assumes a severe and inhospitable aspect.

Before Baltal my sporting escapades came to an end; from that time I only met with wild goats. Had I wished for an expedition, it would have been necessary to leave the high road and to penetrate into the very heart of the mountains. I had neither the time nor the inclination, so I tranquilly continued my route towards Ladak.

A violent transition is effected in passing from the smiling nature and fine population of Kashmir to the arid and sullen rocks and the beardless and deformed inhabitants of Ladak. The country into which I had just penetrated is at an altitude of 11,000 to 12,000 feet; only at Kargil the level descends to 8,000 feet.

The acclivity of Zoji La is very rugged; one has to climb an almost perpendicular wall. In certain places the path winds over projectures in the rock not more than a meter wide, the eye becoming dizzy at the sight of the unfathomable abyss below. At such points as these, heaven preserve the traveller from a false step!

There is one spot where a bridge has been formed by inserting long beams into holes in the rock and covering the same with a layer of earth. Brr! . . . At the thought that a stone rolling from the side of the mountain or that a too great oscillation of the beams might precipitate the earth into the abyss—and with the earth the unfortunate traveller who had hazarded his life upon it—my heart stood still more than once during my perilous journey.

*[*La* means "pass."—ED.]

Our dangers overcome, we halted in a valley where we prepared to pass the night near a post-carrier's hut, a spot which from its close proximity to the ice and snow was not rendered particularly attractive.

Beyond Baltal the distances are determined by means of daks—that is to say, post stations for the mail service. They are low huts, situated at seven kilometers' distance one from another, a guard being left in permanent charge of each.

The postal service between Kashmir and Thibet is still worked on very primitive lines. Letters are enclosed in a leather bag and given to a carrier. This individual, who carries on his back a basket containing several similar bags, rapidly covers the seven kilometers assigned to him. At the end of his journey he makes over his burden to another carrier, who in his turn accomplishes his task in identical manner. Thus letters are carried once a week from Kashmir to Thibet and vice versa, neither rains nor snows hindering their transmission.

For each course a letter-carrier is paid six annas (tenpence), the sum usually given to carriers of merchandise. My coolies only asked a similar recompense for carrying burdens at least ten times as heavy. One's heart aches at the sight of these pale, tired-looking officials. But what can one do? It is the custom of the country. Tea is brought from China in a similar way, this system of transportation being both rapid and economical.

Near the village of Matayan I came again upon the caravan of Yarkandiano whom I had promised to accompany on their journey. They had recognized me from afar and at once begged me to examine one of their band who had fallen ill. I found the poor fellow writhing in the agonies of intense fever. Wringing my hands in sign of despair, I pointed heavenwards, thus endeavoring to make them understand that their comrade's condition was beyond human aid or science and that God alone could save him.

As these people travelled by slow stages, I was obliged to leave them in order to arrive the same evening at Dras, which is situated at the bottom of a valley near a river bearing the same name. Near Dras stands a little fort of very ancient construction—freshly whitewashed—under the guard of three Sikhs of the maharajah's army.

Here my domicile was the posthouse, which is the only station of a single telegraphic line communicating between Srinagar and the interior of the Himalayas. From this time I was no longer able to erect my tent of an evening but had to take shelter in the caravansaries, which, although horribly dirty, were yet well warmed within by enormous logs of lighted wood.

From Dras to Kargil the country is dull and monotonous, if one excepts the marvelous sunrises and sunsets and beautiful moonlight effects. Apart from these the road is flat, endless, and bristling with dangers.

Kargil is the principal town of the district and the residence of the governor of the country. Its site is very picturesque. Two streams of water, the Suru and the Wakka, clatter noisily over the rocks and stones, issuing from their different defiles to unite in forming the river Suru, on whose banks rise the mud constructions of Kargil.

At the break of day, provided with fresh

horses, I continued my route, entering Ladak, or Little Thibet. Here I crossed an oscillating bridge composed, as all those of Kashmir, of two long beams, the ends of which were supported upon the banks, the whole being covered with a layer of fagots and little sticks and giving the illusion of a suspension bridge.

Soon afterwards I was leisurely climbing a little plateau, which covers the route for a distance of two kilometers before descending into the narrow valley of Wakka, dotted with villages, of which Pashkyum, on the left bank, is the most picturesque.

Here my feet trod Buddhist soil. The inhabitants are simple and good-natured; they seem to have no knowledge of what we Europeans call squabbles. Women are somewhat rare. Those I encountered were distinguished from the women I had previously seen in India and Kashmir by the air of gaiety and prosperity apparent on their countenances.

How could it be otherwise, since each woman of this country has on an average from three to five husbands and in the most legitimate manner in the world? Polyandry flourishes here. However large a family may be, there is never more than one woman in it. And if it does not exceed three persons, a bachelor may join it by contributing to the general expenses.

As a rule, the men are of feeble appearance, rather bent, and they seldom live to old age. During my journey in Ladak I did not meet one white-haired old man.

The road from Kargil to the center of Ladak has a much livelier aspect than the one I had just traversed, it being brightened by numerous hamlets, though trees and verdure of any kind are extremely rare.

Twenty miles from Kargil, at the issue of the defile formed by the rapid current of the Wakka, is the little village of Shergol, in whose center rise three brightly painted chapels—*t'horthenes,** to give them the name they bear in Thibet.

Below, near the river, stretch out heaps of stones massed together and forming long, broad walls upon which have been thrown in apparent disorder many flat, varied-colored stones engraved with all kinds of prayers in Ourd, Sanskrit, Thibetan, and even Arabic characters. Unknown to my coolies, I succeeded in carrying away a few of these stones, which are now to be seen in the palace of the Trocadero. From Shergol one meets at every step with these kind of oblong jetties.

Next morning at sunrise, provided with fresh horses, I resumed my journey, halting near the monastery *(gonpa)* of Mulbekh, which appears as if glued to the side of an isolated rock. Below it is the hamlet of Wakka, not far off from which is to be seen another rock of most singular appearance which seems to have been placed in its present position by human hands. On its side has been carved a Buddha several meters long, while it is further ornamented with several prayer girouettes.

These are kinds of wooden cylinders draped with materials yellow and white and attached to staves sunk vertically into the ground. The least breath of wind sets them revolving. The individual who originally placed them on the rock is exempt from the obligation of all prayer, for all that a

*A *t'horthene* is a small mortuary chapel or memorial of the dead.

believer could possibly ask of God is inscribed upon them.

Seen from a distance, this whitewashed monastery has a most weird effect, standing as it does with its skirted and revolving prayer wheels in strong relief against the gray background of the hills.

I left my horses at the hamlet of Wakka and, followed by my interpreter, walked towards the gonpa, to which access is given by a narrow stairway cut in the rock. At the top we were received by a portly lama—with the characteristically scanty beard of the Thibetan people—whose plainness was only exceeded by his affability.

The costume he wore consisted of a yellow frock and a cap of the same color with cloth ears. In his right hand he held a copper prayer girouette, which from time to time, without in any way interrupting our conversation, he set in motion. This action constituted an incessant prayer, communicated to the atmosphere in order that it should the more quickly be wafted to heaven.

We crossed a suite of low-ceilinged rooms whose walls, lined with shelves, displayed various images of Buddha of different dimensions made from all kinds of materials and covered with thick layers of dust. We came out at last upon an open terrace, from which the eye rested upon the surrounding waste of inhospitable country strewn with grayish rocks and traversed by a solitary road, the two extremities of which were lost in the confines of the horizon.

Here we sat down, being at once served with a beer made from hops, brewed in the monastery itself, and called *tchang*. This beverage rapidly imparts embonpoint to the monks, which is considered as a sign of particular favor from heaven.

The Thibetan language is spoken here; its origin is most obscure. One thing, however, is certain, and that is that a king of Thibet, a contemporary of Mahomet, undertook the creation of a universal language for all the followers of Buddha. With this intent he simplified the Sanskrit grammar and composed an alphabet containing a vast number of letters, thus laying the foundation of a language, the pronunciation of which is as easy as its writing is complicated and difficult. In order to represent a sound, no less than eight characters have to be employed.

All the modern literature of Thibet is written in this language, which is only spoken in its purity in Ladak and eastern Thibet. In all the other parts of the country, dialects are used, formed by a mixture of this mother tongue with different idioms taken from the neighboring peoples in one region or another.

In the ordinary life of the Thibetan, two languages are in use, one of which is absolutely incomprehensible to the women, while the other is spoken by the entire nation. It is only in the gonpas that the Thibetan language is found in its integrity.

The lamas much prefer the visits of Europeans to those of Mussulmans. I asked an explanation of this from my host, who replied as follows: "Mussulmans have no point of contact with our religion. Quite recently, in their victorious campaign, they converted by force a part of our coreligionists to Islamism. All our efforts are centered in endeavoring to bring back these Mussulman descendants of

Buddhists to the way of the true God.

"As regards the Europeans, that is quite another matter. Not only do they profess the essential principles of monotheism, but they have almost as much title to be considered worshippers of Buddha as the lamas of Thibet themselves.

"The only error of the Christians has been that, after having adopted the great doctrines of Buddha, they should have completely severed themselves from him in creating for themselves a different Dalai Lama, ours alone having the divine gift of seeing face-to-face the majesty of Buddha and the power of serving as an intermediary between earth and heaven."

"Who is this Dalai Lama of the Christians about whom you speak?" I asked. "We have a 'Son of God,' to whom we address fervent prayers and to whom we have recourse that he should intercede for us with our one and indivisible God."

"It is not of him I speak, sahib. We also respect the one whom you recognize as Son of the one God—not that we see in him an only Son, but a perfect being, elect from among all. The spirit of Buddha was indeed incarnate in the sacred person of Issa, who, without aid from fire or sword, has spread knowledge of our great and true religion throughout the world. I speak rather of your earthly Dalai Lama, him to whom you have given the title of 'Father of the Church.' This is a great sin; may it be forgiven the flocks who have gone astray." Saying which, the lama hastened to turn his prayer girouette.

I now understood that the allusion he had made had been to the Pope.

"You tell me that a son of Buddha, Issa, has

spread your religion over the earth. Who then is he?"

At this question the lama opened his eyes wide, looked at me with astonishment and, pronouncing some words my interpreter could not catch, held forth somewhat unintelligibly as follows:

"Issa is a great prophet, one of the first after the twenty-two Buddhas. He is greater than any one of all the Dalai Lamas, for he constitutes part of the spirituality of our Lord. It is he who has enlightened you, who has brought back within the pale of religion the souls of the frivolous, and who has allowed each human being to distinguish between good and evil. His name and his acts are recorded in our sacred writings. And in reading of his wondrous existence, passed in the midst of an erring and wayward people, we weep at the horrible sin of the pagans who, after having tortured him, put him to death."

I was struck by this recital of the lama's. The prophet Issa, his sufferings and death, our Christian Dalai Lama, the Buddhists recognizing Christianity—all these points made me think more and more of Jesus Christ, and I begged my interpreter to be scrupulous in not omitting a single word the lama might say.

"Where are these writings now to be found? And by whom were they originally written down?" I asked.

"The principal scrolls, whose compilation was effected in India and Nepal at different epochs, proportional to the events, are to be found at Lassa to the number of several thousands. In some of the chief monasteries copies are to be met with, made by the lamas during their sojourns at Lassa at various times and presented by them afterwards to their cloisters in remembrance of their pilgrimages to the home of the great master, our Dalai Lama."

"But you yourselves, have you no copies relating to the prophet Issa?"

"We have none. Our convent is not an important one, and since its formation our successive lamas have only had a few hundred manuscripts at their disposal. The great cloisters own thousands of them. But these are sacred things, which will be shown you nowhere."

Our conversation lasted a few minutes longer, when I left for the encampment, meditating all the time on the lama's narrative. Issa, a prophet of the Buddhists! But how could he have been? Of Jewish origin, he lived in Palestine and in Egypt, and the Gospels contain no word, no allusion to the part Buddhism might have played in the education of Jesus.

I determined to visit every convent in Thibet in the hope of gleaning ampler information concerning the prophet Issa and perhaps of coming across copies of the records relating to his life.

Almost without perceiving it, we crossed the pass of Namika at an altitude of 13,000 feet, whence we descended into the valley of the river Sangeluma. After having turned southwards, we reached Kharbu, leaving behind us on the other bank numerous villages, among which Chagdoom, on the summit of a rock, has an extremely picturesque site.

The houses are white, two or three-storied, and have a very cheerful aspect—a characteristic they share in common with all the villages of Ladak. A European making the round of Kashmir

soon loses all trace of his national style of architecture; while in Ladak, on the contrary, he is
agreeably surprised at the sight of trim little houses
with casements, similar to those of any provincial
town of Europe.

Near Kharbu, on two perpendicular rocks, the
ruins of a little town or village are to be seen. A
storm and earthquake, it is said, demolished its
walls which, however, as regards solidity, seem to
have left nothing to be desired.

The next day I traversed yet another station
and crossed the Fotu La, 13,500 feet, on the summit of which is built a little t'horthene. Thence,
following the completely dry bed of a torrent,
I descended to the hamlet of Lamayuru, which
appears unexpectedly before the eyes of the traveller. A convent, clinging to the side of an isolated
rock and maintaining its equilibrium in miraculous
fashion, dominates the village.

Staircases are unknown in this monastery. One
mounts from one story to another by aid of ropes,
outside communication being effected through a
labyrinth of passages and corridors. Below the convent, whose windows remind one of great birds'
nests, is a little inn which offers to the traveller a
few uninviting rooms.

At once after my arrival here and as I was
preparing to stretch myself out on a carpet, my
apartment was suddenly invaded by a number of
yellow-frocked monks who pestered me with questions as to whence I came, the object of my journey, etc., etc., finally inviting me to ascend to the
monastery.

In spite of my fatigue, I accepted their invitation and began to climb with them a steep path cut

in the rock, so encumbered with prayer cylinders or wheels that every moment I touched and set them whirling. These pious objects had been placed there for this purpose and to prevent the passersby from losing time in their prayers, as if the business of their day was too absorbing to allow of leisure for devotion.

Many pious Buddhists utilize the currents of their rivers with this view. I have seen a whole row of cylinders, provided with their usual formulas, placed along a river bank in such a way that they were kept in continual motion by the water, thus exempting their proprietors from the obligation of prayer.

Having reached our destination, I sat down on a bench in a dimly lighted room, the walls of which were decorated with the inevitable images of Buddha as well as by books and girouettes, my loquacious hosts at once beginning to explain to me the signification of each object.

"And these books you have here," I asked them, "relate, no doubt, to religion?"

"Yes, sahib. They are volumes treating on the first and most important rites of public life. We possess several parts of the words of Buddha, consecrated to the great and indivisible divine Being and to all that has come forth from his hands."

"Among these books is there not some record of the prophet Issa?"

"No," replied the monk. "We only possess a few principal treatises relating to the observance of the religious rites. As for the biographies of our saints, they are collected in Lassa. Even some of the most important of our convents have not yet had time to procure them. Before coming to this gonpa

I lived for several years in a great monastery on the other side of Ladak, and there I saw thousands of books and scrolls copied at different times by the lamas of the cloister."

Having interrogated the monks at still greater length, I learned that the convent in question was near Leh. My repeated inquiries, however, resulted in exciting their suspicions, and it was with undisguised pleasure they reconducted me below, where I retired to rest after a light repast and having charged my Hindu to judiciously question the younger lamas of the gonpa as to the name of the monastery where their chief had lived before his nomination to Lamayuru.

Up at sunrise next morning, I continued my journey, the Hindu having informed me that he had been unable to extract any information from the lamas, who were evidently on their guard. I will not stop here to describe the monastic life of these convents, it being much the same in all the cloisters of Ladak. I saw subsequently the celebrated monastery of Leh, to which visit I shall refer with many details later on.

At Lamayuru commences a steep declivity which, through a narrow and somber defile, leads towards the Indus. Without having any idea of the dangers which this descent presented, I sent my coolies on in advance and set out along a path between hills of brown clay—smooth enough at its commencement but soon leading into a kind of narrow and obscure cutting, winding as a corniche along the side of the mountain and overlooking a frightful precipice.

The way was so narrow that if a rider had met me, we should certainly never have been able to

pass each other. All description would be inade-
quate to convey an idea of the grandeur and wild
beauty of this gorge, the crests of whose summits
dart upwards towards the sky.

At certain points, the passage became so contracted that from my saddle I could with my whip
touch the opposite rock, while at others death
seemed to stare me in the face from the depths of
the abyss below. It was too late, however, to think
of dismounting. I could only regret the rashness of
the step I had taken and proceed as best I could.

This defile is in reality an enormous crevasse,
due to some formidable upheaval of the earth,
which must have violently separated two immense
masses of granite rock. At the bottom of it I could
see a scarcely perceptible white streak. This was an
impetuous torrent whose dull roar filled the gorge
with mysterious sound. Above me wound a narrow
ribbon of blue—the only portion of the celestial
vault visible between the rocks.

The sight of this majestic nature was in itself
an intense pleasure. At the same time, the deathlike
stillness, the awful silence of the mountains broken
only by the melancholy dashing of the waters
beneath filled me with sadness.

For a distance of eight miles I had experienced
these sensations, pleasant and at the same time
depressing, when at a sudden turn to the right
I passed out of the defile and into a valley circled
by rocks, whose summits were reflected in the
Indus. On a bank of the river stands the little
fortress of Khalsi, a famous stronghold dating from
the Mussulman invasions, near to which is the high
road leading from Kashmir to Thibet.

After having crossed the Indus over a kind of

suspension bridge which leads to the door of the fortress, I traversed the valley and then the village of Khalsi, being anxious to pass the night in the hamlet of Snourly situated in the valley of the Indus and constructed in terraces which descend to the river.

The two following days I travelled tranquilly and without any difficulties to overcome along the banks of the Indus through a picturesque country which brought me to Leh, the capital of Ladak.

In crossing the little valley of Saspoula, near the village which bears its name, I came across, for a distance of several kilometers in the neighborhood, stonemounds and t'horthenes. I also passed two monasteries, from one of which floated the French flag. Later on I learned that a French engineer had presented it to the monks, who thus made use of it as a decoration.

I passed the night at Saspoula, not forgetting to visit the cloisters, where for the tenth time I saw the dust-covered images of Buddha, the flags and banners heaped in a corner, hideous masks lying on the ground, books and rolls of parchment piled up without any order, and the usual display of prayer cylinders.

The lamas seem to experience particular pleasure in displaying these objects. They appear to be parading treasures of great importance and are perfectly indifferent as to the amount of interest the spectator may be taking in them. Their idea seems to be, "We must show all we possess in the hope that the sight alone of so many sacred things will force the traveller to believe in the divine grandeur of the human soul."

Concerning the prophet Issa, the same

accounts were given me as I had heard before, and I was informed what I already knew—that the volumes which could enlighten me about him were at Lassa and that only the most important monasteries possessed copies of the same. I thought no more of passing the Karakorum but only of finding this history, which might perhaps give additional light to the inner life of the best of men and amplify at the same time the somewhat vague information which the Gospels give us respecting him.

A little before Leh, at the entrance of the valley which bears its name, the road passes near a lonely rock, on the summit of which is built a fort flanked by two towers (without a garrison) and the little convent named Pintak.

A mountain 10,500 feet high protects the entrance of Thibet. The road then leads abruptly northwards in the direction of Leh, which at a distance of six miles from Pintak stands at a height of 11,500 feet at the bases of immense granite columns whose summits, varying from 18,000 to 19,000 feet, are covered with the eternal snows.

The town itself, girdled by stunted aspen trees, rises in a succession of terraces dominated by an old fort and the palace of the ancient sovereigns of Ladak. Towards evening I made my entrance into Leh, taking up my quarters in a bungalow especially constructed for the use of Europeans who come from India during the hunting season.

LADAK

Ladak originally formed part of Great Thibet. The frequent hordes of invaders from the north who traversed this country to conquer Kashmir and

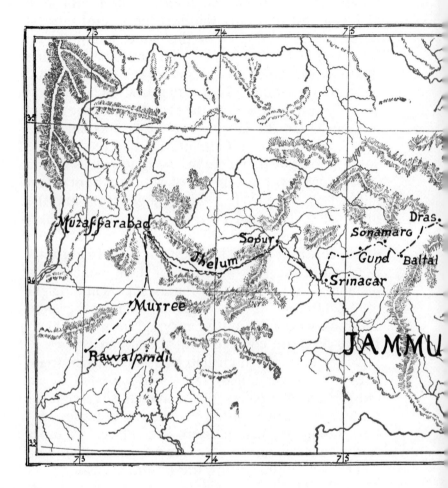

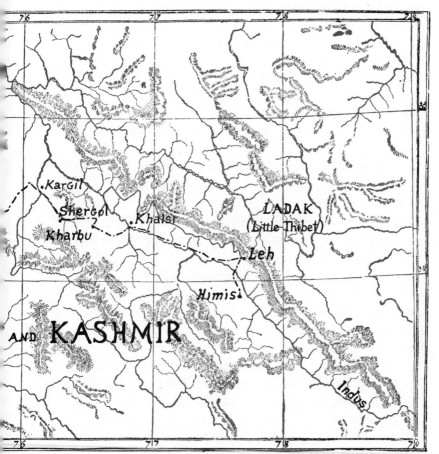

The Author's Itinerary across Kashmir and Ladak

the wars of which it was the theater not only reduced it to misery, but had also the result of depriving it—passing as it did from the hands of one conqueror to another—of the political dominion of Lassa.

The Mussulmans, who took possession at a remote epoch of Kashmir and Ladak, converted by force the feeble inhabitants of Little Thibet to Islamism. The political existence of Ladak terminated with the annexation by the Sikhs of this country to Kashmir, which permitted the Ladakians to return to their ancient beliefs.

Two-thirds of the inhabitants profited by these occurrences to reerect their gonpas and to return to their former mode of living. The Baltistans alone remained Mussulman Shiites, to which sect the conquerors of the country had belonged. Notwithstanding this, however, they have preserved only a very vague semblance of Islamism, which is chiefly revealed in their customs and their practice of polygamy. Several lamas informed me that they had not yet given up hope of bringing them back someday to the faith of their ancestors.

In a religious sense, Ladak is subservient to Lassa, the capital of Thibet and residence of the Dalai Lama. It is at Lassa that the principal khoutoukhtes, or supreme-lamas, are elected, as well as the chogzots, or administrators. Politically it is under the authority of the maharajah of Kashmir, who is represented by a governor.

The inhabitants of Ladak belong to the Chinese-Touranian race and are divided into Ladakians and Tchampas. The Ladakians lead a sedentary existence, build villages along their narrow valleys, live in two-storied houses which they keep carefully, and cultivate large plots of land.

They are exceedingly ugly, of short stature, lean, and bent, with small heads, narrow receding foreheads, prominent cheekbones, and the beady black eyes of the Mongolian race, flat noses, large thin-lipped mouths, weak, scantily bearded chins, and hollow cheeks, heavily furrowed with wrinkles. Add to all this a shaven head, from which depends a diminutive plait, and you will have the general type not only of the inhabitants of Ladak, but of the whole of Thibet.

The women are of equally small stature and have the same prominent cheekbones. But they are of a much more robust constitution, and sympathetic smiles brighten their faces. They have gay and even dispositions and are much given to merriment.

The severity of the climate precludes the Ladakians from wearing rich or many-colored garments. Their shirts are of simple gray linen and coarse cloth which they manufacture themselves; and their pantaloons, which descend as far as the knee, are made of the same material.

People of means still wear the *choga* (a kind of overcoat). In winter a fur cap with earflaps is worn, while in summer the head is protected by a cloth cap, the peak of which folds over on one side. Their shoes are made of felt covered with leather, and from their waistbands hang a whole arsenal of small objects—needle cases, knives, penholders, inkpots, tobacco pouches, pipes, and the inevitable prayer girouettes.

The Thibetans are, as a rule, of such an idle disposition that a plait of hair which has become loose is not replaited before a space of at least three months, while a shirt is not discarded till it

Ladakian Women

falls from the body in rags. The overcoat they wear is always dirty and generally marked on the back by a large oily stain left by their plait, which is carefully greased every day. They take a bath once a year, and then not from their own free will but because they are so compelled by the law. For this reason it will be easily understood that their immediate vicinity is to be avoided.

The women, on the contrary, are great lovers of cleanliness and order. They wash themselves daily and on the smallest pretext. Their costume consists of a short and spotless chemisette, which hides the dazzling whiteness of their skin, and a red jacket draped over their well-rounded shoulders— the hem of which is tucked inside of knickerbockers of red and green cloth. This latter original garment is worn puffed up as a protection against the cold. Red broidered half-boots are worn, lined with fur; and an indoor costume is completed by a wide, many-pleated cloth skirt.

The hair is worn tightly plaited, while to the head is attached with pins large pieces of loose cloth, something after the fashion of the women of Italy. Beneath this headdress are suspended in bizarre fashion various brightly colored pebbles as well as coins and fragments of carved metals.

The ears are covered with flaps of cloth or fur, and sheepskins are worn, protecting the back alone. Poor women content themselves with ordinary skins of animals, while women of position don proper pelisses of red cloth, broidered with gold fringes.

Whether out walking in the streets or calling on friends, the women invariably carry on their backs conical-shaped baskets, the small bases of which are turned towards the ground, filled with peat, which constitutes the chief fuel of the country.

Every woman possesses a certain amount of money which is hers by right, and this she generally spends on jewelry, buying at small cost large pieces of turquoise which she adds to the various ornaments of her coiffure.

The Ladakian woman enjoys a social status envied by all the women of the East, for not only is she free but held in great respect. With the exception of a small amount of field labor, she passes the greater part of her time visiting. And here let it be remarked that idle gossip is to her a thing unknown.

The settled population of Ladak devotes itself to agriculture, but the inhabitants possess so little land (the allotment of each rarely exceeding ten acres) that the income they draw from it is not sufficient to defray either the payment of the taxes or the bare necessaries of life. Manual labor is generally despised. The lowest grade of society bears the name of *Bem,* and an alliance with one of their body is carefully avoided.

During the leisure hours left from their labor in the fields, the inhabitants give themselves up to hunting the Thibetan goat, whose wool is held in high esteem in India. The poorest among the population—those who cannot afford to equip themselves for the chase—hire themselves out as coolies.

This occupation is shared by the women, who bear fatigue very well and who enjoy much better health than their husbands, whose laziness reaches to such a point that in preference to bestirring themselves, they are capable of passing a whole night in the open, heedless of heat or cold and stretched on a bed of stones.

Polyandry (to which I shall return with further details) is a factor in keeping the population united. It creates large families who cultivate the land for the common good, aided by yaks, zos, and zomos (oxen and cows). A member of a family cannot sever himself from it, and if he dies his share reverts to the community.

Little else save wheat is sown, the grains of which, owing to the severity of the climate, are small. Barley is also cultivated and pulverized before sale.

Once the field tasks are terminated, all the men go to gather on the mountains the wild herb *enoriota,* as well as the great thorn *dâma.* From these they make fuel, which is scarce in Ladak, where neither woods nor gardens are ever seen and it is only occasionally one finds on a riverbank a thin clump of willows or poplars. Near the villages, aspen trees are also to be found; but for want of fertile ground, gardening is rendered difficult.

The absence of wood is, above all, apparent in the dwellings, which are sometimes built with bricks dried in the sun but more frequently with medium-sized stones, massed together with a kind of mortar composed of clay and chopped straw. These buildings are two-storied, carefully white-washed in front, and have window sashes painted in showy colors. Their horizontal roofs form terraces, usually decorated with wild flowers, and here during the fine season of the year the inhabitants kill time contemplating nature and turning their prayer wheels.

Each dwelling contains several rooms and amongst these there is always one set apart for visitors, the walls of which are decorated with superb fur skins. In the other rooms are beds and furniture. Rich people possess, moreover, oratories filled with idols and consecrated to prayer.

Life here is very regular. As regards food, there is little choice, Ladakian fare being of the simplest. Breakfast consists of a slice of rye bread. At midday the table is furnished with a wooden bowl filled with flour, into which is poured tepid water. This concoction is stirred with little chopsticks till it assumes the consistency of a thick paste, when finally it is partaken of in little balls with milk.

In the evening, bread and tea are served. Meat is considered a superfluous luxury. Sportsmen alone introduce a little variety into their diet in the form of wild goat, eagles, and white pheasants, with which the country abounds. All day long, and on the smallest pretext, tchang is drunk, a kind of pale beer unfermented.

If it happens that a Ladakian, mounted on a pony (such privileged persons are very rare), starts on an expedition to seek for work in the neighborhood, he provides himself with a small quantity of meal. Dinnertime come, he dismounts near a river or stream, fills a small wooden cup (which he never parts from) with a little flour, kneads it with water, and finally consumes it.

The Tchampas, or nomads, who compose the other half of the population of Ladak, are much poorer and at the same time more uncivilized than the sedentary Ladakians. They are, for the greater part, sportsmen and entirely neglect agricultural pursuits. Although they profess the Buddhist faith, they never frequent the monasteries save when they are in want of meal, which they take in exchange for game.

Ordinarily they camp out on the summits of the mountains, where the cold is intense. While the Ladakians proper are scrupulously truthful, fond of learning, but hopelessly idle, the Tchampas are, on the contrary, very irascible, extremely lively, and great liars—professing, moreover, supreme disdain for the convents.

Among these latter dwell the little people of the Khamba, who come from the outskirts of Lassa and who lead the miserable existence of a troupe of wandering gypsies on the high roads. Unfitted for any kind of work, speaking a different language from that of the country in which they seek their livelihood, they are objects of universal contumely, only tolerated out of pity for their deplorable condition when hunger forces them in bands to seek food in the villages.

Polyandry, which prevails in all Thibetan families, greatly excited my curiosity. It is by no means a consequence of the doctrines of Buddha, it having existed long before his advent. It has assumed in India considerable proportions and constitutes an energetic factor in keeping within limits a population ever on the increase, which result is also aided by the abominable custom of strangling new-born infants of the female sex, the efforts of the English having remained fruitless in their struggle against the suppression of these possibly future mothers.

Manu himself established polyandry as a law, and certain Buddhist preachers, having abjured Brahmanism, introduced this custom into Ceylon, Thibet, Mongolia, and the Korea. Long repressed in China, polyandry, which flourishes in Thibet

and Ceylon, is found also among the Kalmouks
between Todas in southern India and Nairs on the
coast of Malabar. Traces of this bizarre family custom are also to be met with among the Tasmanians
and in the north of America among the Iroquois.

If Caesar is to be believed, polyandry has also
flourished in Europe, for we read in his *De bello
Gallico* (Book V): "Uxores habent deni duodenique
inter se communes, et maxime fratres cum fratribus
et parentes cum liberis."*

The result of all this is that it is impossible
to consider polyandry as an exclusively religious
usage. In Thibet, taking into consideration the
small portion of arable ground falling to the share
of each inhabitant, it is best explained from eco-
nomic motives. To maintain the 1,500,000 inhabitants distributed in Thibet over a surface of
1,200,000 square kilometers, the Buddhists were
obliged to adopt polyandry—each family, moreover, being bound to dedicate one of its members
to the priesthood.

The firstborn son is always consecrated to the
gonpa, which is invariably found on an elevation at
the entrance of each village. As soon as the child
has attained his eighth year, he is entrusted to
passing caravans en route for Lassa, where he lives
for seven years as a novice in one of the gonpas of
the town.

There he learns to read and write, studies the
religious rites, and becomes acquainted with the
sacred rolls written in Pali, formerly the language
of the country of Magadha, the reputed birthplace

---

*["Wives are shared between groups of ten or twelve men, especially
between brothers and between fathers and sons." Julius Caesar, *The
Conquest of Gaul*, trans. S. A. Handford (New York: Penguin Books,
1951), p. 136, n. 1.—ED.]

of the Buddha Gautama.

The eldest brother of a family chooses a wife, who becomes common to all the members of his household. The choice of the fiancé and the nuptial ceremony are of the most rudimentary character.

As soon as a wife and her husbands have decided upon the marriage of one of their sons, the eldest among them is dispatched to call on a neighbor who has a marriageable daughter. The first and second visits are passed in more or less banal conversation, accompanied by frequent libations of tchang; and it is only on the third call that the young man declares his intention of taking a wife. The daughter of the family is then produced, who is generally not unknown to her suitor, women never veiling their faces in Ladak.

A girl may not be married without her own consent. If she is willing, she leaves with her fiancé, becoming his wife and the wife of his brothers. An only son is generally sent to a woman having but two or three husbands, he offering to become her fourth spouse. Such an offer is rarely declined, and the young man is at once installed in his new family.

The parents of a newly married couple usually live with them till the birth of the first child. The day after the arrival of this new member of the family, the grandparents relinquish the whole of their fortune to the young couple and go to live in a small dwelling away from them.

Marriage is occasionally contracted between mere children, who live apart until they have reached a marriageable age. A woman has the right to an unlimited number of husbands and lovers. In this latter instance, if she meets with a young man who pleases her, she takes him home, gives congé

Young People Dressed for a Wedding

to all her husbands, and lives with the one she prefers, announcing that she has taken a *jing-tuh* ("lover"), which piece of news is received by her husbands with perfect sangfroid.

Only the vaguest ideas are entertained here of jealousy. The Thibetan is too cool-blooded to know love. Such a sentiment would mean to him an anachronism, if even he did not see in it a flagrant violation of established usage. In one word, love would pass in his eyes as both selfish and unjustifiable.

In the absence of one of the husbands, his place is offered to a bachelor or widower. These latter are in a great minority in Ladak, wives generally surviving their feeble husbands. Sometimes a Buddhist traveller is chosen, whose affairs detain him in the village. In the same way, a husband who travels or seeks work in the neighboring country profits at each halt by like hospitality from his coreligionists, whose generosity, however, is not always unactuated by ulterior motives.

In spite of the peculiarity of their position, women are held in great esteem and enjoy perfect freedom in the choice of their husbands or jing-tuhs. They are always good-humored, interested in all that takes place, and are free to go wherever they choose—save in the principal prayer chambers of the monasteries, to which access is strictly forbidden them.

Children only regard their mothers. They feel no affection for their fathers, for the excellent reason that they apparently have so many.

Without for one moment approving of polyandry, I cannot condemn it in Thibet; for without it, the population would increase prodigiously and

Leh, Capital of Ladak (Little Thibet), Seen from the Carare

famine and misery overwhelm the nation, bringing in their rear the sinister cortège of theft, murder, and other crimes hitherto absolutely unknown throughout the country.

A FESTIVAL IN A GONPA

Leh, capital of Ladak, is a little town boasting not more than five thousand inhabitants and comprised in two or three streets of houses painted white. In the center of it stands the square "place" of the bazaar, where merchants from India, China, Turkestan, Kashmir, and various parts of Thibet come to exchange their goods for the Thibetan gold brought to them by the natives, seeking not only supplies of cloth gowns for their monks, but even the smallest objects of utility.

An old and uninhabited palace rises on a hill overlooking the town, in the middle of which is found the vast two-storied residence of my friend the Vizir Surajbal, governor of Ladak, a most sympathetic Punjabian who has taken his degree of philosophy in London.

To enliven my stay in Leh, he organized in the square of the bazaar a grand polo* match, while in the evening dances and games were given before the terrace of his house.

Many bonfires threw a brilliant light on the crowds of people who thronged to the entertainment. They formed a large circle, in the midst of which a group of performers, disguised as devils, beasts, and sorcerers, disported themselves, fluttering, jumping, and revolving in a rhythmical dance

---

*Polo, a favorite game of the Mogul emperors, was introduced into India 900 years ago by its Mussulman conquerors.

Portrait of the Governor of Ladak

Inscription on the back of photograph:—*From Pandit Surajbal Manphal (Oxon.) to Nicolas Notovitch at Leh, November 1887. In token of an interesting acquaintance on the northern confines of India.*

to the monotonous music of two long trumpets, accompanied by a drum.

The infernal racket and the continual shoutings of the crowd fatigued me extremely. The entertainment concluded with the graceful dances of the Thibetan women, who, pirouetting and swaying from side to side, made us, on reaching our windows, a profound obeisance, saluting us in crossing their wrists by the jangling of their copper and ivory bangles.

Early next day I started for the great convent Himis which, in a picturesque situation, stands on the summit of a rock dominating the valley of the Indus. It is one of the chief monasteries of the country and is supported by the contributions of the inhabitants and subsidies sent from Lassa.

On the road which leads to it, after having crossed the Indus by a bridge near which nestle numerous villages, one finds endless jetties covered with engraved stones and t'horthenes, which our guides took especial care to pass on the right-hand side. I wanted to turn my horse to the left, but the Ladakians at once made me retrace my steps, leading my horse by the bridle to the right and explaining to me that such was the custom of the country. I tried to find out the origin of this superstition but in vain.

We continued our way towards the gonpa, which is surmounted by a tower with indented parapets visible from afar, and found ourselves before a large door painted in vivid colors, the entrance to a vast two-storied edifice which encloses a courtyard paved with small stones.

To the right, in one of its angles, is another large painted door, ornamented with bands of

Thibetan Lamas

copper. This is the entrance to the principal temple, whose interior is decorated with paintings of the chief idols and where a huge image of Buddha is to be seen flanked by a multitude of minor deities.

To the left is a verandah furnished with an immense prayer wheel, and here on our arrival all the lamas of the convent with their chief were grouped together. Below the verandah were several musicians, who held drums and long trumpets. On the right of the courtyard, a succession of doors led to the rooms of the monks, all furnished with sacred pictures and ornamented with little prayer wheels, surmounted by tridents decked with ribbons and painted red and black.

In the middle of the courtyard rose two large masts, from the tops of which floated yaks' (ox) tails and long, paper streamers inscribed with religious precepts. Along the whole length of the convent walls there were prayer girouettes adorned with ribbons.

A profound silence reigned, everyone anxiously awaiting the commencement of some religious mystery. We took our places on the verandah not far from the lamas. Almost immediately the musicians drew from their long trumpets soft monotonous sounds, accompanying themselves on a curious kind of circular drum attached to a stave fixed in the ground.

At the first notes of the melancholy chant which followed upon this bizarre music, the doors of the convent opened wide, giving access to some twenty persons disguised as animals, birds, devils, and monsters of every kind. On their breasts they bore fantastic devices of demons and death's

Musicians of the Monastery

Trumpets in Thibet are sometimes above six feet long.

heads embroidered in Chinese silk of various colors, while from their headdresses, which took the form of conical hats, hung suspended long multicolored ribbons covered with inscriptions. Over their faces they wore masks, on which death's heads were worked in white silk.

Thus apparelled they slowly made the circuit of the masts, extending their arms from time to time and throwing into the air with their left hands a sort of spoon, a part of which consisted of a fragment of the human skull ornamented with hair, taken, I was assured, from the scalps of enemies.

Their promenade round the masts soon developed into a kind of restless leaping. At a prolonged roll from the drum they came to a sudden standstill, only to start off again, brandishing towards the sky in a threatening manner little, yellow beribboned sticks.

Finally, having saluted the chief lama, they approached the entrance of the temple, whence proceeded at the same moment other masqueraders, their heads covered with copper masks. The costumes they wore were composed of broidered materials of various colors. With one hand they held a tambourine, while with the other they tinkled little bells. From each tambourine hung a ball, which, at the least movement of the hand, rebounded against the sonorous skin of the instrument.

These fresh performers made the tour of the courtyard several times, marking time with their tambourines, with which after each round they created a deafening uproar by striking them all in unison. They ended by running towards the door of the temple and grouping themselves upon the steps before it.

Here a general silence ensued, soon broken by
the appearance of a third company of disguised
men, their enormous masks representing different
deities bearing each on the forehead a third eye.
At their head marched Thlogan-Poudma-Jungnas,
literally "he who was born in the flower of a lotus,"
accompanied by another mask, richly dressed and
holding a large yellow parasol covered with designs.

His suite consisted of various magnificently
attired gods: Dorje-Trolong, Sangspa Kourpo (that
is to say, Brahma himself), and others. These
actors, as a lama seated near us explained, represented the six classes of beings subject to metamor-
phosis—the gods, demigods, men, animals, spirits,
and demons.

On either side of these personages, who
advanced sedately, marched other masks in silken
gowns of startling hues. They wore golden crowns
with six flowered borders surmounted by spires,
and each carried a drum. They made the circuit of
the masts the three prescribed times to the sound
of a braying and incoherent music, ultimately seat-
ing themselves on the ground around Thlogan-
Poudma-Jungnas, who at once inserted with admirable gravity two fingers into his mouth, emitting
a shrill whistle.

In answer to this signal, young men dressed as
warriors came out from the temple. They wore
monstrous green masks adorned with small trian-
gular flags, short shirts, and anklets of beribboned
bells. Making an infernal din with their tambourines and bells, they gyrated round the gods seated
on the ground.

Two big fellows who accompanied them,
dressed in tights, acted the part of buffoons, exe-

Masqueraders with Conical Hats

Copper Masks

cuting all sorts of grotesque movements and comical feats. One of them, dancing all the time, kept striking his companion's drum. This evoked the delight of the crowd, who rewarded his contortions with peals of laughter.

A fresh group of players now joined the throng, personating the greatest powers after Divinity. Their disguise consisted of red miters and yellow pantaloons. They held the usual bells and tambourines and took up their position opposite the gods.

Almost the last performers to enter upon the scene wore red and brown masks and had three eyes painted on their breasts. These, with the preceding players, fell into two ranks, executing to the accompaniment of tambourines and general music a wild dance—advancing, receding, revolving in circles, and forming columns, filling in the pauses with low obeisances.

After a time, this scene of excitement, which wearied us terribly, began to calm down a little. Gods, demigods, kings, men, and spirits rose and, followed by all the other masqueraders, directed their steps towards the entrance of the temple, whence proceeded with utmost gravity a number of men admirably disguised as skeletons. All these sorties had been previously arranged and each had its particular signification.

The cortège of dancers gave place to these funereal-looking beings, who directed their steps gravely towards the masts. There they came to a standstill, manipulating pieces of wood hanging from their sides in such a manner as to imitate to perfection the rattling of jawbones.

They made the round of the courtyard thrice, marching to the rhythm of the intermittent beating of the drums and finally intoning a religious chant. Having once more worked their artificial jaws, they ground their teeth and, making a few more painful contortions, came to a standstill.

At this juncture, an effigy of the enemy of man, made in a kind of plaster of Paris and placed at the foot of one of the masts, was seized and broken to bits, the oldest men among the spectators distributing the pieces to the skeletons as a sign of their resignation to join them anon in the cemeteries.

The performance being now at an end, the chief lama came up to me and begged me to accompany him to the principal terrace to drink tchang which was flowing in honor of the festival. I accepted his invitation with pleasure, for my head was in a whirl through the prolonged spectacle I had just witnessed.

After having crossed the courtyard and ascended a staircase lined with prayer wheels, we passed through two rooms encumbered with idols and came out upon the terrace, when I seated myself on a bench opposite the venerable lama, whose eyes flashed with intelligence. Jugs of tchang were then brought to us by three monks who filled small copper cups which they handed first of all to their chief and then to myself and my attendants.

"Has our little fête pleased you?" the lama asked me.

"I found it very interesting," I replied. "In fact, I am still under the influence of the spectacle. But, to confess the truth, I never had the slightest suspicion that Buddhism in its religious ceremonies

Thlogan-Poudma-Jungnas

Masqueraders in the Suite of the Gods

could be paraded in such extravagant form."

"No religion," replied the lama, "has more theatrical ceremonies than ours. But this ritualistic side of it in no way violates the fundamental principles of Buddhism. We regard it as a practical means of maintaining the ignorant crowd in love for and obedience to the unique Creator, even as with a toy a parent wins the affection and submission of his child. In the people, that is to say the uneducated masses, we see the children of the Father."

"But what signification," I continued, "have all these masks, costumes, bells, and dances—in one word, the entire performance, which appears to be carried out after a fixed program?"

"We have several similar festivals during the year," answered the lama. "Mysteries are represented and actors are invited to take part in them. They have a perfect latitude as regards their movements and gestures and must conform only to the details and limits of a central idea.

"Our mysteries are nothing more than pantomimes, tending to show forth the gods enjoying that high degree of veneration which brings as a reward to man serenity of soul and belief in immortal life.

"The actors receive their costumes from the convents and play after general indications, which allow full liberty of action. The effect they produce is certainly imposing, but our own people can alone appreciate the meaning of their performance. You also have recourse, we understand, to similar proceedings, which, however, do not in any way alter your principle of monotheism."

"Forgive me," I returned, "but surely the mass

of idols which encumber your gonpas is a flagrant violation of this principle?"

"As I have already told you," replied the lama, "man is and ever will be in his infancy. He understands all, sees and feels the grandeur of nature, but is yet incapable of comprehending the Great Soul creating and animating all things.

"Man has always sought after the tangible; he has never succeeded in long believing that which has escaped his material senses. He has ever done his utmost to find a direct means of communication between himself and the Creator, who has worked so much good and at the same time, as he erroneously believes, so much evil upon him.

"For this reason, he has adored every feature of nature having a beneficial influence. We have a striking example of this in the ancient Egyptians, who worshipped animals, trees, and stones, the winds and the rains.

"Other nations equally steeped in ignorance, perceiving that the rains did not always bring forth good harvests and that animals could be disobedient to their masters, sought for direct intermediaries between themselves and the great mysteries and unfathomable might of the Creator. Therefore they made idols, which they regarded as neutral to their surroundings and to whose mediation they had constant recourse.

"From the furthest ages to the present day, I repeat, man has ever leant towards the tangible. The Assyrians, in seeking the way which should lead them to the feet of the Creator, turned their eyes towards the stars, which, although beyond the limits of attainment, they contemplated with adoration. The Guèbres have preserved this same

Masqueraders with Golden Crowns

The God of Animals

belief to the present day.

"Man's nullity and the blindness of his intelligence render him incapable of conceiving the invisible and spiritual tie uniting him to the great Divinity. In this we have the explanation of his attenuation of the divine principle and the reason for his ever seeking after the dominion of things palpable.

"We have a further illustration of this in Brahmanism, whose followers, abandoning themselves to the love of exterior forms, have, not all at once but by degrees, created a whole army of gods and demigods. At the same time, man has never dared to attribute a divine and eternal existence to the visible images wrought by his hands.

"Perhaps the people of Israel have demonstrated in a more flagrant manner than any other, man's love for all that is concrete. For in spite of the series of wonderful miracles worked by their Great Creator—who is the same for all peoples—they could not resist founding a god in metal at the very time when their prophet Moses was in communion with the Most High on their behalf.

"Buddhism has passed through similar modifications. Our great reformer, Sakyamuni, inspired by the Supreme Judge, had a true comprehension of the majesty and indivisibility of the Master. For this reason he openly separated himself from the Brahmans and their doctrine of polytheism, preaching the purity and immortality of the Creator and doing his utmost to put down the images made, it was supposed, in His likeness.

"The success which he and his disciples met with among the people provoked considerable persecution against him by the Brahmans, who, contrary to the laws of the Supreme Being, treated the people with the greatest despotism, creating new gods merely to increase the source of their personal revenue.

"Our first holy prophets, to whom we give the title of Buddhas—that is to say, of wise men and saints, we believing them to be incarnations of the one Great Creator—established themselves of old in various countries of the globe. As their preachings aimed before all at the tyranny of the Brahmans and the sinfulness of their making their religion a mere matter of commerce, they found the greater number of their followers among the lower classes of China and India.

"Among these holy prophets, particular veneration is bestowed on the Buddha Sakyamuni,* who lived three thousand years ago and who by his teachings brought the whole of China into the way of the one true and indivisible God, and also on the Buddha Gautama, who lived two thousand five hundred years ago and who converted nearly half the Hindus to the same belief.†

"Buddhism is divided into several sects, differing from each other only in certain religious ceremonies, the foundation of their doctrine being everywhere the same. We Thibetan Buddhists are called Lamaists,‡ having separated ourselves from the Foistes about fifteen hundred years ago. Till then we formed part of the worshippers of Fô-Sakyamuni, who was the first to collect all the laws made by the various Buddhas at the time of the

---

*known in China under the name of Fô
†[In traditional Buddhism, the name "Sakyamuni" (Sage of the Sakya clan) refers to Gautama Buddha (c. 563–483 B.C.).—ED.]
‡from the word *lama* ("superior")

Youths Dressed as Warriors

Youths Dressed as Warriors

great schism in the Brahmanical religion.

"In later years, a Mongolian khoutoukhte translated into Chinese the books of the great Buddha, receiving as recompense from the emperor of China the title of 'Go-Chi'—preceptor to the king—a title which, after his death, was bestowed upon the Dalai Lama of Thibet and which has ever since been borne by those filling that office.

"Our religion admits of two orders of monks, the red and the yellow. The former—who recognize the authority of the Panchen, who resides at Tashi Lumpo and who is the chief of the civil administration of Thibet—may marry. But we yellow monks have pronounced vows of celibacy, and our direct governor is the Dalai Lama. Beyond this point of difference, the ritual of our two orders is identical."

"Do both have mystery plays similar to the one I witnessed today?"

"Yes, with a very few variations. Formerly these festivals were carried out with most solemn pomp, but since the conquest of Ladak our convents have been more than once sacked and our riches taken from us. Now we have to content ourselves with white vestments and bronze utensils, while in Thibet proper, one only sees golden vessels and tissues of gold."

"During a recent visit that I made to a gonpa, one of the lamas told me about a certain prophet, or, as you would say, a Buddha, of the name of Issa. Can you tell me anything relative to his existence?" I asked, anxious to seize a favorable opportunity of broaching the subject I had so near at heart.

"The name of Issa is held in great respect by the Buddhists," replied my host. "But little is known about him save by the chief lamas, who have read the scrolls relative to his life. There have been an infinite number of Buddhas like Issa, and there are 84,000 scrolls extant replete with details of the lives of each; but few have read more than the hundredth part of them.

"Acting according to established custom, each student or lama visiting Lassa must make a gift of one or more copies to the convent to which he belongs. Our gonpa, among others, already possesses a large number. Among them are to be found descriptions of the life and acts of the Buddha Issa, who preached the holy doctrine in India and among the children of Israel and who was put to death by the pagans, whose descendants have since embraced the tenets he then propagated, which we believe to be yours.

"The great Buddha, Soul of the Universe, is the incarnation of Brahma. He remains almost always in passivity, preserving within himself all things from the beginning of time, and his breath vivifies the world. Having abandoned man to his own resources, he yet at certain epochs comes forth from his inertia, taking upon himself a human form to save his creatures from irremediable ruin.

"During his earthly existence, Buddha creates a new world among his scattered people. And after having fulfilled his task, he leaves the earth to reassume his invisible condition and his life of perfect bliss.

"Three thousand years ago, the great Buddha became incarnate in the celebrated prince Sakyamuni, thus continuing the scheme of his twenty incarnations. Two thousand five hundred years ago, the great Soul of the world again incarnated in

Gautama, laying the foundations of a new kingdom in Burma, Siam, and different islands.

"Soon after, Buddhism began to spread in
China—thanks to the energy of the wise men, who
did their best to propagate the holy doctrine. And
under Ming Ti of the dynasty Han, eighteen hundred and twenty-three years ago,* the precepts
of Sakyamuni received the universal adoption of
the people. Simultaneously with the advent of Buddhism in China, its tenets were diffused amongst
the Israelites.

"Nearly two thousand years ago the perfect
Being, again breaking through his state of inaction,
became incarnate in the newborn infant of a poor
family. It was his will that a child in simple words
should enlighten the ignorant as to the life eternal—
by his own example, bringing men back to the
ways of truth in setting before them the paths most
surely leading to the attainment of moral purity.

"When the holy child was still a boy, he was
taken to India, where until manhood he studied the
laws of the great Buddha who dwells eternally in
heaven."

At this juncture my interlocutor began to show
evident fatigue, commencing to twirl his prayer
girouette as a sign of his desire to end the conversation. I therefore hastily hazarded the following
questions:

"In what language are written the chief rolls
relative to the life of Issa?"

"The documents brought from India to Nepal
and from Nepal to Thibet concerning his existence
are written in the Pali language and are now in

---

*It will be remembered that Mr. Notovitch visited the convent in
1887.

Lassa. But a copy in our language—that is, the Thibetan—exists in this convent."

"How do they regard Issa in Thibet? Has he the reputation of a saint?"

"The people are ignorant of his very existence. Only the chief lamas, who have made a study of the documents bearing on his life, know anything about him. But as his doctrine does not constitute a canonical part of Buddhism—his worshippers not recognizing the authority of the Dalai Lama—the prophet Issa is not accepted in Thibet as a principal saint."

"Would you be committing a sin to recite these copies to a stranger?" I asked.

"That which belongs to God," replied the lama, "belongs also to man. Our duty obliges us to help with all good grace in propagating his sacred word. I am doubtful where the papers are to be found; but if ever you visit our gonpa again, I shall be pleased to show them to you."

At this moment two monks entered, uttered some words unintelligible to my interpreter, and at once retired.

"I am called to the sacrifices," said the lama. "Pray excuse me." Whereupon he bowed and, directing his steps towards the door, disappeared. Having nothing better to do, I retired to the room allotted to me, where I passed the night after partaking of a light supper.

The next day I returned to Leh, thinking under what pretext I could revisit the convent. Two days later I sent by a messenger to the chief lama a present comprising an alarm, a watch, and a thermometer, informing him at the same time of my desire to return if possible to the convent before my departure from Ladak, in the hope that he would permit me to see the book which had formed one of the themes of our conversation.

I had conceived the project of gaining Kashmir and of starting thence at a later period for Himis, but Fate ordained otherwise. For, passing before the hill on the top of which is perched the gonpa of Pintak, my horse stumbled and I was thrown to the ground with such violence that my right leg was fractured below the knee.

It was, therefore, impossible for me to continue my journey, and as I had no desire either to return to Leh or to demand hospitality at the gonpa of Pintak (an unhealthy abode), I ordered my removal to Himis, where I could arrive after half a day's slow travelling.

My fractured limb was bound up in an extemporized splint—an operation which caused me intense suffering—and I was lifted into my saddle, one coolie supporting my leg while another led my horse by the bridle. We crossed the threshold of Himis at an advanced hour in the evening.

Hearing of my accident, everyone came out to meet me. I was carried with great care to the best of their chambers and placed on a bed of soft materials, near to which stood a prayer wheel. All this took place under the immediate surveillance of the superior, who affectionately pressed the hand which I offered him in gratitude for his kindness.

Next day I myself made a better kind of splint for my leg, by the aid of little oblong pieces of wood joined together with strings, and by remaining perfectly motionless the result was so favorable that soon I was in a fit state to leave the gonpa and to start for India in search of surgical aid.

While a youth of the convent kept in motion the prayer wheel near my bed, the venerable superior entertained me by endless interesting stories, constantly taking my alarm and watch from their cases and putting to me questions as to their uses and the way they should be worked.

At last, acceding to my earnest entreaties, he ended by bringing me two large bound volumes with leaves yellowed by time, and from them he read to me in the Thibetan language the biography of Issa, which I carefully noted in my *carnet de voyage** as my interpreter translated what he said. This curious document is written under the form of isolated verses, which very often lack sequence.

In a few days my condition had so much improved that I was able to continue my route. I therefore, after having taken proper precautions regarding my injured limb, retraced my steps, making for India by way of Kashmir. This journey, accomplished by slow stages, lasted twenty days and caused me very great suffering.

Nevertheless, thanks to a litter obligingly sent to me by M. Peychaud (I profit by this occasion to thank him for the gracious hospitality he bestowed upon me) and to a ukase from the grand vizir of the maharajah of Kashmir, which intimated to the authorities an order to furnish me with carriers, I was enabled to reach Srinagar, which place I left almost at once, as I was anxious to reach India before the first falls of snow.

At Murree I met another Frenchman, Count André de Saint Phall, who was making a pleasure trip across Hindustan. During the whole journey we made together as far as Bombay, the young

*[travel notebook—ED.]

Through Bâbû Amar Nâth.

Order to
 Vazir Vazârat
 Pindakhâss.

Signature of Officer,
 Hukm Chand.

You must provide eight palanquin bearers (i.e., sedan carriers) for Mr. Notovitch Sahib, bound for Srî Nagar, through Bâbû Amar Nâth Jî, on hire (i.e., the Sahib is to pay wages for the bearers). There is strict injunction about this order (i.e., there must be no failure in its execution).

Dated 26th Kartik, 1944.

On the back of the order is:

"26th Kartik, 1944."

Translation of the Ukase, or Order, of the Grand Vizir of the
Maharajah of Kashmir

count showed the most touching solicitude for the suffering I endured, caused by my fractured leg and the fever which was then consuming me.

I retain a most grateful remembrance of his kindness, and never shall I forget the friendly care bestowed upon me on my arrival at Bombay by the Marquis de Morès, the Vicomte de Breteuil, M. Monod of the Comptoir d'Escompte, M. Moët, manager of the consulate, and other sympathetic members of the French colony.

At the same time, I take this opportunity of adding a word of sincere thanks to the numerous English friends who during my stay in India honored me with their friendship and hospitality—among others, Colonel and Lady Napier, Mr. and Mrs. O'Connor, Mr. Hume, Mr. E. Kay Robertson of the *Civil and Military Gazette,* and Mr. Rudyard Kipling.

For a long time I have meditated publishing the memoirs of Jesus Christ which I found at Himis. Important matters, however, have absorbed my time and it is only today—after having spent many sleepless nights in arranging my notes, grouping the verses conformably to the sequence of the recital, and giving to the whole work unity of character—that I resolve to give light to the curious document which follows.

The Life of Saint Issa

BEST OF THE SONS OF MEN

CHAPTER I

1 The earth has trembled and the heavens have wept because of a great crime which has been committed in the land of Israel.

2 For they have tortured and there put to death the great and just Issa, in whom dwelt the soul of the universe,

3 Which was incarnate in a simple mortal in order to do good to men and to exterminate their evil thoughts

4 And in order to bring back man degraded by his sins to a life of peace, love, and happiness and to recall to him the one and indivisible Creator, whose mercy is infinite and without bounds.

5 Hear what the merchants from Israel relate to us on this subject.

CHAPTER II

1 The people of Israel, who dwelt on a fertile soil giving forth two crops a year and who possessed large flocks, excited by their sins the anger of God,

2 Who inflicted upon them a terrible chastisement in taking from them their land, their cattle, and their possessions. Israel was reduced to slavery by the powerful and rich pharaohs who then reigned in Egypt.

3 These treated the Israelites worse than animals, burdening them with difficult tasks and loading them with chains. They covered their bodies with weals and wounds, without giving them food or permitting them to dwell beneath a roof,

4 To keep them in a state of continual terror and to deprive them of all human resemblance.

5 And in their great calamity, the people of Israel remembered their heavenly protector and, addressing themselves to him, implored his grace and mercy.

6 An illustrious pharaoh then reigned in Egypt who had rendered himself famous by his numerous victories, the riches he had heaped up, and the vast palaces which his slaves had erected for him with their own hands.

7 This pharaoh had two sons, of whom the younger was called Mossa. Learned Israelites taught him diverse sciences.

8 And they loved Mossa in Egypt for his goodness and the compassion which he showed to all those who suffered.

9 Seeing that the Israelites would not, in spite of the intolerable sufferings they were enduring, abandon their God to worship those made by the hand of man, which were gods of the Egyptian nation,

10 Mossa believed in their invisible God, who did not let their failing strength give way.

11 And the Israelitish preceptors excited the

ardor of Mossa and had recourse to him, praying him to intercede with the pharaoh his father in favor of their coreligionists.

12 Wherefore the Prince Mossa went to his father, begging him to ameliorate the fate of these unfortunates. But the pharaoh became angered against him and only augmented the torments endured by his slaves.

13 It happened that a short time after, a great evil visited Egypt. The pestilence came to decimate there both the young and the old, the weak and the strong; and the pharaoh believed in the resentment of his own gods against him.

14 But the Prince Mossa told his father that it was the God of his slaves who was interceding in favor of these unfortunates in punishing the Egyptians.

15 The pharaoh then gave to Mossa his son an order to take all the slaves of the Jewish race, to conduct them outside the town, and to found at a great distance from the capital another city where he should dwell with them.

16 Mossa then made known to the Hebrew slaves that he had set them free in the name of their God, the God of Israel, and he went out with them from the city and from the land of Egypt.

17 He led them into the land they had lost by their many sins, he gave unto them laws, and enjoined them to pray always to the invisible Creator whose goodness is infinite.

18 On the death of Prince Mossa, the Israelites rigorously observed his laws, wherefore God recompensed them for the ills to which he had exposed them in Egypt.

19 Their kingdom became the most powerful

of all the earth, their kings made themselves
famous for their treasures, and a long peace
reigned among the people of Israel.

CHAPTER III

1 The glory of the riches of Israel spread
throughout the earth, and the neighboring nations
bore them envy.

2 For the Most High himself led the victorious arms of the Hebrews, and the pagans dared
not attack them.

3 Unhappily, as man is not always true to
himself, the fidelity of the Israelites to their God
did not last long.

4 They began by forgetting all the favors
which he had heaped upon them, invoked but
seldom his name, and sought the protection of
magicians and sorcerers.

5 The kings and the captains substituted their
own laws for those which Mossa had written down
for them. The temple of God and the practice of
worship were abandoned. The people gave themselves up to pleasure and lost their original purity.

6 Several centuries had elapsed since their
departure from Egypt when God determined to
exercise once more his chastisements upon them.

7 Strangers began to invade the land of
Israel, devastating the country, ruining the villages,
and carrying the inhabitants into captivity.

8 And there came at one time pagans from
the country of Romeles, on the other side of the
sea. They subdued the Hebrews and established
among them military leaders who by delegation
from Caesar ruled over them.

9 They destroyed the temples, they forced the inhabitants to cease worshipping the invisible God, and compelled them to sacrifice victims to the pagan deities.

10 They made warriors of those who had been nobles, the women were torn away from their husbands, and the lower classes, reduced to slavery, were sent by thousands beyond the seas.

11 As to the children, they were put to the sword. Soon in all the land of Israel naught was heard but groans and lamentations.

12 In this extreme distress, the people remembered their great God. They implored his grace and besought him to forgive them; and our Father, in his inexhaustible mercy, heard their prayer.

CHAPTER IV

1 At this time came the moment when the all-merciful Judge elected to become incarnate in a human being.

2 And the Eternal Spirit, dwelling in a state of complete inaction and of supreme beatitude, awoke and detached itself for an indefinite period from the Eternal Being,

3 So as to show forth in the guise of humanity the means of self-identification with Divinity and of attaining to eternal felicity,

4 And to demonstrate by example how man may attain moral purity and, by separating his soul from its mortal coil, the degree of perfection necessary to enter into the kingdom of heaven, which is unchangeable and where happiness reigns eternal.

5 Soon after, a marvelous child was born in

the land of Israel, God himself speaking by the mouth of this infant of the frailty of the body and the grandeur of the soul.

6 The parents of the newborn child were poor people, belonging by birth to a family of noted piety, who, forgetting their ancient grandeur on earth, praised the name of the Creator and thanked him for the ills with which he saw fit to prove them.

7 To reward them for not turning aside from the way of truth, God blessed the firstborn of this family. He chose him for his elect and sent him to help those who had fallen into evil and to cure those who suffered.

8 The divine child, to whom was given the name of Issa, began from his earliest years to speak of the one and indivisible God, exhorting the souls of those gone astray to repentance and the purification of the sins of which they were culpable.

9 People came from all parts to hear him, and they marveled at the discourses proceeding from his childish mouth. All the Israelites were of one accord in saying that the Eternal Spirit dwelt in this child.

10 When Issa had attained the age of thirteen years, the epoch when an Israelite should take a wife,

11 The house where his parents earned their living by carrying on a modest trade began to be a place of meeting for rich and noble people, desirous of having for a son-in-law the young Issa, already famous for his edifying discourses in the name of the Almighty.

12 Then it was that Issa left the parental house in secret, departed from Jerusalem, and with the merchants set out towards Sind,

13 With the object of perfecting himself in the Divine Word and of studying the laws of the great Buddhas.

CHAPTER V

1 In the course of his fourteenth year, the young Issa, blessed of God, came on this side of Sind and established himself among the Aryas in the land beloved of God.

2 Fame spread the reputation of this marvelous child throughout the length of northern Sind, and when he crossed the country of the five rivers and the Rajputana, the devotees of the god Jaine prayed him to dwell among them.

3 But he left the erring worshippers of Jaine and went to Juggernaut in the country of Orissa, where repose the mortal remains of Vyasa-Krishna and where the white priests of Brahma made him a joyous welcome.

4 They taught him to read and understand the Vedas, to cure by aid of prayer, to teach, to explain the holy scriptures to the people, and to drive out evil spirits from the bodies of men, restoring unto them their sanity.

5 He passed six years at Juggernaut, at Rajagriha, at Benares, and in the other holy cities. Everyone loved him, for Issa lived in peace with the Vaisyas and the Sudras, whom he instructed in the holy scriptures.

6 But the Brahmans and the Kshatriyas told him that they were forbidden by the great Para-Brahma to come near to those whom he had created from his side and his feet;

7 That the Vaisyas were only authorized to

hear the reading of the Vedas, and this on festival
days only;

8 That the Sudras were forbidden not only to
assist at the reading of the Vedas, but also from
contemplating them, for their condition was to
serve in perpetuity as slaves to the Brahmans, the
Kshatriyas, and even the Vaisyas.

9 "'Death only can set them free from their
servitude' has said Para-Brahma. Leave them then
and come and worship with us the gods, who will
become incensed against thee if thou dost disobey
them."

10 But Issa listened not to their discourses
and betook him to the Sudras, preaching against
the Brahmans and the Kshatriyas.

11 He inveighed against the act of a man
arrogating to himself the power to deprive his fellow beings of their rights of humanity; "for," said
he, "God the Father makes no difference between
his children; all to him are equally dear."

12 Issa denied the divine origin of the Vedas*
and the Puranas. "For," taught he to his followers,
"a law has already been given to man to guide him
in his actions;

13 "Fear thy God, bend the knee before him
only, and bring to him alone the offerings which
proceed from thy gains."

14 Issa denied the Trimurti and the incarnation of Para-Brahma in Vishnu, Siva, and other
gods, for said he:

15 "The Judge Eternal, the Eternal Spirit,
comprehends the one and indivisible soul of the universe, which alone creates, contains, and vivifies all.

*Inasmuch as Jesus' closest disciple, John, begins his Gospel with a
quote from the Vedas, "In the beginning was the Word . . .," the authenticity of this passage may be questioned. See p. 393 for discussion.

16 "He alone has willed and created, he alone has existed since all eternity, and his existence will have no end. He has no equal either in the heavens or on earth.

17 "The Great Creator has not shared his power with any living being, still less with inanimate objects, as they have taught to you; for he alone possesses omnipotence.

18 "He willed it and the world appeared. In a divine thought, he gathered together the waters, separating from them the dry portion of the globe. He is the principle of the mysterious existence of man, in whom he has breathed a part of his Being.

19 "And he has subordinated to man the earth, the waters, the beasts, and all that he has created and that he himself preserves in immutable order, fixing for each thing the length of its duration.

20 "The anger of God will soon be let loose against man; for he has forgotten his Creator, he has filled his temples with abominations, and he worships a crowd of creatures which God has made subordinate to him.

21 "For to do honor to stones and metals, he sacrifices human beings, in whom dwells a part of the spirit of the Most High.

22 "For he humiliates those who work by the sweat of their brow to acquire the favor of an idler seated at his sumptuous board.

23 "Those who deprive their brethren of divine happiness shall be deprived of it themselves. The Brahmans and the Kshatriyas shall become the Sudras, and with the Sudras the Eternal shall dwell everlastingly.

24 "Because in the day of the last judgment the Sudras and the Vaisyas will be forgiven much

because of their ignorance, while God, on the contrary, will punish with his wrath those who have arrogated to themselves his rights."

25 The Vaisyas and the Sudras were filled with great admiration and asked Issa how they should pray so as not to lose their eternal felicity.

26 "Worship not the idols, for they hear you not. Listen not to the Vedas, for their truth is counterfeit. Never put yourself in the first place and never humiliate your neighbor.

27 "Help the poor, support the weak, do ill to no one, and covet not that which thou hast not and which thou seest belongeth to another."

CHAPTER VI

1 The white priests and the warriors, becoming acquainted with the discourses of Issa addressed to the Sudras, resolved upon his death and sent with this intent their servants to seek out the young prophet.

2 But Issa, warned of his danger by the Sudras, left the neighborhood of Juggernaut by night, reached the mountain, and established himself in the country of Gautamides, the birthplace of the great Buddha Sakyamuni, in the midst of a people worshipping the one and sublime Brahma.

3 After having perfected himself in the Pali language, the just Issa applied himself to the study of the sacred writings of the Sutras.

4 Six years after, Issa, whom the Buddha had elected to spread his holy word, had become a perfect expositor of the sacred writings.

5 Then he left Nepal and the Himalayan

mountains, descended into the valley of Rajputana, and went towards the west, preaching to diverse peoples the supreme perfection of man,

6 Which is—to do good to one's neighbor, being the sure means of merging oneself rapidly in the Eternal Spirit: "He who shall have regained his original purity," said Issa, "will die having obtained remission for his sins, and he will have the right to contemplate the majesty of God."

7 In crossing pagan territories, the divine Issa taught that the worship of visible gods was contrary to the law of nature.

8 "For man," said he, "has not been permitted to see the image of God, and yet he has made a host of deities in the likeness of the Eternal.

9 "Moreover, it is incompatible with the human conscience to make less matter of the grandeur of divine purity than of animals and objects executed by the hand of man in stone or metal.

10 "The Eternal Lawgiver is one; there is no other God but he. He has not shared the world with anyone, neither has he informed anyone of his intentions.

11 "Even as a father would act towards his children, so will God judge men after their deaths according to the laws of his mercy. Never would he so humiliate his child as to transmigrate his soul, as in a purgatory, into the body of an animal."

12 "The heavenly law," said the Creator by the mouth of Issa, "is opposed to the immolation of human sacrifices to an image or to an animal; for *I* have consecrated to man all the animals and all that the earth contains.

13 "All things have been sacrificed to man, who is directly and intimately associated with me

his Father; therefore he who shall have stolen from me my child will be severely judged and chastised by the divine law.

14 "Man is naught before the Eternal Judge, as the animal is naught before man.

15 "Wherefore I say unto you, Leave your idols and perform not rites which separate you from your Father, associating you with the priests from whom the heavens have turned away.

16 "For it is they who have led you from the true God and whose superstitions and cruelties conduce to the perversion of your soul and the loss of all moral sense."

CHAPTER VII

1 The words of Issa spread among the pagans in the midst of the countries he traversed, and the inhabitants forsook their idols.

2 Seeing which the priests exacted of him who glorified the name of the true God, reason in the presence of the people for the reproaches he made against them and a demonstration of the nothingness of their idols.

3 And Issa made answer to them: "If your idols and your animals are powerful and really possessed of supernatural strength, then let them strike me to the earth."

4 "Work then a miracle," replied the priests, "and let thy God confound our gods, if they inspire him with contempt."

5 But Issa then said: "The miracles of our God have been worked since the first day when the universe was created; they take place every day and at every moment. Whosoever seeth them not is

deprived of one of the fairest gifts of life.

6 "And it is not against pieces of stone, metal, or wood, which are inanimate, that the anger of God will have full course; but it will fall on men, who, if they desire their salvation, must destroy all the idols they have made.

7 "Even as a stone and a grain of sand, naught as they are in the sight of man, wait patiently the moment when he shall take and make use of them,

8 "So man must await the great favor that God shall accord him in his final judgment.

9 "But woe unto you, ye enemies of men, if it be not a favor that you await but rather the wrath of the Divinity—woe unto you if ye expect miracles to bear witness to his power.

10 "For it will not be the idols that he will annihilate in his anger but those who shall have erected them. Their hearts shall be consumed with eternal fire, and their lacerated bodies shall go to satiate the hunger of wild beasts.

11 "God will drive the impure from among his flocks, but he will take back to himself those who shall have gone astray through not having recognized the portion of spirituality within them."

12 Seeing the powerlessness of their priests, the pagans had still greater faith in the sayings of Issa and, fearing the anger of the Divinity, broke their idols to pieces. As for the priests, they fled to escape the vengeance of the populace.

13 And Issa further taught the pagans not to strive to see the Eternal Spirit with their eyes but to endeavor to feel him in their hearts and by purity of soul to render themselves worthy of his favors.

14 "Not only," said he unto them, "abstain

from consuming human sacrifices, but immolate no creature to whom life has been given, for all things that exist have been created for the profit of man.

15 "Do not steal the goods of your neighbor, for that would be to deprive him of what he has acquired by the sweat of his brow.

16 "Deceive no one, so as not to be yourselves deceived. Endeavor to justify yourself before the last judgment, for then it will be too late.

17 "Do not give yourselves up to debauchery, for that would be to violate the laws of God.

18 "You shall attain to supreme happiness, not only in purifying yourselves, but also in guiding others in the way that shall permit them to gain original perfection."

CHAPTER VIII

1 The neighboring countries resounded with the prophecies of Issa, and when he entered into Persia the priests became alarmed and forbade the inhabitants to listen to him.

2 And when they saw all the villages welcoming him with joy and listening devoutly to his sermons, they gave orders to arrest him and had him brought before the high priest, where he underwent the following interrogation:

3 "Of what new God dost thou speak? Art thou not aware, unhappy man, that Saint Zoroaster is the only just one admitted to the privilege of communion with the Supreme Being,

4 "Who ordered the angels to put down in writing the word of God for the use of his people, laws that were given to Zoroaster in paradise?

5 "Who then art thou to dare here to blaspheme our God and to sow doubt in the hearts of believers?"

6 And Issa said unto them: "It is not of a new God that I speak but of our Heavenly Father, who has existed since all time and who will still be after the end of all things.

7 "It is of him that I have discoursed to the people, who, like unto innocent children, are not yet capable of comprehending God by the simple strength of their intelligence or of penetrating into his divine and spiritual sublimity.

8 "But even as a babe discovers in the darkness its mother's breast, so even your people, who have been led into error by your erroneous doctrine and your religious ceremonies, have recognized by instinct their Father in the Father of whom I am the prophet.

9 "The Eternal Being has said to your people through the medium of my mouth: 'You shall not worship the sun, for it is but a part of the world which I have created for man.

10 "'The sun rises in order to warm you during your work; it sets to allow you the repose which I myself have appointed.

11 "'It is to me, and to me alone, that you owe all that you possess, all that is to be found about you, above you, and below you.'"

12 "But," said the priests, "how could a people live according to the rules of justice if it had no preceptors?"

13 Then Issa answered, "So long as the people had no priests, the natural law governed them, and they preserved the candor of their souls.

14 "Their souls were with God, and to com-

mune with the Father they had recourse to the medium of no idol or animal, nor to the fire, as is practiced here.

15 "You contend that one must worship the sun, the spirit of good and of evil. Well, I say unto you, your doctrine is a false one, the sun acting not spontaneously but according to the will of the invisible Creator who gave it birth

16 "And who has willed it to be the star that should light the day, to warm the labor and the seedtime of man.

17 "The Eternal Spirit is the soul of all that is animate. You commit a great sin in dividing it into a spirit of evil and a spirit of good, for there is no God outside the good,

18 "Who, like unto the father of a family, does but good to his children, forgiving all their faults if they repent them.

19 "The spirit of evil dwells on the earth in the hearts of those men who turn aside the children of God from the strait path.

20 "Wherefore I say unto you, Beware of the day of judgment, for God will inflict a terrible chastisement upon all those who shall have led his children astray from the right path and have filled them with superstitions and prejudices;

21 "Those who have blinded them that see, conveyed contagion to the healthy, and taught the worship of the things that God has subordinated to man for his good and to aid him in his work.

22 "Your doctrine is therefore the fruit of your errors; for desiring to bring near to you the God of truth, you have created for yourselves false gods."

23 After having listened to him, the magi

determined to do him no harm. But at night, when all the town lay sleeping, they conducted him outside of the walls and abandoned him on the high road, in the hope that he would soon become a prey to the wild beasts.

24 But, protected by the Lord our God, Saint Issa continued his way unmolested.

CHAPTER IX

1 Issa, whom the Creator had elected to remind a depraved humanity of the true God, had reached his twenty-ninth year when he returned to the land of Israel.

2 Since his departure the pagans had inflicted still more atrocious sufferings on the Israelites, who were a prey to the deepest despondency.

3 Many among them had already begun to abandon the laws of their God and those of Mossa in the hope of appeasing their savage conquerors.

4 In the face of this evil, Issa exhorted his compatriots not to despair because the day of the redemption of sins was at hand, and he confirmed them in the belief which they had in the God of their fathers.

5 "Children, do not give yourselves up to despair," said the Heavenly Father by the mouth of Issa, "for I have heard your voice, and your cries have reached me.

6 "Do not weep, O my beloved ones! For your grief has touched the heart of your Father, and he has forgiven you, even as he forgave your forefathers.

7 "Do not abandon your families to plunge yourselves into debauchery, do not lose the nobility

of your feelings, and do not worship idols who will remain deaf to your voices.

8 "Fill my temple with your hope and with your patience and abjure not the religion of your fathers; for I alone have guided them and have heaped them with benefits.

9 "You shall lift up those who have fallen, you shall give food to the hungry, and you shall come to the aid of the sick, so as to be all pure and just at the day of the last judgment which I prepare for you."

10 The Israelites came in crowds at the word of Issa, asking him where they should praise the Heavenly Father, seeing that the enemy had razed their temples to the ground and laid low their sacred vessels.

11 And Issa made answer to them that God had not in view temples erected by the hands of man, but he meant that the human heart was the true temple of God.

12 "Enter into your temple, into your heart. Illumine it with good thoughts and the patience and immovable confidence which you should have in your Father.

13 "And your sacred vessels, they are your hands and your eyes. See and do that which is agreeable to God, for in doing good to your neighbor you accomplish a rite which embellishes the temple wherein dwells he who gave you life.

14 "For God has created you in his own like-ness—innocent, with pure souls and hearts filled with goodness, destined not for the conception of evil schemes but made to be sanctuaries of love and justice.

15 "Wherefore I say unto you, sully not your

hearts, for the Supreme Being dwells therein eternally.

16 "If you wish to accomplish works marked with love or piety, do them with an open heart and let not your actions be governed by calculations or the hope of gain.

17 "For such actions would not help to your salvation, and you would fall into that state of moral degradation where theft, lying, and murder pass for generous deeds."

CHAPTER X

1 Saint Issa went from one town to another, strengthening by the word of God the courage of the Israelites, who were ready to succumb to the weight of their despair; and thousands of men followed him to hear him preach.

2 But the chiefs of the towns became afraid of him, and they made known to the principal governor who dwelt at Jerusalem that a man named Issa had arrived in the country; that he was stirring up by his discourses the people against the authorities; that the crowd listened to him with assiduity, neglected the works of the state, and affirmed that before long it would be rid of its intrusive governors.

3 Then Pilate, governor of Jerusalem, ordered that they should seize the person of the preacher Issa, that they should bring him into the town and lead him before the judges. But in order not to excite the anger of the populace, Pilate charged the priests and the learned Hebrew elders to judge him in the temple.

4 Meanwhile Issa, continuing his preachings,

arrived at Jerusalem; and, having learnt of his arrival, all the inhabitants, knowing him already by reputation, went out to meet him.

5 They greeted him respectfully and opened to him the gates of their temple in order to hear from his mouth what he had said in the other cities of Israel.

6 And Issa said unto them: "The human race perishes because of its lack of faith, for the darkness and the tempest have scattered the flocks of humanity and they have lost their shepherds.

7 "But the tempest will not last forever, and the darkness will not always obscure the light. The sky will become once more serene, the heavenly light will spread itself over the earth, and the flocks gone astray will gather around their shepherd.

8 "Do not strive to find straight paths in the darkness, lest ye fall into a pit; but gather together your remaining strength, support one another, place your confidence in your God, and wait till light appears.

9 "He who sustains his neighbor, sustains himself; and whosoever protects his family, protects the people and the state.

10 "For be sure that the day is at hand when you shall be delivered from the darkness; you shall be gathered together as one family; and your enemy, who ignores what the favor of God is, shall tremble with fear."

11 The priests and the elders who were listening to him, filled with admiration at his discourse, asked him if it were true that he had tried to stir up the people against the authorities of the country, as had been reported to the governor Pilate.

12 "Can one excite to insurrection men gone

astray, from whom the obscurity has hidden their door and their path?" replied Issa. "I have only warned the unfortunate, as I do here in this temple, that they may not further advance along the darkened way, for an abyss is open under their feet.

13 "Earthly power is not of long duration, and it is subject to many changes. Of what use that man should revolt against it, seeing that one power always succeeds to another power? And thus it will come to pass until the extinction of humanity.

14 "Against which, see you not that the mighty and the rich sow among the sons of Israel a spirit of rebellion against the eternal power of heaven?"

15 The elders then asked: "Who art thou, and from what country dost thou come? We have not heard speak of thee before, and we know not even thy name."

16 "I am an Israelite," replied Issa. "From the day of my birth I saw the walls of Jerusalem, and I heard the weeping of my brothers reduced to slavery and the lamentations of my sisters who were carried away by the pagans.

17 "And my soul was filled with sadness when I saw that my brethren had forgotten the true God. As a child, I left my father's house and went to dwell among other peoples.

18 "But having heard that my brethren were suffering still greater tortures, I have come back to the country where my parents dwell to remind my brothers of the faith of their forefathers, which teaches us patience on earth to obtain perfect and sublime happiness in heaven."

19 And the learned elders put him this question: "It is said that thou deniest the laws of Mossa

and that thou teachest the people to forsake the temple of God?"

20 And Issa replied: "One cannot demolish that which has been given by our Heavenly Father, neither that which has been destroyed by sinners; but I have enjoined the purification of the heart from all blemish, for it is the true temple of God.

21 "As to the laws of Mossa, I have endeavored to establish them in the hearts of men. And I say unto you that you do not understand their real meaning, for it is not vengeance but mercy that they teach; only the sense of these laws has been perverted."

CHAPTER XI

1 Having hearkened unto Issa, the priests and the wise elders decided among themselves not to judge him, for he did harm to no one. And presenting themselves before Pilate, appointed governor of Jerusalem by the pagan king of the country of Romeles, they addressed him thus:

2 "We have seen the man whom thou accusest of inciting our people to rebellion; we have heard his discourses, and we know him to be our compatriot.

3 "But the chiefs of the cities have made thee false reports, for this is a just man who teaches the people the word of God. After having interrogated him, we dismissed him, that he might go in peace."

4 The governor then became enraged and sent near to Issa his servants in disguise, so that they might watch all his actions and report to the authorities the least word that he should address to the people.

5 In the meantime, Saint Issa continued to visit the neighboring towns, preaching the true ways of the Creator, exhorting the Hebrews to patience, and promising them a speedy deliverance.

6 And during all this time, many people followed him wherever he went, several never leaving him but becoming his servitors.

7 And Issa said: "Do not believe in miracles wrought by the hand of man, for he who dominates over nature is alone capable of doing that which is supernatural, whilst man is powerless to stay the anger of the winds or to spread the rain.

8 "Nevertheless, there is one miracle which it is possible for man to accomplish. It is when, full of a sincere belief, he decides to root out from his heart all evil thoughts, and when to attain his end he forsakes the paths of iniquity.

9 "And all the things that are done without God are but errors, seductions, and enchantments, which only demonstrate to what an extent the soul of him who practices this art is full of shamelessness, falsehood, and impurity.

10 "Put not your faith in oracles; God alone knows the future: he who has recourse to diviners profanes the temple which is in his heart and gives a proof of distrust towards his Creator.

11 "Faith in diviners and in their oracles destroys the innate simplicity of man and his childlike purity. An infernal power takes possession of him, forcing him to commit all sorts of crimes and to worship idols;

12 "Whereas the Lord our God, who has no equal, is one, all-mighty, omniscient, and omnipresent. It is he who possesses all wisdom and all light.

13 "It is to him you must address yourselves to be consoled in your sorrows, helped in your works, and cured in your sickness. Whosoever shall have recourse to him shall not be denied.

14 "The secret of nature is in the hands of God. For the world, before it appeared, existed in the depth of the divine thought; it became material and visible by the will of the Most High.

15 "When you address yourselves to him, become again as children; for you know neither the past, the present, nor the future, and God is the Master of all time."

CHAPTER XII

1 "Righteous man," said unto him the spies of the governor of Jerusalem, "tell us if we shall perform the will of our Caesar or await our speedy deliverance."

2 And Issa, having recognized them as people appointed to follow him, replied: "I have not said to you that you shall be delivered from Caesar. It is the soul plunged in error that shall have its deliverance.

3 "As there can be no family without a head, so there can be no order among a people without a Caesar; to him implicit obedience should be given, he alone being answerable for his acts before the supreme tribunal."

4 "Does Caesar possess a divine right?" further asked of him the spies. "And is he the best of mortals?"

5 "There should be no better among men, but there are also sufferers, whom those elected and charged with this mission should care for,

making use of the means conferred on them by the sacred law of our Heavenly Father.

6 "Mercy and justice are the highest attributes of a Caesar; his name will be illustrious if he adhere to them.

7 "But he who acts otherwise, who exceeds the limit of power that he has over his subordinates, going so far as to put their lives in danger, offends the great Judge and loses his dignity in the sight of man."

8 At this juncture, an old woman who had approached the group, the better to hear Issa, was pushed aside by one of the spies, who placed himself before her.

9 Then Issa held forth: "It is not meet that a son should set aside his mother, taking her place. Whosoever respecteth not his mother, the most sacred being after his God, is unworthy of the name of son.

10 "Listen, then, to what I say unto you: Respect woman, for she is the mother of the universe, and all the truth of divine creation lies in her.

11 "She is the basis of all that is good and beautiful, as she is also the germ of life and death. On her depends the whole existence of man, for she is his natural and moral support.

12 "She gives birth to you in the midst of suffering. By the sweat of her brow she rears you, and until her death you cause her the gravest anxieties. Bless her and worship her, for she is your one friend, your one support on earth.

13 "Respect her, uphold her. In acting thus you will win her love and her heart. You will find favor in the sight of God and many sins

shall be forgiven you.

14 "In the same way, love your wives and respect them; for they will be mothers tomorrow, and each later on the ancestress of a race.

15 "Be lenient towards woman. Her love ennobles man, softens his hardened heart, tames the brute in him, and makes of him a lamb.

16 "The wife and the mother are the inappreciable treasures given unto you by God. They are the fairest ornaments of existence, and of them shall be born all the inhabitants of the world.

17 "Even as the God of armies separated of old the light from the darkness and the land from the waters, woman possesses the divine faculty of separating in a man good intentions from evil thoughts.

18 "Wherefore I say unto you, after God your best thoughts should belong to the women and the wives, woman being for you the temple wherein you will obtain the most easily perfect happiness.

19 "Imbue yourselves in this temple with moral strength. Here you will forget your sorrows and your failures, and you will recover the lost energy necessary to enable you to help your neighbor.

20 "Do not expose her to humiliation. In acting thus you would humiliate yourselves and lose the sentiment of love, without which nothing exists here below.

21 "Protect your wife, in order that she may protect you and all your family. All that you do for your wife, your mother, for a widow or another woman in distress, you will have done unto your God."

CHAPTER XIII

1 Saint Issa taught the people of Israel thus for three years, in every town, in every village, by the waysides and on the plains; and all that he had predicted came to pass.

2 During all this time the disguised servants of Pilate watched him closely without hearing anything said like unto the reports made against Issa in former years by the chiefs of the towns.

3 But the governor Pilate, becoming alarmed at the too great popularity of Saint Issa, who according to his adversaries sought to stir up the people to proclaim him king, ordered one of his spies to accuse him.

4 Then soldiers were commanded to proceed to his arrest, and they imprisoned him in a subterranean cell where they tortured him in various ways in the hope of forcing him to make a confession which should permit of his being put to death.

5 The saint, thinking only of the perfect beatitude of his brethren, supported all his sufferings in the name of his Creator.

6 The servants of Pilate continued to torture him and reduced him to a state of extreme weakness; but God was with him and did not allow him to die.

7 Learning of the sufferings and the tortures which their saint was enduring, the high priests and the wise elders went to pray the governor to set Issa at liberty in honor of an approaching festival.

8 But the governor straightway refused them this. They then prayed him to allow Issa to appear before the tribunal of the ancients so that he might be condemned or acquitted before the festival, and

to this Pilate consented.

9 The next day the governor assembled together the chief captains, priests, wise elders, and lawyers so that they might judge Issa.

10 They brought him from his prison and seated him before the governor between two thieves to be judged at the same time as he, in order to show unto the crowd that he was not the only one to be condemned.

11 And Pilate, addressing himself to Issa, said unto him: "O man! is it true that thou incitest the people against the authorities with the intent of thyself becoming king of Israel?"

12 "One becomes not king at one's own will," replied Issa, "and they have lied who have told thee that I stir up the people to rebellion. I have never spoken of other than the King of Heaven, and it is he I teach the people to worship.

13 "For the sons of Israel have lost their original purity; and if they have not recourse to the true God, they will be sacrificed and their temple shall fall into ruins.

14 "As temporal power maintains order in a country, I teach them accordingly not to forget it. I say unto them: 'Live conformably to your station and your fortune, so as not to disturb the public order.' And I have exhorted them also to remember that disorder reigns in their hearts and in their minds.

15 "Wherefore the King of Heaven has punished them and suppressed their national kings. Nevertheless, I have said unto them, 'If you become resigned to your destinies, as a reward the kingdom of heaven shall be reserved for you.'"

16 At this moment, the witnesses were

brought forward, one of whom made the following deposition: "Thou hast said to the people that the temporal power is as naught against that of the king who shall soon deliver the Israelites from the pagan yoke."

17 "Blessed art thou," said Issa, "for having spoken the truth. The King of Heaven is greater and more powerful than the terrestrial law, and his kingdom surpasses all the kingdoms of the earth.

18 "And the time is not far off when, conforming to the divine will, the people of Israel shall purify them of their sins; for it has been said that a forerunner will come to proclaim the deliverance of the people, gathering them into one fold."

19 And the governor, addressing himself to the judges, said: "Dost hear? The Israelite Issa confesses to the crime of which he is accused. Judge him, then, according to your laws, and pronounce against him capital punishment."

20 "We cannot condemn him," replied the priests and the elders. "Thou hast just heard thyself that his allusions were made regarding the King of Heaven and that he has preached naught to the sons of Israel which could constitute an offense against the law."

21 The governor Pilate then sent for the witness who, at his instigation, had betrayed Issa. The man came and addressed Issa thus: "Didst thou not pass thyself off as the king of Israel when thou saidest that he who reigns in the heavens had sent thee to prepare his people?"

22 And Issa, having blessed him, said: "Thou shalt be pardoned, for what thou sayest does not come from thee!" Then, addressing himself to the governor: "Why humiliate thy dignity, and why

teach thy inferiors to live in falsehood, as without doing so thou hast power to condemn the innocent?"

23 At these words the governor became exceeding wroth, ordering the sentence of death to be passed upon Issa and the acquittal of the two thieves.

24 The judges, having consulted together, said unto Pilate: "We will not take upon our heads the great sin of condemning an innocent man and acquitting thieves. That would be against the law.

25 "Do then as thou wilt." Saying which the priests and the wise elders went out and washed their hands in a sacred vessel, saying: "We are innocent of the death of this just man."

CHAPTER XIV

1 By the order of the governor, the soldiers then seized Issa and the two thieves, whom they led to the place of execution, where they nailed them to crosses erected on the ground.

2 All the day the bodies of Issa and the two thieves remained suspended, terrible to behold, under the guard of the soldiers; the people standing all around, the relations of the sufferers praying and weeping.

3 At sunset the sufferings of Issa came to an end. He lost consciousness, and the soul of this just man left his body to become absorbed in the Divinity.

4 Thus ended the earthly existence of the reflection of the Eternal Spirit under the form of a man who had saved hardened sinners and endured many sufferings.

5 Meanwhile, Pilate became afraid of his

action and gave the body of the saint to his parents, who buried it near the spot of his execution. The crowd came to pray over his tomb, and the air was filled with groans and lamentations.

6 Three days after, the governor sent his soldiers to carry away the body of Issa to bury it elsewhere, fearing otherwise a popular insurrection.

7 The next day the crowd found the tomb open and empty. At once the rumor spread that the supreme Judge had sent his angels to carry away the mortal remains of the saint in whom dwelt on earth a part of the Divine Spirit.

8 When this rumor reached the knowledge of Pilate, he became angered and forbade anyone, under the pain of slavery and death, to pronounce the name of Issa or to pray the Lord for him.

9 But the people continued to weep and to glorify aloud their Master; wherefore many were led into captivity, subjected to torture, and put to death.

10 And the disciples of Saint Issa abandoned the land of Israel and scattered themselves among the heathen, preaching that they should renounce their errors, bethink them of the salvation of their souls and of the perfect felicity awaiting humanity in that immaterial world of light where, in repose and in all his purity, the Great Creator dwells in perfect majesty.

11 The pagans, their kings, and their warriors listened to the preachers, abandoned their absurd beliefs, and forsook their priests and their idols to celebrate the praise of the all-wise Creator of the universe, the King of kings, whose heart is filled with infinite mercy.

Chapter Three

ON THE TRAIL TO HIMIS

Selections from Swami Abhedananda's
In Kashmir and Tibet *with his*
translation of the Himis manuscript

SWAMI ABHEDANANDA

Editor's Note

In 1922, Swami Abhedananda traveled to the Himis monastery in order to determine whether Nicolas Notovitch did in fact obtain a translation of an ancient Buddhist manuscript describing Jesus' sojourn in the East as he claimed in his *Unknown Life of Jesus Christ.* He reported that a lama who gave him a tour of the monastery verified Notovitch's story, showed him the book that became the basis for Notovitch's *Life of Saint Issa,* and helped him translate a part of the text.

Abhedananda published an account of his journey, along with a portion of the text he wrote down while at Himis, in a book written in Bengali entitled *Kashmir O Tibbate—In Kashmir and Tibet.*

This work was composed in stages, partly by Abhedananda and partly by Brahmachari Bhairav Chaitanya, an assistant who worked from the Swami's diary and original notes. Abhedananda later updated an early version of the manuscript. Since the literary style of the text is far less polished than that of his other writings, and Abhedananda is often referred to in the third person as "Swamiji," it appears that he did not revise the entire text. In 1954, fifteen years after Abhedananda's passing, the volume was edited once more by Swami Prajnananda and published in a revised second edition.

With the publication of this collection of eye-witness reports documenting Jesus' travels in the East, we are pleased to announce that the following passages from chapters 13 and 15 of *In Kashmir and Tibet* have been translated into English for the first time by three devotees of the ancient wisdom who desire to see this information reach the Western student in its purest form: Prasun Kumar De, a native of Calcutta now living in Los Angeles, Per Sinclair, an American translator deeply interested in Indian culture and religions, and Jayasri Majumdar, a language instructor and translator from Calcutta now living in Los Angeles. To these friends of Truth the author and publisher extend their profound appreciation.

Himis Monastery

At dawn, Swamiji went with the lamas to visit the monastery. He sat down with the head lama in his office.* The lamas brought in a big register (visitor's book) and noted our names and addresses. Swamiji signed in English as follows: "Swami Abhedananda, Vice President of the Ramakrishna Mission, Belur Math, near Calcutta."† Out of curiosity, Swamiji read all the names in the book but did not find one single Bengali name.

The room was big. There was a spacious mattress [thick gymnasium-type of mat] spread out on the floor, in the style of the Marwari people. A number of lama clerks were writing letters or keeping accounts. The main temple and the courtyard in front of the monastery were under repair. About thirty Tibetan laborers and masons were at work. Earth, stone, and wood were being used for the repair work. Many boys and girls and lama women were the carriers for the masons. The headmason appealed to Swamiji for a contribution for the

*Thirty-four years ago (1888 in the year of Christ) the honorable Swami Akhandananda, one of the sannyasi (monk) disciples of Sri Ramakrishna, came from the Barahanagar Temple to visit this monastery.
†At that time (1921–1924) Swami Abhedananda was the vice-president of Ramakrishna Math and Mission.

laborers, and Swamiji gave them some money. Having received the donation, the happy workers began singing mountain songs [folk songs] in their unintelligible Tibetan language.

I was told that the late Maharaj Pratap Singh of Kashmir had donated thirty thousand rupees for the work of restoration. When Pratap Singh of Punjab attacked this province, the head monk of the monastery sided with the Maharajah of Kashmir and promised six months' rations and lodging for his entire army. Since then, this monastery has been bound in eternal friendship with the royal family of Kashmir.

Prayer wheels had been installed all over the monastery. In some places, the large prayer wheel continually rotates by the force of water from a nearby spring. A bell attached to the wheel rings constantly. At other places, smaller prayer wheels in the shape of small drums are arranged in rows.

Some ten to twelve rooms contain images of gods and goddesses. We have already seen these gods and goddesses in other temples and described them. One dark room contains the likeness of a lama guru, Stag-Sang-Rom-Chen. His divine beauty, noble figure, and broad forehead indicate distinction. He is the founder of the monastery. We have already mentioned that many people call him the "tiger lama."

Most of these images are made of gold and silver. There are not many images here which are made of other metals. The stupas on which they stand are crafted entirely of silver and inlaid with precious stones and gold ornamental work. The ornaments on the bodies of the deities are all of gold and precious stones. The main ornaments are bangles on the wrists and arms, necklaces, and golden crowns.

There is one image of a goddess, Mandara or Kumari, which we had not seen in any other place before. She is the wife of Padma Sambhava (Guru Rinpoche) and sister of Shanti Rakshita.* In 749 A.D. she left Udyan, a place in northern India, with her husband and went to preach Buddhism in Tibet. They used to preach the Mahayana school of Buddhism. In monasteries such as Sang-Ye, Ching-Fook, etc., their images are worshiped daily with devotion. The lamas consider Padma Sambhava an incarnation of Mañjuśri.

In the Himis monastery, there reside nearly 150 Gyē-Loang, or monks, belonging to the Dug-Pa order. Their caps are red. Each has his separate room. In a room on the roof lives the Khang-Po, or the head of the monastery. He speaks a little English and Hindi. Except for the person who is looking after us, no lama can speak any language other than Tibetan. We would have faced a lot of difficulties if we had not brought an expert interpreter with us from Leh.

The monastery here is situated on about two acres of land. Except on the east, the monastery is surrounded by high mountains. Some extensions have been built directly connecting the monastery with the mountain slopes.

Under this monastery, there are quite a few temples, both large and small, as well as villages and farm land. The Kushak, or head monk, of the

*A well-known anthology of theories written by him has recently been published by the State of Baroda.

monastery has innumerable disciples and devotees who are householders. Once a year, he visits all his disciples and receives large donations as tithes. Besides this, if anybody falls ill or is frightened by evil spirits, he visits them and is handsomely paid for his services. All expenses of the monastery are met from such earnings.

A few years back, Dr. Nicolas Notovitch, a Russian traveler who was on a tour of Tibet, fell down a hill near this hermitage and broke his leg. The villagers brought him to the guesthouse of the monastery and the lamas gave him medical aid. He recovered about a month and a half later. At that time, he came to know from one of the lamas of the monastery that Jesus Christ came to India and that this was described in one of the hand-written manuscripts in the library of the monastery. With the help of one lama, he managed to obtain it and had it translated into English. After returning home, he wrote a book entitled *The Unknown Life of Jesus.* In his book he discussed this topic in detail.

Swamiji read the book when he was in America and felt very enthusiastic about it. In order to verify the descriptions, he took the trouble to come up and see the Himis retreat for himself. Swamiji inquired of the lamas and learned from them that the account was indeed true. Swamiji wanted to see the book in which this subject was written about.

The lama who was showing Swamiji around took a manuscript off the shelf and showed it to Swamiji. He said that it was a copy and the original was in a monastery at Marbour near Lhasa. The original was written in Pali, but this was a transla-tion into Tibetan. It consisted of 14 chapters and

224 verses. With his help, Swamiji got a part of it translated.

Only those verses which describe the activities of Jesus Christ when he was in India are quoted here.*

---

*[In chapter 13 of *In Kashmir and Tibet,* Swami Abhedananda described his experiences at Himis and reproduced only the portion of the Himis manuscript covering Jesus' trek to India. He placed the other verses from the Himis manuscript in chapter 15 of his work. We have taken the excerpt from chapter 15 and inserted it into chapter 13 in order to put the verses in their original, and chronological, order. Abhedananda's version of the Himis manuscript almost exactly parallels Notovitch's *Life of Saint Issa* through chapter 5, verse 4. Following that, Abhedananda excerpted parts of the Himis manuscript corresponding to scattered verses of *The Life of Saint Issa* through chapter 9, verse 1.—ED.]

Jesus Christ, the Leader of Men

CHAPTER I

1 The Jews, descendants of Israel, committed such heinous sins that the earth trembled and the gods in heaven wept,

2 Because they infinitely tortured and killed Issa, the great soul in whom the Divine Soul rested.

3 To render good to all and remove all sinful thoughts from their minds, the Divine Soul descended on him.

4 And to offer peace, happiness, and love of God to the sinners and to remind them of the infinite grace of God, It descended.

5 Thus describe the traders who came to this country from the land of Israel.

CHAPTER II

1 The tribes of Israel used to live in a very fertile land which yielded two crops in a year. They had several herds of sheep and goats. By their sinful act, they incurred the wrath of God.

2 For this reason, God confiscated all their property and placed them into the slavery of the pharaoh, the powerful ruler of Egypt.

3 But the pharaoh inflicted inhuman oppres-

sion upon the descendants of Israel. He put them in chains, inflicted wounds upon their bodies, deprived them of their livelihood, and engaged them in hard labor,

4 So that they would ever remain fearful and not declare themselves as free men.

5 The sons of Israel, thus exposed to extreme hardship, prayed to the Father of the Universe, the Saviour of their forefathers, and begged Him for mercy and help.

6 At that time a rich pharaoh, known for his conquests, became the ruler of Egypt; his palaces were handcrafted by the slaves.

7 The pharaoh had two sons. The younger of the two was called Mosa. He was versed in science and arts,

8 And he endeared himself to all by virtue of his good character and his compassion for the suffering.

9 He saw that the descendants of Israel suffered extreme hardships but had not lost faith in the Father of the Universe nor started worshiping the many small gods of the Egyptians.

10 Mosa believed in one God.

11 The teacher-priests of the Israelites brought this plea to Mosa, that if he asked his father, the ruler pharaoh, to help their co-workers, it would lead to the good of all.

12 When Mosa brought this plea to his father, his father grew very angry and started oppressing his subjects further like slaves.

13 But within a short time, Egypt was visited by a great plague that began to kill young and old, rich and poor. The ruler pharaoh thought that the gods were angry and that he was being thusly punished.

14 At that time Mosa told his father that the Father of the Universe was punishing the Egyptians as an act of grace on the poor oppressed subjects.

* * *

In due course of time, by the grace of the Father of the Universe, the sons of Israel began to find prosperity and freedom.

CHAPTER IV

1 The Supreme God, Father of the Universe, out of great compassion for sinners, desired to appear on earth in human form.

2 That Incarnation appeared as a soul separate from that Supreme Soul who has no beginning, no end, and is above all consequence.

3 [He] descended to show how a soul can unite with God and realize eternal bliss,

4 And assumed a human form to demonstrate in his own life how a mortal can achieve righteousness and separate the soul from the mortal body in order to gain immortality and proceed to that heaven of the Father of the Universe, where there exists eternal bliss.

5 [He] appeared as an immaculate child in the land of Israel. The child became the spokesman of the Father of the Universe to explain the transient nature of the body and the glory of the soul.

6 The parents of this child were poor but very devout and of high birth. They disregarded earthly possessions in order to proclaim God's name and his glory and believed that the Lord of the Universe had made them suffer only to test them.

7 The Lord of the Universe blessed this firstborn

child to reward their patience and sent him to save the sinners and cure the afflicted.

8   This divine child was named Issa. During his childhood he exhorted people to be devoted and respectful to the one Lord of the Universe and sinners to abstain from sinful acts and to repent.

9   People from everywhere came to listen to the wise sayings from the mouth of this child, and the sons of Israel unanimously proclaimed that the infinite, merciful Supreme Soul who knows no beginning, no end, existed in the child.

10   In the course of time, Issa entered his thirteenth year. The Israelites, according to their national custom, get married at this age. His parents used to live like ordinary householders.

11   That humble cottage of theirs grew clamorous with the arrival of the rich and aristocratic. Everyone was eager to have Issa as their son-in-law.

12   Issa was unwilling to marry. He had already attained fame by his expositions of the nature of God. At the proposal of marriage, he decided to leave his father's house in secret.

13   At that time the desire was very strong in his mind to attain perfection through devotional service to God and that he should study religion with those who had attained enlightenment.

14   He left Jerusalem, joined a group of traders, and set out for the land of Sind [the lower Indus valley, South Pakistan] where they used to purchase merchandise for export to various countries.

CHAPTER V

1   He (Jesus), at the age of fourteen, crossed northern Sind and entered the sacred land of the Aryans. . . .

2   While traveling alone along the land of the five rivers [the Punjab], his majestic features, peaceful face, and broad forehead prompted the devoted Jains to recognize him as one who had received the mercy of the Lord.

3   And they asked him to stay in their temples. But he did not accept their invitations, because he did not want any attention from others at that time.

4   In due course he arrived at the home of Jagannath, the country of Vyasa-Krishna's mortal play,* and became a disciple of the Brahmins. He endeared himself to everyone and it was there that he began reading, learning, and expounding the Vedas.

* * *

Next he lived for six years in Rajagriha, Kasi, and other holy places. Then he set out for Kapila-vastu, the birthplace of Lord Buddha.

Having lived there for six years with the Buddhist monks, he learned Pali thoroughly and began studying the Buddhist scriptures....

From there he toured Nepal and the Himalayas... and then proceeded westward.

Gradually he arrived in Persia, where the doctrines of Zarathustra were followed.†...

...Soon his fame spread everywhere....

Thus he returned to his homeland at the age of twenty-nine and began spreading the word of peace amongst his oppressed countrymen.

---

*[*Mortal play* describes the action of a god who plays a role—i.e., takes a mortal form, which begins with birth and ends with death—for a specific purpose, such as the incarnations of Krishna.—TRANS.]
†At that time Jesus halted at a wayside pond near Kabul to wash his hands and feet, and rested there for a while. That pond still exists. It is known as "Issa-pond." To mark the event, every year a fair is held at this place. This is mentioned in an Arabic book, *Tariq-A-Ajhan.*

The reverend lama said. . .three or four years after he [Jesus] left his body, the original manuscript was compiled in Pali from descriptions of all those Tibetans who met him at that time, as well as from descriptions of the traders who, with their own eyes, witnessed his crucifixion by the king of his country.

There is no doubt that if all the scholarly opinions that are current in various places regarding Christ's sojourn in India are collected and published in a book, it would prove to be a valuable document.

Chapter Four

LEGENDS OF THE EAST

Nicholas Roerich
Excerpts from Altai-Himalaya, Heart of Asia,
and Himalaya, *with original texts on Saint Issa*

NICHOLAS ROERICH

Roerich the Man, His Expedition and Finds

ONE would have to look far and wide to find a greater diversity of talent resident in one man: archaeologist, anthropologist, explorer, hunter, diplomat, mystic, poet, author and lecturer, artist, set and costume designer, conservator of culture—Nicholas Roerich, the consummate Renaissance man.

His life was a quest for Truth. Twice that quest took him to Central Asia—on the first expedition (1924–28) to Sikkim, through Punjab, Kashmir, Ladakh, Karakoram, Khotan, Kashgar, Karashahr, Urumchi, Irtysh, the Altai Mountains, the Oyrot region, Mongolia, Central Gobi, Kansu, Tsaidam, Tibet, and, secretly, to Moscow.

Born in St. Petersburg, Russia, on October 10, 1874, Nicholas Konstantinovich Roerich spent much of his youth near Gatchina, twenty-five miles southwest of the city, at his family's rural estate, Iswara.[1] There he developed a passion for hunting and a fascination with natural history and archaeology. He wrote adventure stories and epics for hunting magazines and, at the age of fifteen, illustrated a story about a chance (and dangerous) encounter he had with a bear. Michail O. Mikeshine, an artist, saw his drawings, encouraged his art work, and gave him his first painting lessons.

Nicholas wanted to pursue a career in art but his father, a prominent barrister, determined that he should study law. So he studied both, enrolling in the Academy of Fine Arts and the University of St. Petersburg in 1893.

In 1898, he was appointed to a professorship at the Imperial Archaeological Institute, and in 1901 he married Helena Ivanovna Shaposhnikov, a niece of the famous composer Modest P. Musorgski and grandniece of Field Marshal Mikhail I. Kutuzov, the Russian general whose strategy of indefinite retreat helped defeat Napoleon in 1812. They had two sons—George, a scientist, and Sviatoslav, an artist.

Helena was a distinguished and most gracious lady of letters, spiritually profound, intellectually brilliant—an accomplished pianist and a prolific writer in the esoteric tradition of Eastern religion. Besides the books credited to her, she reportedly authored works under as many as five pseud-onyms, including Josephine Saint-Hilaire and Natalie Rokotoff.[2] From time to time, it is possible to catch glimpses of her activities. She carried on a correspondence with President Franklin D. Roose-velt in 1934, for example—which suggests the important nature of her work.[3] But on the whole, not much is known about her because she was deliberately self-effacing.

Not only were the Roerichs enormously gifted, but they were also affectionate and inspiring. "I want to say that no other people have ever radiated such light and unconscious joy as Roerich and Madame Roerich," wrote George Grebenstchi-koff, an author and friend. "The days of our meeting were days of the highest uplift of spirit both for my wife and myself; at the bidding of one of the Roerichs either of us would have been ready to make any sacrifice."[4]

In the early 1900s, while the Roerichs traveled widely throughout Russia and Europe, Professor Roerich painted, undertook archaeological excavations, studied architecture, lectured, and wrote lucidly on art and archaeology. At the invitation of ballet impresario Sergei P. Diaghilev, he became a member of the famous St. Petersburg World of Art (Mir Iskusstva) society and served for a time as its president. Through its journal, the society "sought to express the ideal of Art for Art's sake," a concept in which "Art was seen as a form of mystical experience, a means through which eternal beauty could be expressed and communicated—almost a new kind of religion."[5]

In 1906, Roerich was appointed director of the School for the Encouragement of the Fine Arts in Russia. In 1907, he began applying his talents to stage and costume design, and later designed sets for Diaghilev and for Igor Stravinsky's ballet *The Rite of Spring*. The following year he became a member of the Board of the Imperial Society of Architecture and in 1909 was elected academician of the Russian Imperial Academy of Fine Arts.

Roerich led a productive and adventurous life and was often at the forefront of important events. At the start of the Bolshevik Revolution in March 1917, Maxim Gorki called his countrymen involved in the arts to a meeting in St. Petersburg. They elected a Council of Art Affairs which met at the Winter Palace. Roerich served as its chairman for two months.

At that time he was a candidate for the office of minister of fine arts and was asked to serve in the government in this or some other capacity. In discussing a lost collection of valuable old paintings belonging to Roerich, the *American Magazine of Art* (June 1921) noted that the fate of the paintings was "unknown, because he would not accept the high post offered him by the Bolsheviks."[6] Sensing the impending catastrophe, he took his family to Finland, thus drawing the curtain on his early career in Mother Russia.

At the invitation of Dr. Robert Harshe, director of the Chicago Art Institute, Roerich came to the United States in 1920. He had already executed more than 2,500 paintings and was an internationally acclaimed artist. Nonetheless, he created an immediate artistic sensation.

"Roerich's paintings are so great because of their affirmation, their great surety, in this restless day," wrote noted art critic Olin Downes. "In the midst of our modern society, so positive and so limited, he gives to his fellow-artists a prophetic example of the goal they must reach—the expression of the Inner Life."[7]

His work contains scenes of nature, themes inspired by history, architecture, religion—many in the style of the ancient Russian church paintings, others mystical, allegorical, epic, or sublime, and some which, like *The Last Angel,* are prophetic. He was influenced by a great many artists—from Arhip I. Kuindjy, his instructor at the Academy of Fine Arts, to Gauguin and Van Gogh—and a variety of schools of art. But his was a school of his own making.

His style, however, is difficult to describe because, as architect Claude Bragdon put it, he belongs to an elect fraternity of artists that includes da Vinci, Rembrandt, Blake—and, in music, Beethoven—

whose work has "a unique, profound and indeed a mystical quality which differentiates them from their contemporaries, making it impossible to classify them in any known category or to ally them with any school, because they resemble themselves only—and one another, like some spaceless and timeless order of initiates."[8]

Roerich was an artist of incredible empire whose paintings—often alive with exhilarating color—make a tangible impact on the viewer. Henry A. Wallace (secretary of agriculture 1933–40, vice president of the United States 1941–45) said Roerich's paintings "gave him a smooth feeling inside."[9] And some claimed they were literally transported to other realms by his artistry, or at least had visions thereof: "The genius of Roerich's fantasy reaches the border of clairvoyance," wrote the great Russian novelist Leonid Andreyev.[10]

In his essay "The Inner Meaning of Roerich's Art," Ivan Narodny proclaimed, "The very moment when I saw the paintings of Nicholas Roerich exhibited at the Kingore Galleries in New York, I felt they lured my eyes into an unknown wonderland, by evoking my soul to hear the sounds of chimes, choruses, organs, orchestras and aeolian harps. . . . Looking at Roerich's pictures I have been lured to meditations, dreams and spiritual tears—emotions experienced by pilgrims while kneeling in prayer before the wonder-working ikons."[11]

In support of the verisimilitude of those who report such lofty visions—or exclaim that "Roerich's art is *out of this world!*"—while in orbit, Yuri A. Gagarin, the first man in space (April 12, 1961), wrote in his journal: "Rays were blazing through the atmosphere of the earth, the horizon became bright orange, gradually passing into all the colors of the rainbow: from light blue to dark blue, to violet and then to black. What an indescribable gamut of colors! Just like the paintings of the artist Nicholas Roerich." [12]

In America, Roerich traveled widely, exhibited his works, circulated in the best circles, lectured at the most exclusive girls schools and at Marshall Field's department store, where he taught on the "spiritual garment" and harmonizing the human aura with clothing. [13]

He founded Cor Ardens (the International Society of Artists) and the Master Institute of United Arts in 1921, and Corona Mundi (International Art Center) in 1922. After planning the first of his expeditions to Asia, he embarked for India in 1923 to prepare for the journey.

The trustees of the Master Institute of United Arts founded the Roerich Museum in 1923. The museum housed a great number of Roerich's paintings but, reflecting Roerich's concept of the unity of art, it quickly became, in the words of historian Robert C. Williams, "a genuine cultural enterprise, sponsoring exhibits, lectures, and concerts by distinguished artists, musicians, and writers throughout the late 1920s and early 1930s." [14]

In 1928, Roerich founded the Urusvati Himalayan Research Institute in the lovely Kulu Valley in Nagar, India, which was a center for the study of ethnographic and archaeological materials.

In the course of his life, Roerich produced an astonishing number of paintings—about 7,000— wrote more than 1,200 works of all kinds, was *a* if not *the* (sometimes unseen) force behind placing the Great Seal of the United States on the dollar bill, and was nominated for the Nobel Peace Prize in 1929 and 1935 for his efforts to promote international peace through art and culture and to protect art treasures in time of war.

As early as 1904, Roerich proposed a treaty to protect the world's cultural endowment, suggested the idea to Czar Nicholas II in 1914 and formally drafted it into the language of international law in 1929.

The Third International Roerich Peace Banner Convention, November 1933, was a turning point in the campaign to ratify what became popularly known as the Roerich Pact. In effect, the pact obligated nations to respect museums, universities, cathedrals, and libraries as they did hospitals. Where hospitals flew the Red Cross flag in time of war, cultural institutions would fly Roerich's "Banner of Peace"—a white field with three red spheres enclosed by a red circle.

Efforts to promote the pact were spearheaded by the secretary of agriculture, Henry A. Wallace— at that time an admirer and, some say, spiritual disciple of Roerich. The meeting was no small affair among the Washington elite; Senator Robert F. Wagner served as the honorary chairman and fourteen U.S. senators, two congressmen, sixteen governors, the superintendent of the U.S. Military Academy, and several college presidents were honorary members of the convention.[15]

On April 15, 1935, Roerich finally saw a Pan-American treaty embodying the pact signed at the White House by representatives of the United States and twenty Latin American nations.[16]

Biographers have written a great deal about all phases of Roerich's life, except one: the capstone of his endeavors, the force which gave direction, unity, and meaning to his multiple activities—his spiritual life.

Somewhere along the line, the Roerichs acquired a profound understanding of the literature and traditions of esoteric religion—especially esoteric Buddhism. No doubt Nicholas Roerich's intimate knowledge of the ways of the East, combined with his diverse experience and great learning, explains why he was received with honor almost everywhere he went on his first Central Asian expedition, why the Chinese marveled at his learning and referred to him as "the Initiate," and why the Mongolians reportedly said, "Such great universal personalities as Roerich are walking the path of the Bodhisattvas of the highest order as absolute lights of the century. . . . Therefore, our country considers the visit of Professor Roerich. . . a great honor and a joy." [17]

It is not easy to trace the development of Roerich's spiritual life. The veil of obscurity, according to some of his followers, is the result of an intentional effort by the Roerichs to retain a reverent circle of privacy around their personal lives and inner experiences.

One of Roerich's biographers, Dr. Garabed Paelian, believed the first stirrings began in Nicholas' early childhood with the appearance of a white-robed figure in his dreams. [18] Some of Roerich's followers claim that his painting instructor Kuindjy, a man with Saint Francis-like qualities, was for a time his guru. In a tribute to Kuindjy, Roerich recalled, "I was happy to have as my first teacher an extraordinary man. The eminent Master Kuindjy was not only a remarkable artist, but also a great Teacher of life." [19]

Some believe that Kuindjy might have introduced Roerich to esoteric ideas and literature. Just what Kuindjy taught Roerich other than painting is shrouded in mystery, and whether he was his guru is a matter of considerable debate. Nevertheless, in an essay, "Guru—The Teacher," published in *Shambhala* (1930), Roerich says Kuindjy was "a real Guru for his pupils in the high Hindu conception." He speaks of Kuindjy having "the authority of the Guru" but states: "from where his [Kuindjy's] conception of real Guruship in the refined eastern understanding arose, I do not know." [20]

In any case, the Roerichs were briefly members of the Theosophical Society, studied its literature, eventually translated Helena P. Blavatsky's *Secret Doctrine* into Russian and in 1919 or 1920, according to the reports of some of their followers, made contact with the great Mahatmas of the East, Morya and Koot Hoomi.

While the Roerichs lived in the United States, a group of devotees familiar with their spiritual activities recognized Nicholas as a guru. Over the years, the Roerichs authored a large number of books on a wide variety of spiritual topics. Most have no biographical information at all. Some do not even identify the author, and others, at least in the case of Helena Roerich, were written under pseudonyms.

Drawn by their undying love of the Orient and the many secrets it held for them, the Roerichs departed in 1923 for a four-and-a-half-year epic tour of Asia. The expedition included Nicholas, Helena, their son George (the scientist), and several other Europeans. Their son Sviatoslav (the artist) and Lama Lobzang Mingyur Dorje, a scholar of

Tibetan literature, joined the party for a leg of the journey. They traveled through Sikkim, India, Kashmir, Ladakh, Tibet, China, Mongolia, and Russia. In short, their route encircled Central Asia.

"Of course, as an artist my main aspiration in Asia was towards artistic work," Roerich wrote in *Heart of Asia,* a synopsis of his travel diary, "and it is even difficult to estimate how soon I can embody all my artistic impressions and sketches—so generous are these gifts of Asia. No knowledge acquired in literature or in museums empowers one to express Asia or any other country, unless he has seen it with his own eyes and unless he has made at least some notes and sketches on the sites themselves. Conviction, this magic and intangible property of creation, comes only in the continuous cumulation of real conceptions. It is true, mountains everywhere are mountains, water everywhere is water, sky everywhere is sky, and men everywhere are men. But nevertheless, if seated before the Alps, you attempt to picture the Himalayas, something inexplicable but convincing will be lacking.

"In addition to its artistic aims, our Expedition planned to study the position of the ancient monuments of Central Asia, to observe the present condition of religions and creeds, and to note the traces of the great migrations of nations."[21] The expedition fulfilled its aims abundantly.

For much of the time, the Roerichs were out of touch with the West. After a long silence, this telegram reached New York on May 24, 1928. Its terse sentences impart a flavor of the journey:

"Roerich American Expedition after many hardships has reached Himalayas. Thus ended big Central Asiatic Expedition. Many artistic and scientific results. Already sent several series of paintings to New York. Hope last sending from Mongolia safely reached you. Many observations regarding Buddhism.

"Expedition started in 1924 from Sikhim through Punjab, Kashmir, Ladak, Karakorum, Khotan, Kashgar, Karashahr, Urumchi, Irtysh, Altai Mountains, Oyrot region, Mongolia, Central Gobi, Kansu, Tsaidam, Tibet.

"Peaceful American flag encircled Central Asia. Everywhere warmly greeted except Khotan and Lhasa Governments. Further movement Expedition from Khotan assisted by British Consul at Kashgar. On Tibetan territory have been attacked by armed robbers. Superiority of our firearms prevented bloodshed. In spite of Tibetan passports Expedition forcibly stopped by Tibetan authorities on Oct. 6, two days north of Nagchu. With inhuman cruelty Expedition has been detained for five months at altitude of 15,000 feet in summer tents amidst severe cold about 40 degrees below Centigrade.

"Expedition suffered from want of fuel and fodder. During stay in Tibet five men, Mongols, Buriats and Tibetans died and ninety caravan animals perished. By order of authorities all letters and wires addressed to Lhasa Government and Calcutta British authorities seized. Forbidden to speak to passing caravans. Forbidden to buy foodstuffs from population. Money and medicines came to an end. The presence of three women in caravan and medical certificate about heart weakness not taken into consideration. With great difficulties on March 4, Expedition started southward. All nine European members of the Expedition safe. Courageously bore hardships of exceptionally severe Winter. Greetings."[22]

During the trek, despite overwhelming obstacles,

Roerich executed some 500 paintings. In this book we have reproduced sixteen of his works done in tempera—some of which were completed on the expedition—and a portrait of the artist in oil by his son Sviatoslav. Roerich also kept a diary on the journey, later published under the title *Altai-Himalaya*. It is a loosely stitched tapestry of thoughts on science, archaeology, and religion combined with a swift-moving travelogue. A compilation of Roerich's "thoughts upon horseback and in the tent," it was once characterized as "the Symphony of Asia."[23] We know of no comparable work in existence. It is every whit a monument of beauty as his breathtaking, soul-effusing paintings.

In the course of his observation of religious practices, Roerich accumulated a great deal of evidence, both oral and written, not merely corroborating Notovitch's findings but adding new texts to the body already collected. Fortunately for students of the lost years, of world religions and mysticism in twentieth-century art, the search for Saint Issa will take them to the unexplored archives of Nicholas and Helena Roerich and a world of transcendent beauty that beckons spiritual pilgrims seeking to enter the twenty-first century with integrity and the strength to meet world chaos with knowing and calm.

"The expedition left New York in May, 1923, and in December of the same year reached Darjeeling in British Sikkim," George Roerich noted in his diary, *Trails to Inmost Asia*. "Here a base was established and several trips were conducted into Sikkim. The whole of 1924 was spent in Sikkim in preparation for the more extensive journey into inner Asia."[24]

The Roerichs left Darjeeling on March 6, 1925, and headed for Srinagar, Kashmir. There they commissioned skilled artisans to prepare the tremendous amount of gear they would need because "a journey such as that from Kashmir to Chinese Turkestan over the highest mountain route in the world," wrote George, "requires unusual forethought and careful consideration."

"The winter outfit for the cold weather on the mountain passes and the winter in Chinese Turkestan consisted of fur coats lined with *pashmina,* Gilgit fur boots, fur caps, fur socks, and fur sleeping bags. We also ordered several tents of waterproof Willesden canvas with warm pattoo lining. These tents had to be specially constructed to withstand the rough traveling and the mountain gales. They consisted of two flies, the outer fly reaching the ground to prevent the strong wind of the higher uplands from penetrating beneath and lifting the tent. The tent poles were of thick bamboo with strong metal joints, and the tent pegs of galvanized iron." [25]

On April 15, the family moved to Kashmir's hill station, Gulmarg, where they spent the rest of April, May, June, and July. On August 8, they started their journey along the Leh Treaty Route, eighty-two ponies in tow.

"Flies, mosquitoes, fleas, earwigs! All possible gifts has Kashmir. Our departure was not without bloodshed," wrote Roerich in *Altai-Himalaya.* "In Tangmarg a band of ruffians attacked our caravan and began to beat our men with iron rods; seven of our men were hurt. It was necessary to preserve order with revolvers and rifles. In Ghund, our hostlers fed the horses with poisonous grass; the horses began to shiver and finally lay down. The entire night they had to be walked up and down. My horse, Mastan, suffered especially, and also Sabsa, that of George. The drivers made fires around the ammunition box. A wildcat crept into the tent under George's bed."[26]

In *Heart of Asia* he recorded: "The ancient caravan road from Srinagar to Leh is covered in a seventeen days' march. But it is usually advised to take a few days more. Only cases of extreme need can induce the traveler to make this journey without interruption. Such unforgettable places, as Maulbeck, Lamayuru, Basgu, Kharbu, Saspul, Spithug, arrest one and retain themselves forever in one's memory, both from an artistic and a historical point of view.

"Maulbeck—now already a declining monastery, to judge by the ruins—must have once been a real stronghold, boldly occupying the summit of a huge rock. Near Maulbeck, on the main road, you are startled by an ancient gigantic image of Maitreya. You feel that not a Tibetan hand, but probably a Hindu, carved this image at the time of Buddhist glory. . . .

"One must have a sense of beauty and of fearless self denial to build strongholds on such heights. In many such castles, long subterranean passages, leading to a river, were hewn in the rocks, so that a loaded donkey could just manage to pass there. This fairy-tale of subterranean passages, as we shall see, has created many of the best sagas. As in Sikkim, the Ladaki lamas turned out to be kind, tolerant of other faiths and hospitable to travelers, as Buddhists should be. . . .

"In Nimu, a small village before Leh, 11,000 feet high, we had an experience which can under no circumstances be overlooked. It would be most interesting to hear of analogous cases. It was after a clear, calm day. We camped in tents. At about 10 p.m. I was already asleep, when Mrs. Roerich approached her bed to remove the woolen rug. But hardly had she touched the wool, when a big rose-violet flame of the color of an intense electric discharge shot up, forming a seemingly whole bonfire, about a foot high. A shout of Mrs. Roerich, 'Fire, fire!' awoke me. Jumping up, I saw the dark silhouette of Mrs. Roerich and behind her, a moving flame, clearly illuminating the tent. Mrs. Roerich tried to extinguish the flame with her hands, but the fire flashed through her fingers, escaping her hands, and burst into several smaller fires. The effect of the touch was a slightly warming effect, but there was no burning, nor sound, nor odor. Gradually the flames diminished and finally disappeared, leaving no traces whatsoever on the bed cover. We had occasion to study many electric phenomena, but I must say that we never experienced one of such proportions.

"In Darjeeling, a spheroidic lightning passed only two feet from my head. In Gulmarg, in Kashmir, during an uninterrupted thunderstorm of three days, when hail fell as big as a pigeon's egg, we studied a great variety of lightning. In the Trans-Himalayas, we repeatedly experienced the effect upon ourselves of different electric phenomena. I remember how in Chunargen, at an altitude of 15,000 feet, I awoke at night in my tent, and touching my bedrug, was surprised at the blue light flashing from my fingertips as though enwrapping my hand. Believing that this could occur only in contact with woolen material, I touched the linen pillowcase.

The effect was again the same. Then I touched all kinds of objects—wood, paper, canvas; in each case the blue light flashed up, intangible, soundless and odorless.

"The entire Himalayan region offers exceptional fields for scientific research. Nowhere else, in the whole world, can such varied conditions be concentrated: peaks up to almost thirty thousand feet; lakes at an elevation of fifteen thousand feet; deep valleys with geysers and all types of hot and cold mineral springs; the most unsuspected vegetation—all this vouches for unprecedented results in new scientific discoveries. If one could compare scientifically the conditions of the Himalayas with the uplands of other parts of the world, what remarkable analogies and antitheses would arise! The Himalayas are a veritable Mecca for a sincere scientist. When we recalled the book of Professor Millikan, 'The Cosmic Ray', we imagined the wonderful possibilities which this great scientist would find on these Himalayan heights. May these dreams become true, in the name of true science!"[27]

In only eighteen days, the Roerichs' caravan arrived in Leh. George wrote, "Our expedition remained in the capital of Ladak from August 26 to September 19, 1925, except for several days spent on a journey to the famous Hemis Monastery and other places of interest round the town. Much of the time during this stay was occupied by preparations for the next difficult portion of the journey across the great mountain route to Chinese Turkestan."[28]

The interlude at Himis was not a pleasant one. Professor Roerich was unimpressed by the monastery. He did, however, find evidence of the Issa manuscripts, although he does not specify whether the texts he later published were copied there. Otherwise disappointing, the Himis experience is outlined in his notes in *Himalaya,* a monograph published in 1926 from portions of his diary mailed home:

"One must also see the reverse side of Buddhism—let us go to Hemis. Already approaching one feels the strange atmosphere of darkness and dejection. The stupas are with strange fearful images—ugly faces. Black ravens fly above and black dogs are gnawing at the bones. And the canyon tightly incloses itself. Of course, the temple and the houses are all huddled together. And the objects of service are heaped together in dark corners like the loot of robbers. The lamas are half-literate. Our guide laughs, 'Hemis, a big name, but a little monastery.' Of course small, not according to size, but to inner meaning. Here is apparent prejudice and greed. The only fine thing about it was that upon the neighboring sharp rocks, at morning, the deer appeared and, standing long upon the cliffs, turned their heads to greet the sun."

"It is an old monastery founded by a great lama who left a book about Chambhalla and these manuscripts are lying down below, out of sight, probably feeding the mice."

"Regarding the manuscripts of Christ—first there was a complete denial. Of course denial first comes from the circle of missionaries. Then slowly, little by little, are creeping fragmentary reticent details, difficult to obtain. Finally it appears—that about the manuscripts, the old people in Ladak have heard and know."

"And such documents as manuscripts about Christ and the Book of Chambhalla lie in the 'darkest' place. And the figure of the lama—the compiler of the book—stands like an idol in some sort of fantastic headgear. And how many other relics have perished in dusty corners? For the tantrik-lamas have no interest in them. It was necessary to see this other side of Buddhism."[29]

"And how simple it is to brush aside this grime and dust of fanaticism! How simple to restore the stirring mural paintings! How easy to purify and to cleanse the finely wrought statues! Nor is it difficult to bring the monastic organizations back to the full meaning of the working order, according to the teachings of the greatest Lion (Sinha)—Buddha."[30]

Leh received the Roerichs with much greater honor. They were invited to stay in the king's crumbling but majestic seventeenth-century palace which dominates the horizon. "The entire atmosphere at Ladak seemed to be under benevolent signs for us," recalled Roerich.

"The city of Leh, the residence of the former Maharajah of Ladak, now conquered by Kashmir, is a typical Tibetan town, with numerous clay walls, temples and long rows of Suburgans, which lend a solemn silence to the place. This city, on a high mountain, is crowned by the eight-story palace of the Maharajah. At the latter's invitation, we stopped there, choosing for our dwelling the top floor of the stronghold, which trembled under the violent gusts of wind. During our occupancy a door and part of the wall collapsed. But the wonderful view from the roof made us forget the instability of the castle.

"Below the palace, lies the whole city: bazaars crowded with noisy caravans, fruit orchards and, around the city, great fields of barley from which garlands of merry songs resound at the close of the day's work. The Ladaki women walk about picturesquely in their high fur caps, with turned up earpieces. Down their backs hang long head-bands decorated with a great amount of turquoise and small metal ornaments. Across the shoulders, like an ancient Byzantine korsno, is generally worn the skin of a yak, fastened on the right shoulder with a fibula. Among the richer women, this korsno is of colored cloth, resembling still more the real Byzantine ikons. And the fibulae on their right shoulder might have been excavated in Nordic and Scandinavian tumuli.

"Not far from Leh, on a stony hill, are ancient graves, believed to be prehistoric and recalling Druidic antiquities. Not far away is also the place of the old Mongolian Kham, which tried to conquer Ladak. In this valley also are Nestorian crosses, once more recalling how widely spread in Asia was Nestorianism and Manicheism."*[31]

---

*Nestorianism: doctrine set forth by fifth-century bishop of Constantinople Nestorius which stated that there were two separate persons—human and divine—in the incarnate Christ as opposed to the orthodox teaching that Christ was a divine person who assumed a human nature. After Nestorius' views were condemned in 431 by the Council of Ephesus, supporters of his theology formed a center of resistance at the famed theological school in Edessa. The school was closed in 489 by imperial order and a small remnant of Nestorians

And among the riot and color of the Asian bazaar, the arrival and departure of caravans, the bustling merchants, the breathtaking beauty of the Himalayas, the ancient traditions surrounding the city of Leh, arose the legends of Issa.

"In Leh, we again encountered the legend of Christ's visit to these parts. The Hindu postmaster of Leh and several Ladaki Buddhists told us that in Leh not far from the bazaar, there still exists a pond, near which stood an old tree. Under this tree, Christ preached to the people, before his departure to Palestine. We also heard another legend of how Christ, when young, arrived in India with a merchant's caravan and how He continued to study the higher wisdom in the Himalayas. We heard several versions of this legend which has spread widely throughout Ladak, Sinkiang and Mongolia, but all versions agree on one point, that during the time

---

migrated to Persia (Iran). In 637, following the Arab conquest of Persia, the Nestorians were recognized as a religious community and their scholars became influential in the formation of Arab culture. Today most of their members, usually referred to as Assyrian Christians, live in Iraq, Syria, and Iran. *Manichaeism:* religion founded in Persia in the third century by Mani (c. 216–276). Mani, who claimed apostleship under Jesus, believed himself to be the instrument of the promised Paraclete and messenger of the Holy Spirit in the line of succession of prophets or messengers of God, chief among them Zoroaster, Buddha, and Christ. Mani's followers were vegetarians, believed in reincarnation, and followed a ritual of prayer several times a day. Their religious practices also included frequent fasting, almsgiving, and confession. Mani's syncretistic movement was an early rival of the Christian church, which treated his doctrine as heresy. He was persecuted by orthodox Zoroastrians as well and was martyred in Persia by Zoroastrian priests. Manichaeism spread west through Egypt, North Africa, and the Roman Empire—disappearing in the sixth century after fierce persecution—and penetrated eastward as far as Chinese Turkestan, where it lasted until about the tenth century.

of His absence, Christ was in India and Asia. It does not matter how and from where the legend originated. Perhaps it is of Nestorian origin. It is valuable to see that the legend is told in full sincerity." [32]

Altai-Himalaya adds more: "A good and sensitive Hindu spoke meaningfully about the manuscript of the life of Issa. 'Why does one always place Issa in Egypt during the time of his absence from Palestine? His young years of course were passed in study. The traces of his learning have naturally impressed themselves upon his later sermons. To what sources do these sermons lead? What is there in them of Egyptian? And why does one not see traces of Buddhism—of India? It is difficult to understand why the wandering of Issa by caravan path into India and into the region now occupied by Tibet, should be so vehemently denied.'

"The teachings of India were famed far and wide; let us even recall the description of the life of Appolonius of Tyana and his visits to Hindu sages.

"Another speaker reminds us that in Syria there was found a slab with an inscribed governmental edict about the persecution of the followers of Jesus as enemies of the government. This archaeological find must be curious for those who deny the historicity of Jesus the Teacher. And how does one explain the tiny coins used by the early Christians in the catacombs? And the first catacombs themselves still exist. There are always those who love scornfully to deny when something difficult enters their consciousness; but then, knowledge is transformed into seminaristic scholasticism and slander is cultivated as a fine art. In what possible way could a recent forgery penetrate into the consciousness of the whole East? And where is the scientist who could write a long treatise in Pali and Tibetan? We do not know such an one....

"Leh is a remarkable site. Here the legends connected the paths of Buddha and Christ. Buddha went through Leh northwards. Issa communed here with the people on his way from Tibet. Secretly and cautiously the legends are guarded. It is difficult to sound them because lamas, above all people, know how to keep silent. Only by means of a common language—and not merely that of tongue but also of inner understanding—can one approach their significant mysteries. One becomes convinced that every educated Gelong knows much. Even by his eyes one cannot guess when he agrees or inwardly laughs at you, knowing more than yourself. How many stories these silent ones can tell of the passing 'savants' who have found themselves in the most ridiculous positions! But now has come the time of the illumination of Asia."[33]

Living in the palace of Ladakh, Roerich gained inspiration for his paintings. "From this site of the sermons of Issa, from its high terraces, one must paint a series of all that can be seen from here. In these high places, purified by winds, occurred the signs of great communions. Of course the places have changed. Destructions and constructions succeeded one another. The conquerors have brought new accumulations, but the basic silhouette remains unchanged. The same heavenly frames as formerly are crowning the earth—the same glowing stars and the tides of sand like a sea congealed. And the deafening winds, sweeping up from the earth...."

Then a further confirmation of the manuscripts arose unsolicited.

"The old King Lama came himself. In spite of his poverty he brought with him about ten accompanying lamas and relatives. From the conversation it became apparent that the family of the king knows of the manuscripts about Issa. They also informed us that many Mohammedans would like to possess this document. Then followed conversation about prophecies connected with Shambhala, about the dates and about that which fills reality with beauty. The old King Lama departs and the crowd in white kaftans bow before him in reverence, simply and beautifully."

"How wonderful that George knows all necessary Tibetan dialects. Only without a translator will people here speak about spiritual things. Now one must absorb, with full knowledge, with clear, true approach. Curiosity is not fitting. Only insistent love of knowledge!"

"The eighth of September [1925]. Letters from America. Many messages will miss us here. The letters traveled for six weeks—but successfully reached the steamer."

"Upon the walls of the room chosen as the dining-room are painted vases with many-colored plants. On the bedroom walls are all the symbols of Chintamani—the stone of the treasure of the world. And the carved pillars, black from age, support the dusky ceiling with its big Berendey-like balusters. Little doors are above a high threshold and the narrow windows are without glass. And before

nightfall the wind blows freely through the passage-
ways. The floor is covered with bright felting from
Yarkand. And upon the lower terrace a black dog
barks—Tumbal, and the white dog, Amdong, are
our new fellow travelers. During the night the wind
whistles and the old walls shake.

"I am painting in the upper chamber which
has its exit upon all the roofs. Its doors have broad
carved casements and the pillars have intricately
frescoed capitals. Stairs, steps and dark ceilings are
patterned by age. Where have I seen this chamber
before? Where have these bright colors sparkled?
Of course in the 'Snowmaiden'* in the Chicago
setting. My dear ones enter and say: 'Well, here is
verily the true Berendey in his own chamber.'

"*Berendeyevka* ended sooner than we thought—
the fall does not tarry. One must pass Karakorum
before the autumn northeast wind approaches. The
way to Shayok is passable only a week longer.
Moreover, the people already have taken the
bridges apart for fuel, and the water has risen to
the height of a man. There remains the path
through the Khardong and Sasser passes. Many
varied imperative considerations cause us to hasten
the date of departure. With a large caravan one
becomes a subject."

"Karakorum—the black throne. Beyond lies
China—again the old patrimony of Buddha."

"In the courtyard they complete the loading of
the yaks. We are now setting out! And the day is
sparkling.   September 18th, 1925." [34]

-----

*Roerich designed the stage settings and costumes for the 1921 Chi-
cago Opera Company production of Rimski-Korsakov's *Snow Maiden*.

Roerich mailed the foregoing portion of his diary, along with the paintings thus far completed, back to America. But the caravan did not leave until September 19, and he wrote more about Issa:

"We learned how widespread are the legends about Issa. It is important only to know the substance of these legends. The sermons related in them, of unity, of the significance of woman and all the indications about Buddhism, are so remarkably timely for us. Lamas know the significance of these legends. And why do people resent and slander these legends? Every one knows how to slander the so-called 'Apocrypha.' For slander does not need a high intelligence. But who can fail to recognize that many of the so-called 'Apocrypha' are far more basically true than many official documents? The Kraledvorsky manuscript which was accepted by every one happened to be a forgery—while many genuine documents do not enter into any one's consciousness. It is enough to remember the so-called Evangel of the Ebionites. Such authorities as Origen, Jerome and Epiphany speak about the existence of this biography. Irenaeus, in the second century, knows of it—and where is it now? It is better, instead of useless discussions, humanly to reflect on the facts and thoughts which are communicated in the legends of Issa, 'the best of human sons.' Appreciate how close to contemporary consciousness is the substance of these legends and be astonished how widely all the East knows of them and how persistent is the repetition of them.

"For a long time we loaded the yaks, horses, mules, donkeys, sheep, dogs—a complete biblical procession. The caravaneers are like a case of an ethnographical museum. We passed the pool where, according to tradition, Issa first taught. To the left remain the prehistoric tombs. Behind them, the place where Buddha, the ancient founder of the Order, went northward through Khotan. Farther on, ruins of structures and the garden which speaks so much to us. We passed by stony reliefs of Maitreya, which on the way, convey to distant travelers their parting word of hope for the future. The palace remained behind the rock, with the temple Dukar— the illumined, many-armed Mother of the World. The last sign from Leh was the farewell of the women of Ladak. They went out upon the road carrying the blessed milk of yaks. They sprinkled the milk on the foreheads of the horses and travelers in order to give them the power of yaks, so needed on the steep inclines and upon the slippery ribs of the glaciers. The women bade us farewell."[35]

Thus Roerich and his family departed for the next leg of their pilgrimage—up the Khardong La to follow the highest caravan route in the world. For the next three years they were swallowed up in the Heart of Asia.

One parting tale of Issa reached them after they had crossed Khardong La September 23:

"The evening ends with an unexpected encounter with a Moslem. At the frontier of the desert there proceeds a talk about Mohammed, about the domestic life of the Prophet and about his reverence for woman. The talk continues about the movement of the Achmadis, and about legends saying that the tomb of Jesus is in Srinagar and the tomb of Mary in Kashgar. Again about the legends of Issa! Moslems are especially interested in these legends. . . .

"Young friends, you must know all conditions

of the caravan life in the desert. Only upon such ways will you learn to fight with the elements, where each uncertain step is already an actual death. There you will forget the number of days and hours. There the stars will shine for you as heavenly runes. The foundation of all teachings is fearlessness. Not in bitter-sweet, summer suburban camps, but on the severe heights, learn keenness of thought and resourcefulness of action. Not only during lectures, in well-heated auditoriums, but upon the cold glaciers, realize the power of the work of matter and you will understand that each end is but the beginning of something still more significant and beautiful.

"Again the piercing gale. The fire becomes dim. The wings of the tent are flapping noisily—they want to fly."[36]

The Ancient Texts
on Christ in India, Nepal,
Ladakh, and Tibet

MUCH of the account of Jesus' journey to the East
which Professor Roerich published from an unnamed 1,500-year-old document bears a striking
resemblance to Notovitch's *Life of Saint Issa.* The
chapter in which the verses appear, written in 1925,
is a compilation of Roerich's observations about
religion, sandwiched between entries describing his
journey in Sikkim and arrival in Kashmir and a
chapter about his departure from Kashmir and travels through Ladakh. He may have found the manuscript at Himis, some other monastery in Ladakh, or
possibly even in Sikkim. But the place of the find
is not nearly so significant as the fact that a good
portion of his text is parallel to sixty of those
precious verses published in Paris thirty-one years
earlier by another Nicholas and fellow Russian by
the name of Notovitch.

Following are the entries about Jesus from
Himalaya and *Altai-Himalaya,* including the legends, ancient texts, and Roerich's own reflections.
They are reproduced here, just as they appear in
his original commentary on religion dated laconi-
cally, Mountains 1925.*

*The chapter and verse cross-references to *The Life of Saint Issa* are
noted in the margin.

"If behind the present image of Buddha it is difficult sometimes to recognize the lofty image of Buddha the Teacher, then it is still more unexpected to find in Tibetan mountains beautiful lines about Christ. Yet, a Buddhist monastery preserves the teachings of Christ and Lamas pay reverence to Christ, who passed and taught here."

"Lamas know that Christ, passing through India and Tibet, turned not to the Brahmins and the Kshatriyas, but to the Sudras—to the working and humbled ones. The writings of the lamas recall how Christ extolled woman—the Mother of the World. And lamas point out how Christ regarded the so-called miracles." [37]

"There have been distinct glimpses about a second visit of Christ to Egypt. But why is it incredible that after that, he could have been in India? Whoever doubts too completely that such legends about the Christ life exist in Asia, probably does not realize what an immense influence the Nestorians have had in all parts of Asia and how many so-called Apocryphal legends they spread in the most ancient times. And then, how much truth is veiled in the so-called Apocryphal legends!

"Many remember the lines from the book of Notovitch, but it is still more wonderful to discover, on this site, in several variants, the same version of the legend of Issa. The local people know nothing of any published book but they know the legend and with deep reverence they speak of Issa. One might wonder what relation Moslems, Hindus or Buddhists have with Issa. But it is still more significant

to see how vital are great ideas and how they penetrate even the most remote places. Never may one
discover the source of such legends. But even if they
originated from ancient Nestorian Apocrypha,* at
present it is instructive to see the widespread and
deep consideration paid to the subject. It is significant to hear a local inhabitant, a Hindu, relate how
Issa preached beside a small pool near the bazaar
under a great tree, which now no longer exists. In
such purely physical indications you may see how
seriously this subject is regarded."[38]

"The writings of the lamas say that Christ was
not killed by the Jews but by the representatives of
the government. The empire and the wealthy killed
the Great Teacher who carried light to the working
and poor ones. The path of attainment of light!"[39]

"Let us hearken to the way in which, in the
mountains of Tibet, they speak of Christ. In the
documents which have the antiquity of about 1500
years one may read:

IV:12–13   Issa secretly left his parents and together
with the merchants of Jerusalem turned
towards Ind to become perfected in the
Divine Word. And for the study of the laws
of the Great Buddha.

*In *Trails to Inmost Asia* (pp. 28–29), George Roerich says, "It seems
very probable that there existed a floating Nestorian Christian population in Ladak during the eighth to tenth centuries A.D. when
Nestorian colonies were numerous along the trade routes of Turkestan and other regions of central Asia. Whether the Nestorian visitors
to Ladak were merchants or pilgrims, it is impossible to determine at
present. In the country round Ladak and Kashmir are found curious
legends of a Christian character, which are at present current among
the Mohammedan population of the two provinces."

He passed his time in Djagernath, in V:5
Rajagriha, in Benares. All loved him because
Issa dwelt in peace with Vicias and Sudras,
whom he instructed.

But the Brahmins and Kshatriyas told V:6–8
him that Brahma forbade those to approach
who were created out of his womb and feet.
The Vicias were allowed to listen to the Vedas
only on holidays and the Sudras were not only
forbidden to be present at the reading of the
Vedas but could not even look at them. Sudras
were destined to serve eternally as slaves to
the Brahmins and Kshatriyas.

But Issa listened not to the speeches of V:10–11,
the Brahmins, but went among the Sudras to 20–23
preach against the Brahmins and Kshatriyas.
He denied with his full force the right of man
to take upon himself the power to deny his
fellows of human dignity. Issa preached that
man had filled the temples with his abominations. In order to revere metals and stones,
man sacrificed his fellows in whom dwells a
spark of the Supreme Spirit. Man demeans
those who labor in the sweat of their brow, in
order to gain the good will of those sluggards
who sit at the lavishly set board. But they
who deprive their brothers of the common
blessings shall be themselves stripped of
them. And Brahmins and Kshatriyas shall
become the Sudras of Sudras, with whom the
Supreme Spirit shall abide unto eternity.

Vicias and Sudras were struck with aston- V:25–27
ishment and asked what they could perform.
Issa bade them "Worship not the idols. Do not
consider yourself first. Do not humiliate your

neighbor. Help the poor. Sustain the feeble. Do evil to no one. Do not covet that which you do not possess, but which is possessed by others."

VI:1–2   The Brahmins and warriors, learning of the words which had been told to the Sudras, decided to kill Issa. But Issa, forewarned by the Sudras, departed from this place by night.

Afterwards, when he had learned the scrolls, Issa went into Nepal and into the Himalaya mountains.

VII:4, 5, 9   "Well, perform for us a miracle," demanded the priests of him. Then Issa replied to them: "Miracles made their appearance from the very day when the world was created. He who cannot behold them is deprived of the greatest gift of life.—But woe to you, enemies of men, woe unto you, if you await that He should attest his power by miracle."

VII:13   Issa taught that men should not strive to behold the Eternal Spirit with one's own eyes but to feel Him with the heart, and to become a pure and worthy soul.

VII:14–16   "Not only shall you not perform human offerings, but you must not slaughter animals, because all is given for the use of man. Do not steal the goods of others, because that would be usurpation from your near one. Do not cheat, that you may in turn not be wronged.

VIII:9   "Do not worship the sun—it is but a part of the universe.

VIII:13   "As long as the nations were without priests, they were ruled by the natural laws and preserved the purity of their soul.

"And I say: Beware, ye, who divert men VIII:20-21
from the true path and who fill the people
with superstitions and prejudices, who blind
the vision of the seeing ones, and who preach
subservience to material things."

Issa had reached his twenty-ninth year IX:1
when he arrived in the land of Israel.

Issa preached, "Do not be subject to IX:5, 7-9
despair, do not desert your homes, do not
defile the nobility of your feelings, do not
worship idols but be imbued with hope and
with patience. Raise up the fallen and sustain
the hungry, succor the ailing, in order that
you be entirely pure and just upon that last
day which I am preparing for you.

"If you would perform deeds of benevo- IX:16–17
lence and love, perform them with a generous heart. And let there not be in thy deeds
the hope of gain or any calculations of profit.
For deeds of gain or of profit will not bring
you nearer."

Then Pilate, ruler of Jerusalem, gave X:3
orders to lay hands upon the preacher Issa and
to deliver him to the judges without, however,
arousing the displeasure of the people.

But Issa taught: "Do not seek straight X:8, 9
paths in darkness and possessed by fear. But
gather force and support each other. He who
supports his neighbor strengthens himself.

"Do you not see that the rich and the X:14
powerful ones are sowing the spirit of revolt
against the eternal consciousness of heaven?

"Lo, I tried to revive the laws of Moses in X:21
the hearts of the people. And I say that you do
not understand their true meaning because
they do not teach revenge but forgiveness. But

the meaning of these laws is distorted."

XI:4   But the ruler, waxing wroth, sent to Issa his disguised servants that they should watch his actions and report to him about his words to the people.

XII:1   "Thou just man," said the disguised servant of the ruler of Jerusalem approaching Issa, "teach us, should we fulfill the will of Caesar or await the approaching deliverance?"

XII:2   But Issa, recognizing the disguised servants, said, "I have not said unto you that you would be delivered from Caesar; but I said that the soul which was immersed in sin would be delivered from sin."

XII:8,
10-16   At this time, an old woman approached the crowd, but was pushed back by one of the disguised ones. Then Issa said, "Reverence woman, mother of the universe. In her lies the truth of creation. She is the foundation of all that is good and beautiful. She is the source of life and death. Upon her lies the life of man, because she is the succor of his labors. She gives birth to you in travail, she watches over your growth. Until her very death you bring anguish to her. Bless her. Honor her. She is your only friend and sustenance upon earth. Reverence her. Defend her. Love your wives and honor them, because tomorrow they shall be mothers, and later—the mothers of the human race. Their love ennobles man, soothes the embittered heart and tames the beast. Wife and mother—invaluable treasure. They are the adornments of the universe. From them issues all which peoples the universe.

"As light divides itself from darkness, so   XII:17-21
does womankind possess the gift to divide in
man good intent from the thought of evil.
Your noblest thoughts shall belong to woman.
Gather from them thy moral strength, which
you must possess to sustain your near ones. Do
not humiliate her, for therein you will humiliate yourselves. And through this shall you
lose the feeling of love without which naught
exists upon earth. Bring reverence to thy wife
and she shall defend you. And all which you
will do to mother, to wife, to widow or to
another woman in sorrow—that shall you also
do for the Spirit."

So taught Issa, but the ruler Pilate, fright-   XIII:3
ened by the devotion of the people to Issa,
who, if his enemies may be believed, wanted to
cause the uprising of the people, ordered one
of his spies to make accusation against him.

Issa, who taught only of the salvation of   XIII:5, 18
his fellowmen, endured all sufferings. Said
Issa: "Not far hence is the time when by the
Highest Will the people will become purified,
because then shall come the proclamation of
the deliverance of the peoples and *their union
into one family.*" [emphasis Roerich's]

And then turning to the ruler he pro-   XIII:22
claimed: "Why to demean thy dignity and
teach thy subordinates to live in deceit, when
even without this, thou couldst have also had
the means of accusing an innocent one."[40]

After quoting these manuscripts, Roerich
wrote in *Altai-Himalaya:*
"Thus the legends of Asia weave such an image

of Jesus, so ennobled and near to all nations. And Asia preserves in its mountains such legends. And it is not astonishing that the teachings of Jesus and Buddha are leading all nations into one family. But beautiful it is, that the light-giving idea of unity is expressed so clearly. And who shall be opposed to this idea? Who will lessen the simplest and most beautiful decision of life? And the earthly Unity is so easily and scientifically merging into the great Unity of all worlds. The commandments of Jesus and of Buddha lie upon one shelf. And the signs of ancient Sanskrit and of Pali unite all aspirations."[41]

The author continues in *Himalaya:*

"Another source—historically less established—speaks also about the life of Jesus in Tibet:

Near Lhassa was a temple of teaching, with a wealth of manuscripts. Jesus wanted to acquaint himself with them. Ming-ste, a great sage of all East, was in this temple. After much time, with utmost dangers, Jesus with a guide reached this temple in Tibet. And Ming-ste and all teachers widely opened the gates and welcomed the Jewish sage.

Often Ming-ste conversed with Jesus about the future era and about the sacred duty accepted by the people of this century.

Finally Jesus reached a mountain-pass and in the chief city of Ladak, Leh, he was joyously accepted by monks and people of the lower class. And Jesus taught in the monasteries and in the bazaars, wherever the simple people gathered—there he preached.

Not far from this place lived a woman whose son had died and she brought him to

Jesus. And in the presence of a multitude, Jesus laid his hand on the child, and the child rose healed. And many brought their children and Jesus laid his hands upon them, healing them.

Among the Ladakists, Jesus passed many days, teaching them to heal and to transform the earth into a heaven of bliss. And they loved him and when the time of his departure came they sorrowed as children. And at morning came a multitude to bid him farewell.

Jesus said to them, "I came to show human possibilities. What has been created by me, all men can create. And that which I am, all men will be. These gifts belong to all nations and all lands—for this is the bread and the water of life."

Said Jesus of skilled singers: "Whence is their talent and their power? For in one short life they could not possibly accumulate a quality of voice and the knowledge of harmony and of tone. Are these miracles? No, because all things take place as a result of natural laws. Many thousands of years ago these people already molded their harmonies and their qualities. And they come again to learn still more from varied manifestations." [42]

Picking up the thread in *Altai-Himalaya,* we read:

"After the vital conception of general well-being indicated by Jesus and preserved by Buddhists, one cannot but recall the words of Eusebius in his book, 'Life of Constantine': 'In order to attach to Christianity greater attraction in the eyes of the nobility, the priests adopted the outer garments and adornments which were used in pagan cults.' Every one who knows the cult of Mithra can appreciate the justice of this remark. A devout neo-Platonist and worshiper of the ancient philosophy, Clement of Alexandria, taught Christian bishops."

"Ignorance! Russian princes perished in the tents of Khans for their refusal to reverence the image of Buddha—yet at the same time the monasteries of Tibet were already preserving the wonderful lines about Jesus. Cyril of Alexandria brought about the destruction of the woman ascetic Hypatia, but it was to her own pupil, Cinesius, that the bishopric of Ptolemy was offered even before he accepted baptism.

"Superstition! Jerome advised the newly converted Christians to trample upon the body of their pagan mother.

"Cynicism! Pope Leo X exclaimed, 'How useful to us is this allegory of Christ!'"

"It should not be forgotten that Origen, who knew the meaning of the ancient mysteries and understood the true significance of the teaching of Jesus, even he could speak in the words of 'The Acts': 'And all the believers were together and held everything in *united possession.* And the estates which were sold and all properties were distributed to each according to his need. And each day, dwelling unitedly and breaking bread in their homes, they partook of their food with joy and simplicity of the heart.'

"Origen understood why this general well-being was important and saw profoundly into the truth. Because of this, the Church, sometimes extremely liberal in bestowing the title of saint, refused him this title; but even enemies did not refuse to call Origen a teacher. For he approached the teaching scientifically and did not fear to speak of what was evident to him.

"Of what was Origen accused? 'Lives of the Saints' thus speaks of him: 'Origen, the wonder of his age by reason of the prodigiousness of his mind and the profundity of his erudition, was condemned for heresy in two Alexandrian Councils and, after his death, in the Council of Constantinople. Origen did not think correctly about many truths of the Christian Church. Expounding the non-gentile teachings of the preexistence of the soul, he did not reflect properly upon Christ, believing that a certain number of spiritual beings of equal worth were created, of whom one strove with such flaming love that he became united with the Highest Word and became its bearer upon earth. Holding to the heretical belief in the incarnation of the God-Word and the creation of the world, Origen did not rightly comprehend the death of Christ by crucifixion, representing it as something which had its spiritual counterpart in a spiritual world. He attributed too much to the acts of natural forces with which our nature is gifted . . . .'— Admirable were the councils which could speak against the infinite cosmic meaning of matter!"

"Amid strife and in the manifestation of truth, upon the chariots of time ascend the law-givers of human welfare: Moses, the untiring leader; Amos, the austere; Buddha, lion-conqueror; Confucius, justice of life; Zoroaster, flaming poet of the sun; Plato, transfigured and reflected in his 'Shadows'; Blessed Issa, great in the immortal sacrifice; solitary Origen, the wise commentator; Sergius, great teacher and ascetic. All walked untiringly; all fell victim to the persecution of their day; all knew that the teachings of general well-being would inevitably come to pass; all knew that each sacrifice for the sake of the general well-being was but the approach of the way."

"On the mountain they tell of these teachings and listen to them simply. And in the deserts and upon the steppes people sing in their daily life about eternity and about the same general well-being. The Tibetans, the Mongols, the Buriats, all remember about this happiness."[43]

Chapter Five

"THESE BOOKS SAY YOUR JESUS WAS HERE!"

*Elisabeth Caspari's testimony
on the texts at Himis*

ELISABETH CASPARI

The Parchment in Hand

MANY of the world's great scientific and historical breakthroughs have been made by people searching for something entirely different. Columbus was looking for the Indies when he found the Bahamas, Roentgen was experimenting with cathode rays when he discovered the X ray, and Fleming was studying bacteria when he stumbled upon penicillin.

One seldom knows what lies around the bend or over the next pass. The necessary ingredients seem to be only the inquiring mind, perseverance, the daring to follow one's hunches—the intuitive faculty of the heart—and ultimately to rely on the promise "Seek and ye shall find," which in no way guarantees *what* one shall find but only that *something* will be forthcoming as a reward for noble effort—if one is faithful to the end.

Take the case of Elisabeth Gétaz. Her plans did not include taking the high road to Ladakh and rediscovering the manuscripts purportedly found by Nicolas Notovitch, Swami Abhedananda, and possibly Nicholas Roerich. For one thing, a bone disease in her foot left her unable to walk during much of her childhood. Her immediate goals lay more in getting up out of bed than in traveling up and down steep mountain passes to a remote

Buddhist monastery in the Himalayas. But then, pre-science of our fate might prove overwhelming; one step at a time our lives unfold. And for Elisabeth, the first step was just that—taking a step.

Things did not look promising. A string of surgeons tried unsuccessfully to operate on her foot and her minister concluded that it was not the will of God for her to regain her health and run and play like other children. But, against all odds, she would not give up.

Her family finally located a physician who thought he could help her. His treatment was novel. Under the circumstances, it was the only thing that even offered a glimmer of hope—in more than one way. He prescribed sun treatments, and they worked! Within four years she could walk.

On the road to recovery, Elisabeth began to study the piano. It was an instrument she could play with her foot propped up. She fell in love with it and became an excellent pianist; her services as a piano tutor began to be in great demand around her native village of Château d'Oex, Switzerland.

Not unexpectedly, Mlle. Gétaz decided that her vocation was to teach music to children. She studied hard and received a Diplôme de Perfectionnement from the Institut de Ribaupierre at Montreux, Switzerland. Then she went on to the École Normale de Musique de Lausanne and there received two advanced degrees in music pedagogy. Upon graduation, she founded a music school in Château d'Oex and developed a unique teaching method which took the drudgery out of practice and made her school an immediate success. From all over Europe both beginning piano students and aspiring music teachers flocked to her Alpine school.

In 1929, M. Charles Caspari came to Château d'Oex to be restored by the fresh mountain air and sunshine. Not only did he regain his health, but he met and courted Mlle. Gétaz. After their marriage he took over many of the administrative details of the school, leaving Madame more time for the calling she loved—music. They worked together at Château d'Oex for eight years.

But the finger of destiny was not content to leave Madame Caspari in the Alps. In the spring of 1937, a chance remark set in motion a chain of events that was to lead her all over India and finally to the rooftop of Himis monastery in the Himalayas. "There is a great teacher coming to France to give lectures on science and religion," a friend said to her one day. "You really ought to go."

"Why not?" the Casparis thought. So they crossed Lake Geneva to Evian where the lecture was being held. It was sponsored by the Swiss members of Mazdaznan,* the Western Zoroastrian movement. Madame Caspari was taken with the teaching and joined the organization soon after. At the lecture she met the leaders of Mazdaznan. When they discovered she was soon going to London, they made a seemingly unportentous request. "Would you be so kind, Madame, to convey our greetings to our beloved Mother Superior?" Happily she agreed.

The rendezvous was more than she expected. Riding in a cab through the streets of London to the address given, she imagined that the head of the movement would be a prim English matron. Much

---

Mazdaznan: in Avestan (ancient Iranian language), divine thought or knowledge of God in man. *Mazda* 'wisdom', also God or Light; *znan* 'worshipful' or 'to be worshiped'.

to her surprise, the driver pulled up to a building as impressive as Buckingham Palace. Madame Caspari was ushered into a Louis XIV salon where she found herself standing before an imposing lady—who turned out to be an American called Mother Gloria by Mazdaznan followers—the regal Mrs. Clarence Gasque.

In the ensuing conversation, Madame Caspari learned that Mrs. Gasque was also the head of the World Fellowship of Faith, formed for the unity and cooperation of those engaged in the spiritual search. Mrs. Gasque, delighted to discover that Madame Caspari was a musician, explained that she was planning a lecture tour of the cities of northern England. In her direct and charming manner she said, "I need a pianist. You must come with me."

"But I have a husband and a school of music," Madame Caspari replied. "I cannot just fly away like this, I have to go home."

Mrs. Gasque handed her the telephone. "Talk to Monsieur."

Charles told her to follow her heart, and so she accepted the invitation. Thus began a long friendship between Mme. Caspari and Mrs. Gasque.

At the end of the lecture tour, Madame Caspari returned to her music school. But not for long.

One Monday morning in December 1937, she received a letter from Mrs. Gasque saying she was planning a trip to Tibet with stops in Ceylon, India, and Kashmir. In the course of her journey, she proposed a study of Buddhism and a pilgrimage to Mount Kailas, a sacred Tibetan mountain. She closed with, "You and Monsieur are coming with me. . ."

The offer was too tempting. The Casparis, also interested in the religions of the East, knew by this time that a request from their dear friend was not to be denied. They had only three short weeks to tie up their affairs, pack, and set sail on the steamer *Orontes* for Ceylon.

In every country Mrs. Gasque and her party of nine were received with utmost respect and even ceremony by religious leaders. One morning their train arrived in Madras at 6:00 a.m. Madame Caspari woke up and peeked out the window. The Maharajah of Pithapuram, head of India's World Fellowship of Faith, was in attendance with his retinue—complete with red carpet. He insisted that Mother Gloria and Madame Caspari stay at his Palace of the Roses.

Here the travelers sojourned in an elegant guesthouse surrounded by the fabled splendor of the East. This same sort of elaborate hospitality became par for the course throughout much of their journey.

After passing through Madras, Bombay, and New Delhi, they headed north to Kashmir. In the spring of 1938, Mrs. Gasque rented a bungalow in Srinagar, the capital of Kashmir, where they could prepare their gear for the Tibetan path. They spent the better part of a year there. Everything had to be thought of—food, equipment, and servants, not to mention medicine, batteries, and cream to protect them from the elements. The Himalayas were not to be tackled lightly.

They started out on a spring day in 1939. First they traveled by bus as far as it could go. Beyond that point, no wheels but prayer wheels could

venture into the fortress of the Himalayas.* They
added to their caravan twelve servants, one translator, and 112 ponies plus guides and pony wallahs,
or drivers.

Their aims were extensive but not unheard of.
They planned to stop at several monasteries on the
way to Mount Kailas to observe the practices of
Buddhism, the customs and daily life of the people
for whom this teaching was the moving force. They
also had high hopes of getting to Himis in time for
the famed "devil dance" renowned for its beautiful
costumes of rich brocade. Little did they know that
they would return enriched beyond all expectations
with an experience very different from the traditional pilgrims' path. After spending their first night
under the stars, they awoke at dawn and were early
in the saddle—riding hard to make camp.

Due to the skill of their servants—the very best
to be found in Kashmir—and foresight in packing,
the journey was less arduous than it had been for
Nicolas Notovitch nearly fifty-two years before.
While they got acquainted with their mounts, the
servants galloped ahead to prepare the first camp at
the meadow of Sonamarg. In what became their
daily routine, they set up the tents and began cook-
ing a hot meal for the hungry travelers. Wizards at
mountain cookery, in no time they had built make-
shift ovens and baked fresh bread. And so the
pilgrims settled into this comfortable ritual.

Traveling ever upward towards the first high
pass, the Zoji La soaring to 11,580 feet, they found

---

*When the Chinese Communists invaded Ladakh in 1962, the Indian
government hurriedly completed a 270-mile (434-kilometer) road
from Srinagar to Leh to repel them. Jeeps, tourist buses, and trucks
now make the journey in two days.

The beauty of the Himalayas is characterized by its contrasts. M. et Mme.
Charles Caspari captured this juxtaposition of green trees against icy peaks in
their 1939 pilgrimage to Mount Kailas, Tibet. The onset of World War II cut
short the journey, however, forcing them to turn back, but not before visiting the
great monastery of Himis.

Sponsor of the 23-man journey to Mount Kailas, Mrs. Clarence Gasque was the head of the World Fellowship of Faith.

A hundred and twelve ponies were required to carry all of the equipment, food, baggage, and 23 people.

The last "civilized" bridge.

On the first night the pilgrims camped in the fragrant meadow of Sonamarg.

A typically rugged Himalayan trail. Madame Caspari and the party became accustomed to traveling through barren lands, overshadowed by the mountain sentinels wrapped in snow.

Such narrow bridges were par for the course in Ladakh.

Dubbed "Robin Hood" because of his ragged appearance, this man is returning from his pilgrimage to Leh, Ladakh—on foot!

The ponies took everything in stride (horizontal and vertical) as the pilgrims climbed ever upward towards the Zoji La—the first high pass.

Chortens, tombs or shrines of important people, line the road before towns and villages.

Glacial runoff paints a high plateau near Mulbekh emerald green. In spite of the high altitude and arid climate, barley, apricots, apples, and even wild flowers thrive here.

Smiling faces at Lamayuru.

Lamayuru perched precariously at the edge of a cliff. It is a refreshing sight for travelers descending from icy Fotu La, a 13,432-foot pass.

The path winds back up into the mountain heights as the journey continues.

Giving the ponies a bath in the Indus River at Nimu.

*At last, Leh, Ladakh. One of the highest cities in the world sprawls over a
plateau of 11,500 feet!*

Monks at Himis come out to greet the party.

This 26-mile stretch of desert must be crossed to reach the monastery of Himis where the famed "devil dance" takes place. To Madame Caspari, it seemed the harshest territory that they had crossed yet. All day they struggled in the blazing sun. As night fell, they finally reached an oasis. It was at the foot of the gorge which led up to Himis.

The party ascended up to the monastery high above and a deafening bray assailed their ears. Later they found that this was the resident "orchestra," blaring a greeting.

The play at Himis. Lama-actors garbed in grotesque masks and brilliant costumes of rich brocade for a Buddhist portrayal of Armageddon.

Ten-foot trumpets, cymbals, and yak-hide drums of every size make up the "orchestra." It accompanied the whirling, gyrating actors in a cacophony effected to scare demons away.

The roof at Himis. In fine weather much of the activity at the monastery takes place on the roof.

A tanka at Himis portraying the life of the Buddha.

In the temple.

At the beginning of the sojourn at Himis, a welcoming committee escorted the visitors to their guesthouse.

Shortly before the pilgrims departed, the librarian, carrying ancient manuscripts, approached Mrs. Gasque and Madame Caspari as they were seated on the roof: "These books say your Jesus was here."

upon arrival that snow covered the ground although it was July. Their guides made them travel single file in complete silence. "Do not speak," they said, "you will bring down an avalanche."

As they descended, the snow ended as suddenly as it had begun and they were assailed by the sweet smell of wild-rose hedges. Down treacherous defiles, along the edges of gorges, across scorching deserts which became freezing at sundown as the winds swept off the glaciers, braving chasms spanned by bridges impossibly narrow—the travelers pushed on.

Despite the large caravan, it was not uncommon for wild beasts to prowl close to the tents of Mrs. Gasque and the Casparis. On some welcome nights, the two ladies stayed in dak bungalows built for official use.

Traveling towards Leh, they encountered inhabitants of this seemingly inhospitable land. The friendly, open, and ingenuous Ladakhis were always ready with a big smile, a cry of *"joolay, joolay"* ("hello, hello"), and a big welcome for Mrs. Gasque.

Greeted by the head lama or chief villager at every stopping point, they would be served, with great ceremony, Tibetan tea. The souplike beverage was flavored with rancid yak butter—the more important the guest, the more rancid the butter. Hence, the most rancid lump was always saved for Mrs. Gasque!

Slowly traversing the ancient caravan route, they visited Mulbekh, Lamayuru, and other monasteries. Most striking was the constant contrast characterizing the countryside. Freezing winds that changed to gentle breezes in a few hundred feet. Smiling lamas living in enchanted palaces juxtaposed against wasteland. Seemingly endless high plateaus, barren in every direction, interrupted by rich green oases surrounded by groves of trees.

Moving midst the all-pervading spirit of the Buddha, they talked to monks and toured monasteries. The faces of the lamas, many of them young, expressed a childlike curiosity and a joviality. It seemed to the pilgrims that while traditions had survived, much of the real wisdom was buried away in aging manuscripts. The parchments and tankas (tapestries depicting the lives of saints and Buddhas), sculptures and statues they saw along the way were carefully preserved, though in some monasteries the once-vibrant frescoes were fading with the years.

Although the people revered Gautama Buddha, it seemed as if their religion, now but a ritual, was transmitted to them more through majestic mountains, even their collective unconscious memory, than through ancient texts. But the traditions were scrupulously followed. Prayer flags flapped from nearly every available point. Prayer wheels—cylinders either containing or inscribed with prayers—could be found embedded in walls, especially in monasteries, in the hands of pilgrims, or fitted with paddles and set in streams to keep a never-ending vigil.

They believed that the spin of a wheel or the flutter of a flag was equivalent to uttering the inscribed prayer. Perhaps it was their solution to the injunction "Pray without ceasing!"

These myriad impressions, like many hands sketching scenes on a mural, combined to make up Madame Caspari's story of Ladakh. As the first and what was destined to be the only leg of their Tibetan journey was drawing to its close, the caravan reached Nimu, a village just before Leh. Here they paused to wash their clothes—and ponies—in the river. Camping in the warm sun beside the Indus, they had a chance to contemplate the ice-covered peaks—glaciers shining in the sun, gentle river at their feet.

The next day they reached Leh, which at 11,500 feet is one of the highest cities in the world.* At the entrance of the city, they encountered a chorten† standing as a silent sentinel. A quarter-mile wall studded with stones carved with a token of centuries' devotion—OM MANI PADME HŪM‡—bade them welcome.

The narrow streets were characteristic of a town that had never known a car. Its crowded bazaars were a meeting place for Chinese, Indians, Kashmiris, Arabs, and Tibetans. The king's palace where Roerich had stayed presided over all. They visited the ancient monastery and soon pressed on for Himis and the pageant.

Leaving the city, they started out across the great desert plateau separating Leh and Himis. All of a long hot day they traversed this "desert of the pink stones," as their fellow traveler Cyrano called it. As dusk fell, then night, they still had not reached Himis. Then suddenly they were in a cool, fragrant oasis right at the foot of a steep gorge. High above, the invisible monastery clung to the face of the rock.

They received their usual reception the next morning when the welcoming party arrived. The

---

*Wenchuan in China is the highest at 16,732 feet.
†shrine or tomb of a saint or holy man
‡Buddhist mantra: *Hail to the Jewel in the Lotus* (the sacred fire pulsating within the chakra)

abbot himself and two chief assistants came down to provide Mrs. Gasque escort up to Himis.

The monks had prepared a beautiful guesthouse for Mrs. Gasque and Madame Caspari. The rest of the group camped in tents near a little stream. But, alas, the pilgrims found that because of the difficulties and delays of their journey, they had just missed the sacred festival.

As luck would have it, before they had a chance to be disappointed, the abbot told them that the paraphernalia hadn't been packed away yet and offered to give Mrs. Gasque a command performance of the entire three-day pageant!

The next day it began with a panoply of brilliant costumes and animated lama-actors. A dramatic portrayal of Armageddon unfolded before them. The power of Good was personified as Buddha in the form of a lion, symbolizing the strength and courage needed to drive the Evil One out of the world. He was beset by demons, skeletons, and animals in grotesque masks played with great glee by the junior lamas. All whirled and gyrated to the braying of the Eastern orchestra—ten-foot trumpets, cymbals, and drums of every size—increasing in volume to the final climax, the casting out of the evil spirits and the triumph of the Buddha.

After the festival, they lingered at the lamasery for four days touring the temple and the library,* chatting with the monks and enjoying the view from Himis' high rooftop.

---

*When asked about the difference between her account of Himis and that of Roerich (Madame Caspari recalls the Himis library as clean, well-kept, and small, while Roerich says the manuscripts were stored in "dusty corners"), Madame Caspari answered that Himis was probably cleaned up quite a bit at festival time when she was there. Furthermore, there was a fourteen-year difference between

On the third day Mrs. Gasque and Madame Caspari were sitting on the roof, watching a traveling tanka painter. Nearby, the monks' letter writer, cross-legged before a small table, was painting beautiful Tibetan script with delicate brushes.

In the midst of this scene, the librarian and two other monks approached the ladies carrying three objects. Madame Caspari recognized them as Buddhist books made of sheets of parchment sandwiched between two pieces of wood and wrapped in brocades—green and red and blue seeded with gold.

With great reverence, the librarian unwrapped one of the books and presented the parchments to Mrs. Gasque:

"These books say your Jesus was here!"

One sentence.

Madame Caspari looked at them in awe. In a few suspended seconds the last verse of the book of John swept through her mind like an endless river. As a child in Sunday school in Château d'Oex she had listened in wonderment: "And there are also many other things which Jesus did, the which, if they should be written every one, I suppose that even the world itself could not contain the books that should be written."

Did the apostle of Christ's love know that his Jesus had been here? Did the Master recount his fateful journey to his beloved disciple—with whom

---

their visits. Another explanation for this discrepancy may be found in an account by Marco Pallis, a Greek who visited Himis in 1936. He noted that Himis had two "libraries": a small one with a well cared-for collection of manuscripts, and a larger, less-organized room where piles of books were stored in disarray (*Peaks and Lamas* [London: Cassell and Co., 1942], p. 304). It is also possible that a new, more careful librarian had taken over since Roerich's visit.

he had also shared the mysteries of the kingdom? If
so, had someone deliberately suppressed this historical information which would be so meaningful,
so precious to Christians? Wouldn't Jesus want us
to know how he spent the most important seventeen years of his life—the preparation for his universal and triumphant message?

"Your Jesus was here."

It was incomprehensible that such an earth-
shaking event should have been kept secret from
all of Christendom for all these centuries. Why
didn't the whole world know about Jesus' journey
to Ladakh?

She and Mother Gloria looked at one another,
exulting in their joy and amazement. Together they
examined the manuscripts more closely, covered as
they were with elegant Tibetan script.

Searching her memory, Mme. Caspari recalled
hearing a legend that Jesus had been in India and
Alexandria, but never in her wildest imaginings
had it occurred to her that "her Jesus" had come
so far, so high—here to the Himalayas. At that
moment she was completely unaware of the fifty-
year-old Nicolas Notovitch controversy, nor could
she guess the import of her eyewitness account to
the ongoing debate.

She observed that the librarian was speaking
out of a conviction born of the monastery's ancient
tradition. His words rang with the authority of an
exact knowledge handed down with the manuscripts
from head lama to head lama. It was not hearsay, no
mere oral tradition, because the writings were in
hand—*and for a moment in her hand.* The evidence
was there, kept intact by the unbroken continuity of
a religious order. Here was the parchment. There

was the script. Here was the treasured record that
Jesus had come on a mission to India. And here were
Buddhist monks who revered "her Jesus" as one of
the greatest spiritual teachers of all time.

Mrs. Gasque looked at the unknown heralds of
the mystery of mysteries: Christ in Tibet two thousand years ago! She, too, saw that they handled the
parchment with great devotion. It was transparent
that the lamas had no other motive for revealing
their secret to the two ladies except love and a sense
of kinship with souls who had ventured so far from
home to study the path of their Buddha. The
librarian, with the permission, no doubt, of the
abbot of Himis, derived profound pleasure in
bringing the good news that would cause only
rejoicing to those who recognized in the teachings
of Buddha statements of the Universal One who
spoke through Issa, great messenger of Truth.

"My Jesus *was* here! In Himis!" Mme. Caspari
thought. Maybe he even sat on one of these very
rooftops—here or at Leh—or studied in one of the
ancient libraries. She pondered the implications of
the find. Her mind whirled, reeled as she thought
of Jesus traveling, perhaps, all over the world. She
realized that up until that hour, Jesus had been to
her, as to most Christians, a product of Palestine.
He was born there, he lived and died there. Any
religious training he received was a part of the
Jewish tradition. To place Jesus in Tibet or in India
would mean that he had studied their customs,
their languages, *their religion!*

Why did Jesus feel compelled to undertake this
journey, just as she had, prior to his Palestinian mission? And to what manifold purposes did our Father
send him? Indeed, this casual encounter atop the

world had far-reaching theological implications. Maybe the teachings of Jesus told to John substantiated in turn the teachings of Gautama or the Vedas.

And we who also ponder these questions may wonder, too, why Mother Gloria and Elisabeth Caspari were selected by the monks. Many Europeans had visited Himis, some skeptical, others sincere, but only a handful—as far as our own research has been able to discover—were told of the documents. Why were Mrs. Gasque and Madame Caspari put in the singular position of adding their voices to the few known confirmations of the existence of the Issa documents at Himis?

Perhaps the monks saw that these pilgrims were different, that here were people devoted to the study of their religion, reverent and accepting of their heritage of spiritual knowledge, who did not view Buddha as a heathen idol or a piece of Oriental art. Evidently they knew that these two devotees posed no threat and would not try to confiscate the documents or walk off with "souvenirs" from their libraries. For whatever reason, on that momentous occasion in the summer of 1939, Mrs. Gasque and Madame Caspari joined the small group of pilgrims who had been chosen by Providence to testify regarding some of the best-kept secrets of the life of Jesus Christ.

Each member of this select group journeyed to Himis in a different state of mind, with varying levels of expectation, and each uncovered the same story: Nicolas Notovitch, who had heard rumors of it and went in search of the documents. Swami Abhedananda, who went to see for himself and to verify Notovitch's story. Nicholas Roerich, who had heard Issa legends recounted all over Ladakh and expected to find corroboration in some form. And finally Mrs. Clarence Gasque and Madame Elisabeth Caspari, who were served the ancient books on a silver platter without having so much as lifted a finger of the mind, and most certainly unaware of the legend or of the finds of Notovitch, Abhedananda, and Roerich.

Madame Caspari descended the slope to the plain with the rest of the party. Camping in the oasis that night, she and Charles listened to his short-wave radio. World War II had been declared. They had to get back to Switzerland as soon as possible. They decided not to go on to Mount Kailas as planned.

Though they made haste down the trail, they arrived in Srinagar too late to get a seat on the last civilian transport. They were stuck. In India. For nine long years! Wondering what was happening to their home, their world.

Madame Caspari tucked her precious treasure away in her memory, only volunteering it many years later at a Summit University Forum interview after having heard of the beautiful verses about Jesus reportedly copied by Nicolas Notovitch from ancient Tibetan manuscripts at the monastery of Himis.

From Srinagar, the Casparis went to see a friend in New Delhi. There Madame Caspari decided to go back to Madras to attend the course of famed educator Maria Montessori, whom she had met in India prior to the start of the pilgrimage. It was a good way to occupy one's time and creative resources during the war. Dr. Montessori was delighted with Madame

Caspari's music methods. "You were a Montessorian before you met me," she declared. Madame Caspari stayed with her new-found teacher and they became lifelong friends.

After the war, the Casparis went to the United States, planning to stay only a short time. Then Richert and Lowell Fillmore, sons of Unity founder Charles Fillmore, became intrigued with Montessori's message. Richert encouraged Madame Caspari's efforts and in 1949 helped her to begin her own Montessori school in Lee's Summit, Missouri, named Wee Wisdom Garden. It was the first Montessori school in the United States since Dr. Montessori's departure in the early 1900s. Soon Madame Caspari had three schools and over ninety students. Working as a team, the Casparis devoted the rest of their lives to the advancement of the Montessori message in America, lecturing all over the country.

Elisabeth Caspari has organized Montessori schools in California, Missouri, Kansas, Florida, South Carolina, and Mexico. Several hundred Montessori preschools have been established through the Pan-American Montessori Society which she founded with Dr. Feland Meadows. In the last five years, Madame Caspari, now eighty-five, has completed training courses for teachers, interested professionals, and parents in Denver, Savannah, and Los Angeles. Active in spreading the Montessori revolution in education, she has most recently received invitations to teach her course in India, Australia, the Philippines, Switzerland, and Senegal.

Presently she is living on Summit University's beautiful Malibu campus where she trains Montessori teachers and assists in the direction of Montessori International. In this private school, preschool through twelfth grade, students and teachers from all over the world benefit from the miracles of the Montessori method. Here, too, Madame Caspari has found the unity of the teachings of Christ and Buddha which form the basis of community life—a search which has taken her and many other students of the unknown life of Christ around the world and Home at last.

Chapter Six

LADAKH TODAY – IMPRESSIONS OF A CULTURAL ANTHROPOLOGIST

*Dr. Robert S. Ravicz
traces the traditions of life and
worship to the present*

Village or forest, water or land,
holy is the place where saints dwell.

Holy is the forest.
Holy is the place where the senses are at peace,
where the saint finds refuge and simple delight.

The Dhammapada

Colorful Crossroads
of an Ancient Culture

TIME, history, culture, and place possess their own integrity in Ladakh. Time is patterned of a different quality in this land; it seems collapsed. Past and present are more surely together than in the world we know.

Centuries-old monasteries and fortified village walls now in ruins peering down on us are curious addenda or historical cues as we pass by in jeep or local bus—private cars are virtually not present—or afoot or in caravan. Yes, camels and mules loaded with grain, wool, merchandise, and objects of today's factories, yesteryear's handwork, and cottage industries ply the main road.

The camels bespeak millennia of domestication and movement of peoples and cultures, ideas and objects between the Mediterranean shores and this high-lying land route into Central Asia and China. Standing on the roof atop hill-protected Himis monastery, one is told that Mongol invaders swept through the Indus and Leh valleys below, unknowing of the existence or location of Himis.

In this Buddhist-majority place not so far west of Tibet, Muslim boy and Christian girl are wedded in a dazzling two-day ceremonial observance. A few details may enlighten.

Surrounded by her female kin and dowry objects, the bride cries and wails during a several-hour period, awaiting the arrival of the groom and male kin at her father's house. She is expressing sadness at leaving her father's home. Her father, in a large room at the top of his three-story home in Leh, receives gifts and congratulations—of sympathy—at the loss of his daughter. These are delivered with expressions of respect and white prayer scarves of the kind used as offerings or blessings by Buddhists.

The shouting outside signals the arrival of the groom and kin. As they approach the house they are showered with epithets and are ritually, but fairly soundly, struck by the girl's stick-wielding kin and servants standing on either side of the path to the house.

At the two feasts, hosted on successive days by the two fathers, festivities take place in huge tents—the ground underneath layered three or four deep in Oriental carpets, rich in color and texture and association of place: China, Afghanistan, Tibet, and the geometry of Yarkand and Central Asia.

For the first feast, the girl's father provides food and wine. Seated at tables, only the Christian guests drink the wine and eat with spoon and knife; Muslim guests drink tea and eat with the right hand, seated on the carpeted ground. No alcoholic beverage is served at the meal of the second night, sponsored by the groom's father. Before the meal is served, informal groups of five or six ladies sedately dance to the wind instruments.

The wedding festivities, as other social and ceremonial occasions, provide the opportunity for the display of the best in women's finery; especially notable are striped silken capes, turquoise-studded

*A **Moslem village*** *west of Mul-bekh built in the settlement pattern found throughout Ladakh—a series of ascending terraces rising from river or stream to fields for culti-vating barley, wheat, and other foodstuffs, and then to the dwell-ings. Buddhist settlements have a* gompa, *or monastery, above the rest of the village. Moslem pasto-ralists pause near Dras to rest and smoke tobacco. They are "transhu-mants," whose regular movements are patterned by the seasons, rather than nomads. Each summer they drive their animals, primarily sheep and goats, from Jammu and Kargil toward the Mulbekh Valley and back to warmer climes before the snows. Appearances to the con-trary, most of them are well-off. A few are wealthy.*

A majestic 24-foot rock-carving of Maitreya executed at Mulbekh around the tenth century in the Chamba style of Indian art. At the annual celebration commemorating the founding of Mulbekh, villagers drink chang, *a barley beer, and dance to flutes and drums in front of the image of the Coming Buddha. Unseen by the celebrants, a villager makes the dangerous climb up the back of the rock to place new prayer flags on the summit. Inside the structure, lamas make offerings of prayers and* tormas—cone-shaped dough balls used in Buddhist rituals.*

NOACK

RAVICZ (3)

Lamayuru (left), established in the eleventh century, is the first major Buddhist monastery in Ladakh east of Mulbekh, the gateway to the world of Tibetan Buddhism. Suspended between heaven and earth, it occupies a sublime station in the Himalayas halfway down the Fotu Pass (13,432 ft.) to Khalatse in the Indus Valley (c. 9,700 ft.). Its monks serve the spiritual needs of the villagers—they teach, offer solace, perform exorcisms and cure illnesses, receiving food and other material necessities in return. Perched atop a high knoll east of Leh, Tikse monastery (above) commands a magnificent view of the heartland of Ladakh. Four-hundred-year-old shrine at Alchi (center), 25 miles west of Leh. Brilliant yellow and coral prayer banners (bottom) hang from towering poles in the courtyard at Himis.

*(a) **Mural at Himis,** typical of artwork found at gompas throughout the Tibetan Buddhist world. (b) Monks playing trumpets. The deep, resonant, Om-like sound is used to greet dignitaries and call the monks to worship. (c) Wheel of life, depicting the realms of existence in symbolic form, found at the entrance to gompas. (d) Monks at Himis make* tormas, *or dough offerings, that will be used in a Buddhist ritual. (e) Image of Duk-kar, a Tara-like goddess invoked for protection from misfortune and illness, at Shey, a gompa near Leh. (f) Monk at Himis reading sutras and sounding mantras. In a day's long ritual, he will chant* Om Mani Padme Hum, *"Hail to the Jewel in the Lotus," and other mantras perhaps a hundred thousand times. (g) The abbot and monks at Matho monastery listen to (h) the head of the Sakyapa sect of Buddhism, His Holiness Sakya Trizin. Unlike most monks, as leader of the Sakyapa sect he is expected to marry. His two young sons (g) listen attentively. (i) Monks at Himis use hand-carved wood blocks to print prayers on paper. (j) A typical Tibetan Buddhist religious text such as would have been used to record the history of Saint Issa. (k) Votive butter lamps on a gompa altar are lit daily as an offering to the Buddhas.*

j

k

Chortens (top), *found all over Ladakh, enshrine sacred relics such as jewelry, gems, prayers, or the ashes of important lamas. These are located outside of Leh.* Mani *walls, or prayer walls* ***(right),*** *built of mounds of earth covered by stones* ***(above)*** *bearing the inscription* Om Mani Padme Hum, *are a common sight in Ladakh. This one, built on the outskirts of Leh, is a quarter of a mile long. Others are as long as a mile. The Indus River* ***(facing page)*** *winds through the mountains of Ladakh.*

*(a) **Villagers en route** to Likir in sharp relief against the stark, barren lands of Ladakh's desert plateau and Himalayan peaks. (b) Ladakhi woman dressed in her finery. The cobra-like turquoise headpiece, or* perak, *shows wealth and status. (c) Ladakhis believe turquoise and other stones have healing powers. But there is no turquoise to be found anywhere in Ladakh today and the* perak *is handed down from mother to daughter. Turquoise used in the* perak *may have come from ancient Persia. Ladakhis also use pearls, coral, gold, silver, "zi-stones" prized for their protective and curative powers, and occasionally diamonds and rubies in their jewelry. (d) Archer at Spituk shoots arrows at a tiny target during the annual celebration of the founding of the gompa. (e) The main street of Leh becomes a vegetable bazaar during June, July, and August. Most businesses in Leh close for the winter due to temperatures which are often 20 to 40 degrees below zero and because many of the shopkeepers are Moslems who spend the winter in Srinagar and Kargil. (f) Participants at an archery contest near Spituk pause to drink* chang. *(g) Flute player in Zanskar enjoys a moment of merriment and song during the annual celebration of the founding of his village of about 300 people near Karshan gompa. In Zanskar, located in a remote series of valleys south of Leh, Buddhist culture remains almost untouched by outside forces. (h) Ladakhi women at the Himis festival. (i) Ladakhi funeral. After four days of mourning, lamas walk in procession from the home of the deceased to dispose of the body by cremation.*

NOACK

Decked out in prayer flags,
*Himis monastery **(facing page)**
is the scene of the* cham—*a
sacred historical dance—dedicated to Padma Sambhava.
Entertaining and didactic, it
is also a ritual of purification.
The 3-day celebration contains
some pre-Buddhist religious
elements, such as the masked
demon dancers, and uses the
forces of Good in an attempt to
control the demonic forces in
order to destroy Evil. Thus it
blends earlier Bon traditions
with aspects of Buddhism such
as group dancing by lamas and
the reading of religious texts.
Each of the dancing demons
has a third eye empowering him
with the knowledge of all things
in all directions. Other dancers
include clowns, animals and, of
greatest importance, the deer
and the tantric officiants who,
through special learning, control the more dangerous powers
represented by the skull worn
on the front. The deer is the
most ecstatic of the dancers
and ultimately destroys Evil.
Three-hundred-fifty-year-old
Buddha **(bottom)** at Shey
gompa is Ladakh's largest
bronze statue.*

JESUS' JOURNEY TO THE EAST *(Possible Routes)*

It is not certain what route Jesus took on his journey to the East. Here is one possible itinerary via ancient roads and trade routes, reconstructed from the Notovitch, Abhedananda, and Roerich texts and legends: Jesus departed **Jerusalem** (follow the yellow line), took the Silk Road to **Bactra,** headed south to **Kabul,** crossed the **Punjab** and proceeded to a Jain area on the Kathiawar peninsula where Jain temples were later built near the town of **Palitana.** He crossed India to **Juggernaut (Puri),** made trips to **Rajagriha (Rajgir), Benares,** and other holy cities and, fleeing his enemies, went to **Kapilavastu**—birthplace of Gautama Buddha. Jesus took a trail just west of Mt. Everest to **Lhasa** (where the palace of the Dalai Lama was built in the 17th century). On the return trip (follow the violet line), he took the caravan route to **Leh,** went south to the state of **Rajputana** and then north to **Kabul.** He proceeded on the southern trade route through Persia where Zoroastrian priests abandoned him to wild beasts. Jesus survived and arrived unharmed in **Jerusalem.**

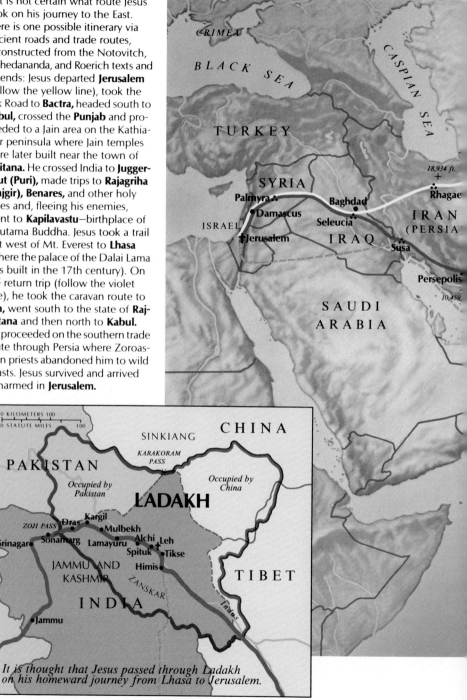

It is thought that Jesus passed through Ladakh on his homeward journey from Lhasa to Jerusalem.

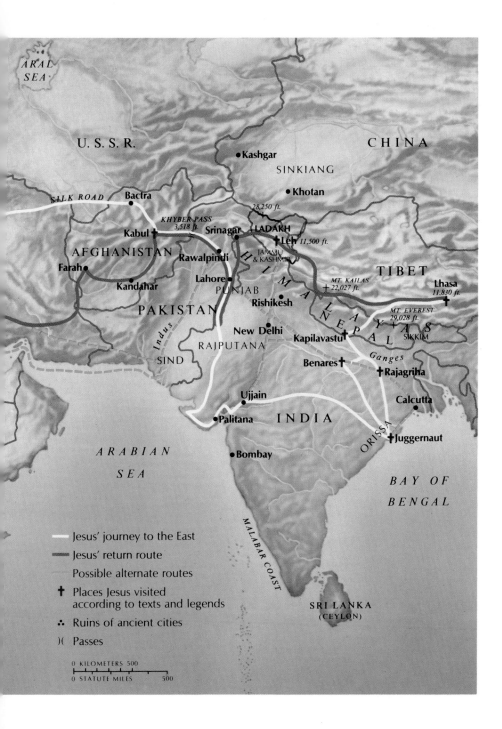

ARAL
SEA

U. S. S. R.

CHINA

●Kashgar

SINKIANG

●Khotan

SILK ROAD ●Bactra

28,250 ft.

KHYBER PASS
3,518 ft. Srinagar LADAKH

Kabul✝ ✝Leh 11,500 ft.

AFGHANISTAN Rawalpindi● JAMMU
& KASHMIR

Farah● TIBET

Kandahar Lahore● MT. KAILAS
✝ 22,027 ft. Lhasa
11,830 ft.✝

PUNJAB Rishikesh

PAKISTAN *Indus* New Delhi Kapilavastu MT. EVEREST
29,028 ft.✝

RAJPUTANA SIKKIM

SIND Benares✝ *Ganges* ✝Rajagriha

Ujjain

●Palitana INDIA Calcutta

ARABIAN
SEA ✝Juggernaut

●Bombay BAY OF
BENGAL

MALABAR COAST

─── Jesus' journey to the East

─── Jesus' return route

─── Possible alternate routes

✝ Places Jesus visited
according to texts and legends

∴ Ruins of ancient cities

)(Passes

SRI LANKA
(CEYLON)

0 KILOMETERS 500

0 STATUTE MILES 500

Edward F. Noack and his wife Helen spend an afternoon falcon hunting in the garden of the Wali of Swat in northwest Pakistan. In the late seventies, a monk at Himis (above) told Mr. Noack, "There are manuscripts in our library that describe the journey of Jesus to the East." Dr. Robert S. Ravicz, cultural anthropologist, with lamas at Mulbekh. It is a local custom to take a twig from a tree to clean one's teeth. Here Dr. Ravicz gains firsthand knowledge of this practice under the watchful eye of Maitreya. While at Himis in 1975, Dr. Ravicz was told about the Issa manuscripts by an eminent Ladakhi physician.

headdresses *(perak),* and gem-encrusted prayer boxes suspended from coral-and-pearl necklaces.

In addition to the Moravian church east of this city of ten thousand, a large mosque is situated in the center of town near the heart of the commercial district, perhaps the axis of the former Silk Route—north to Central Asia and China, and the Wool Road from Tibet south and west to Kashmir and the markets of India and then to the Western world, where in England was loomed the finest of Tibet's wool. Elsewhere in the city, and for hundreds of square miles about, there rise the shrines and monasteries attesting centuries of the Buddhist presence.

The new presence comes not as traders, but as visitors—the foreign tourists who require goods and services of a new kind and thus commercialize interpersonal relations and begin to turn the Buddhist ceremonies they come to witness into entertainment rather than an expression of intrinsic values. With their sound and visual recording equipment, they represent the complex societies of East and West. Eschewing the two-humped Bactrian and horse, they often opt for the rapid trip by air during the summer months.

Walking for many weeks and during several voyages makes one singularly aware of the nature of a place. The color scheme of Ladakh is somewhat muted, but cheery. Grey, white, and brown indicate mountains, with added tones of mauve and purple. Whitewashed reliquaries, or chortens, and similarly colored houses match monastery facades, which add blue or reddish-colored frames to the windows.

For the women, coral red and turquoise blue stones on headdresses and neck ornaments of pearls provide their favorite expression: the aesthetic match of wealth and ornamentation. High red color in the cheeks characterizes nearly everyone. Wild flowers seem small, and delicate shades of pink and yellow predominate. The blue of the sky appears unmatched by any other blue or any other sky; the finest of turquoise is graded for quality against the sky color.

There is immensity and restriction: the sky expands limitlessly upward, but the high peaks prevent wide-angle views. The valleys are miniscule, limiting numbers and density of population. Among the people, there appears a boundless sense of humor, hardiness, and openness.

Physical space is zoned. There is the verdant green of the riverine terraces, with barley, wheat, cabbage, radishes, and onions, all of large size, yielding well.

Next come the residences—a village rising above the fields—and, still higher, the monastery, above which the arid land rises to the snows interspersed with occasional green meadows where the herds of yak and sheep feed. This is desert, high desert whose forms and life are patterned by the great mountains—these Himalayas, upthrust from the South Asia continental mass through land movements and geological pressure.

The mountains prevent the southward flow of wintry winds and climate from Central Asia, making most of South Asia tropical, even that portion lying north of the tropic of Cancer. Rain hardly ever falls into the valley villages as the mountains high above catch the monsoon precipitation. There is arctic cold in the winter to be faced, but with little or no ice and snow, temperatures 20 to 40 degrees below zero: dry cold. Some of the waterways freeze, affording footpaths for those who need to travel, as walking into the mountains is impossible and the passes freeze all exit from or access to Ladakh.

People spend much of the wintry cold in a large kitchen-family room containing an enormous stove. Since there is little wood in this arid world, fuel consists mainly of animal dung. Architecture also fits this highly defined ecology—house and monasteries built, when possible, against hillsides. Animals are confined on the ground floor, and an opening above them allows their body heat to rise and warm the residents in the second and third floors.

Ecology and subsistence shape social patterns. As there is little arable land, it is desirable to keep its ownership and use within the family. Younger sons may enter the monastery. If they remain at home or return home, they may become part of a fraternal polyandrous household. Between monastery and village there occurs an exchange of goods and services; lamas take care of the spiritual life and they own perhaps half of the land. Villagers donate food and labor.

In traveling, too, one becomes aware of the control of the environment on daily activity; thus, crossing a stream must be planned for morning, because by afternoon the melting snows turn it into a raging torrent. It is the rhythm of this natural process that gives rise to the great river systems of South Asia providing the possibility of life for millions of people.

The Indus River in Ladakh runs now placid, now wild, joining other Himalayan waters to nourish the cultures to the south and west. It is the same river which supported the development of the Indus civilizations of Harappa and Mohenjo-daro five thousand years ago.

What look like ponies to us are small, hardy horses adapted during several thousand years to the rigors of the mountain terrain and the needs of pastoral people. They yield milk and butter and serve with amazing dexterity and maneuverability the arduous task of herding yaks along the broken and steep-sided mountain slopes.

When marriage occurs between persons of different villages, the groom and family bring the bride ceremoniously to their village. Riding ponies, accompanied by lamas in ritual dress, they take a rest stop in a mountain meadow; all dismount to watch the lamas dance, then proceed to their destination— bride and groom tied together on one horse, symbolically associated in life.

The sound of a chime through passes or on a mountain path or in valleys comes from a bell made of a blend of metals suspended round the horse's neck, and it arouses our awareness that it is one of the few sounds in this dramatic landscape.

Chapter Seven

EPILOGUE

A Tale of Two Worlds

J. MICHAEL SPOONER

JESUS APPROACHING LADAKH AS A YOUTH

A Few Final Questions

To recapitulate: Notovitch said he was told by a lama at Mulbekh in 1887 that there were records of the life of Saint Issa at Lhasa and other principal monasteries. He then claimed to have seen such a document at Himis and in 1894 published the verses allegedly read to him, as translated by his interpreter. The book created a controversy which appeared to be resolved when Professor J. Archibald Douglas went to Himis and took a deposition from the head lama, who claimed that all the salient points of Notovitch's story were completely false.

In 1922, Swami Abhedananda went to Himis, inquired about Notovitch and his discovery, and was told just the opposite. Not only did the lama confirm Notovitch's story, but in turn he also helped Abhedananda translate the same verses, which the Swami later published in Bengali in *In Kashmir and Tibet* along with a part of Notovitch's English rendition of the text. In addition, Abhedananda verified many of the particulars of Notovitch's story which were under question.

In 1925, while leading an expedition through Central Asia, Nicholas Roerich visited Himis. He later published writings he discovered at the monastery and/or elsewhere which paralleled Notovitch's.

He also reported finding throughout his journey many other accounts, both written and oral, of Issa's sojourn in the East. He was well aware of Notovitch's book but in no way was he dependent upon it for his material. His son George Roerich, who was a noted Orientalist and spoke Tibetan, no doubt would have noticed if they had been presented with a fraudulent document.

Finally, in 1939, with no prior knowledge of the Issa legends or of Notovitch's book, Elisabeth Caspari was shown three books by the librarian at Himis who explained, "These books say your Jesus was here!"

It is usually about this time in the story that the detective is sitting—or pacing slowly back and forth if he is the type—in a large, mahogany-paneled study. There is a roaring fire in the large stone fireplace. The dialogue may differ slightly, but the questions are always the same. Why? What does it all mean?

Could all three men—Notovitch, Abhedananda, and Roerich—have fabricated their stories or been fooled by various lamas? Highly unlikely. And what about Elisabeth Caspari? And then Justice Bill Douglas and world traveler Ed Noack and Professor Bob Ravicz and others like them who may yet turn up? Could there be some self-perpetuating conspiracy to play a joke on the Western world going on at Himis? Again, not likely. As Professor Roerich put it, "In what possible way could a recent forgery penetrate into the consciousness of the whole East?"

Well, reasons our ruminating detective, the whole notion of Jesus going to India, while improbable to many in the West, is still alive in the East.

He recalls that in *The Lost Years of Jesus Revealed,*
Dr. Charles Francis Potter observed that his book
about Jesus and the Essenes was popular in India. "It
seems," Potter wrote, "that many Hindus believe
that Jesus' 'Lost Years' were, partly at least, spent in
India, getting much of his best teaching from the
Vedas.¹ Didn't he say, 'Take my yoga upon you and
learn of me, for my yoga is easy'?"²

Suppose, then, the text (or texts) exists and the
story is true? Then what? At this point, the detective
leans against the mantle and looks intently into the
flames. A burning log pops, sending sparks up the
flue, and slowly the sine qua non of every working
detective—a theory—begins to emerge:

Jesus, he reflects, is generally thought to have
learned everything from Moses and the prophets
and was otherwise God-taught. And yet *The Life of
Saint Issa* and other jewels from the heart of Asia
say just the opposite—i.e., that he went east "with the
object of perfecting himself in the Divine Word and
of studying the laws of the great Buddhas."

During the course of his travels, Jesus seems to
have met with Eastern holy men—for a purpose. It
appears that he sought them out and planned his
itinerary around extended sojourns at the most
notable spiritual communities of the day—to investigate, observe, and gather notes for a work he was
to write—penned with his lifeblood.

According to the texts and legends, there
among those of like mind (those whose probings
beyond the tangible were provocative of the new era
heralded by the birth of Christ) he prayed, meditated, practiced yoga, studied, and taught. Clearly
he is remembered by both worlds as having healed
the sick, raised the dead, exhorted the people to

Love, and challenged their entrenched oppressors. He exposed the same hypocrisy he was to denounce in the priest class of Palestine, pronouncing deprecatory woes upon Brahmans, Kshatriyas, and lawyers alike, casting out all manner of possessing demons; in sum, doing all those things for which he would later pay dearly with his life—the life with which he narrowly escaped the Eastern theatre.

And if we read between the lines and consider his extraordinary acts—most certainly not denying but fulfilling the laws of material and spiritual physics—it is also quite clear that he sought and attained adeptship over the elements and elemental forces as well as control of the heartbeat and body functions. And that he mastered the arts of bilocation and alchemy—observable later in his sudden appearances and disappearances,[3] in his transmutation of ordinary water into the finest wine,[4] and in his conversion of lukewarm 'omnidirectional' souls into one-pointed fiery devotees.

All this he did and more, not as a god but in fulfillment of a known path of self-mastery, a natural soul-evolution unto the unleashing of the imprisoned splendor within. He seems to have been making a strong statement, etched in every footprint, that his was a path preordained by the Father, obtainable by all of His sons—if they will but keep on keeping on, with gusto and good cheer.

Was it a dress rehearsal for his Palestinian mission? Or was it that and more?

Was he the wise student in search of the wiser Teacher? Had he probed the periphery of knowledge in his home country only to go forth pushing back, mile upon mile (the Father's sheer will empowering his own)—yes, pushing back the barriers

of the mind well beyond the horizon of his childhood tutors' time and space?

Was he the real *Revolutionary*—rabble-rouser
as he was to be called—*of the Spirit* in search of His
Kingdom, truly His own Higher Consciousness? Is
this what he found at the Top of the World—his
own Shangri-la? Both *without* in the sacred shrines
and mystic mountains and lush valleys cradling
those peculiar people with the shining eyes so full
of soul fire? And *within* in the secret chamber of his
own precious heart where burns the threefold
flame? And was his Self-discovery the key to his
strength that endured, as none other has endured,
while carrying the full weight of world karma—the
Piscean cross?

Did he meet Maitreya face to face, as Moses
before him had talked with his Hierarch?

Did he know Gautama in his innermost being?

Did he ascend the crystal cord and through the
crown chakra embrace Sanat Kumara?

Coming down from the clouds with a mental
thud—having gone about as far out, and farther,
as a self-possessed chap such as he might venture
without going completely off the deep end (Scot-
land Yard notwithstanding)—our detective waxes
methodical, even empirical: There are still some
loose ends. After all, he reminds himself, he doesn't
know what became of Notovitch. Or of Douglas,
for that matter. Nor can he verify by his own witness the actuality or the authenticity of the manuscripts either in the past or the present. "So what
have I proven?" he chastises himself for allowing
himself to get so carried away with the Jesus mystery.

Despite his self-doubt, whose shadow flickers

on the wall, he scratches his head and dares to list A Few Final Questions:

Why do you suppose, really, that the vast majority of people in the West are unfamiliar with the theory, so widely accepted in the East, that Jesus Christ, the avatar of the Piscean age, went to India and Tibet during the so-called lost years?

Have the facts been intentionally suppressed? By himself? (Until the time appointed?) By the Gospel writers? (According to his prophecy, that the Holy Ghost should first come ere the secrets be revealed?[5]) Or by devilish design—by later editors? (To suppress the imitation of Christ and His Path by future generations of His spiritual seed?) Are there yet to be unearthed in the Vatican sixty-three manuscripts, or parts thereof, dealing with this very subject, as the Russian journalist was given to believe?

Did Jesus journey elsewhere during the course of his life? To Britain as a youth with his Uncle Joseph (of Arimathea) to be educated in the well-established schools of the ancient Druids who, we hear tell, took their lessons from Pythagoras? ("This is a bit much, old boy—even for the most progressive detective I know!" he remonstrates. *"However,"* retorts the other side of himself, "the legend *has* persisted among the Britons for centuries!")

No wonder the Jews marveled, saying, "How knoweth this man letters, having never learned?"[6] Maybe it was *they* who never learned that he had traversed many worlds and had been taught, as Enoch was, by the Father and his angelic emissaries, some robed in flesh, some not.

Exactly how long *did* he live, *physically,* after the resurrection!

If I'm not mistaken, our sleuth carries on, unable to stop the spinning wheels of the mind, didn't Paul and Peter meet him in the way numerous times and talk with him easily—*after* the Bethany 'disappearance' generally pinpointed as *the* Ascension?[7] How many "goings and comings" were there anyway!

And which one was the final one?

Did the Master demonstrate his apparent adeptship both in surviving the crucifixion and in disappearing from their sight in that 'Cloud' atop Bethany's hill? *Did he* (our detective summons his most courageous posture) thus exit the Palestinian scene, his point made, and go on to preach and teach his disciples, as Church Father Irenaeus wrote—spending his final years in the magical land of Kashmir, as some say? Maybe he never even died! Maybe he just transcended earthly life in stages—just like that—only to disappear from sight forever in a final, as they say, *Mahasamadhi* called by theologians the Ascension.

But, then, for the last almost two thousand years his followers in great numbers have claimed to have seen him, talked with him, heard his voice, been healed by him, and even supped with him!

He seems to recall, his mind now racing, sweat beaded on his brow, there are strong traditions indicating that following the crucifixion Martha with Mary Magdalene, other Marys, and Lazarus went to France to propagate the Faith. The church of her ministry still stands in Tarascon, the repository of her relics.

Were these chief disciples of the Lord in Gaul tending the needs of the World Teacher and his disciples? If indeed he were alive, they could only be, if they had any choice in the matter, where their Lord was. "For wheresoever the carcase is, there will the eagles be gathered together."[8]... Was Jesus dropping a hint—if you are looking for me, look for my chief disciples? Did Jesus *actually* intend, as some have attempted to prove, to establish both a kingdom and a lineage of the sons of God? And, having done so, did he then move on, the eternal Youth, to new circumstances and other sheep in the Far East?

Could he be like le Comte de Saint Germain— the Wonderman of Europe (who came after him yet was before him)—the man who never dies, knows everything, and moves from place to place bearing his elixir of liquid Light to all who believe the Truth and take up the Cross and follow him?...

Just when you think you're getting a handle on the case, an undisclosed source comes up with another yellowed folder. The information now on our desk is beginning to piece together—from the pages of history, the records of akasha, and the indelible race memory of the ever-living profile of the best of the sons of men... evidence that must be saved for the next volume.

Where will it all end? You shake your head, pick up your file and, Diogenes' lantern in hand, go out into the night looking for the only one who really knows the answer.

Chapter Eight

CREDITS

After the Final Curtain
A Tribute to the Scriptwriter and the Cast

All the world's a stage,
And all the men and women merely players:
They have their exits and their entrances,
And one man in his time plays many parts . . .

Shakespeare, As You Like It

Acknowledgment of Collaborators

THIS Divine Mystery has been in the making for two thousand years and longer. All the players and their parts have passed before us on the screen of life. And the drama of those sent by the angels to trace the footsteps of Christ—though some knew not the holy ground they trod—was in some ways as suspenseful as that of the original Teacher and his apostles.

The events that transpired during the hitherto unknown life of Christ, the so-called missing years, were scripted by God long before our minds could capture their reality in the Word made flesh. He, too, authored the lines of the supporting cast whose steps we herein retrace—those other pilgrims who came upon the scene, and anonymous, haloed scribes who in their own time and place cherished his blessed feet. . . and recorded their peregrinations.

This is the strong meat of the Word[1] whose time has come! The long-lost 'missing' chapters in the Greatest Story Ever Told and the Greatest Life Ever Lived. It could not remain hidden;[2] for his people, his very own—they must know. By the hand of God the evidence has been kept. Untold numbers have played their parts sometimes altogether unconscious of the flame in that invisible torch they were passing hand to hand, mouth to mouth, heart to heart of the memory of this Son of God, this Saviour who so changed the world that neither it nor we shall ever be the same.

We who have joined forces to pull the threads together, piece the pieces of the puzzle, and organize the chapters are the least of the players in this two-thousand-year cast of torchbearers in the night. The strokes of our pen and our musings must be a monument to the Father and his recording angels who held it all together and kept it for the appointed time.

"Behold, now is the accepted time; behold, now is the day of salvation!". . . So the apostle cried.[3]

I believe that today as never before followers of the Messiah from every walk of life are ready to consider an unorthodox approach to the life and mission of the one God-man above all others who, if he has not already done so, may yet make the greatest impact on their lives and spirits.

The ramifications of Jesus' journey to the East are staggering. Dare we finally consider that he who humbled himself as a man[4] *for our sakes* also took up the role of student under his predecessors, the great Lights of antiquity, demonstrating *for our sakes* that he who would be Master must first be servant?[5] That he who would teach must first study—to show himself approved unto God?[6] And that the Saviour of *all men* is bound by the One who sent him to provide a message and an example relevant to *all men*—that through the very fabric and language and ritual of their own religious traditions, they, too, might "behold his Glory"?[7]

How could Hindu or Buddhist or Zoroastrian or Confucian, then or now, find relevancy to the Son of God (or to His vessel, the Son of man) against the backdrop of Torah or Talmud or Hebrew prophets? He who was the embodiment of the consummate Light of history—the best of all the sons of men— must also be the embodiment of the summum bonum of every world religion, the epitome of its teaching and example anticipated, *looked forward to,* both by its doctrine and its body of believers.

Did he come only for the Jews? If so, did he go to the East in search of the lost tribes who had migrated there? And more? Those "other sheep" he said were his, yet "not of *this* fold"?[8]

All had been done before—India was a dress rehearsal for the great play *(lila),* the epic of the millennia. Surely, this youth, wise among the scholars of Jerusalem before his departure for the East,[9] would have no difficulty in outsmarting the Brahmans in their own conceit or exposing their deceptions to the people[10]—precisely as he was to overturn the money-changers in the temple upon his return to Palestine.[11]

It was the conspiring of Father and Son to use the Eastern stage as the trial run for the all-time hit— the classic number-one drama of the Son's triumph over the forces of Evil, portraying a brief but magnificently directed ministry (directed by the Divine Director who sent him) that would make plain the essential truths, in parable and sign and wonder, of the Eastern repository of wisdom.

Jesus' weaving of the threads of eternity into a life and scripture to be uniquely savoured by the Western mind is his great legacy to souls born to a civilization unawakened to the memories of the Motherland[12]—realities that dance easily, a priori, in the hearts of India's children. The clues are there, if one will look for them with a willingness to see, in every fragment remaining from Gospel writers, Gnostics, apocryphal accounts, Church Fathers and a few historical notations—and in much that has been taken from us by evildoers, tamperers with Holy Writ, who, uncommissioned by us, have probated our spiritual inheritance—Christ's last will and testament.

Today the Lord would return to us the forgotten and lost books, a vast Teaching for the liberation of our spirits. And Comfort for our trials of karma in these latter days. Through unseen hands and many unsung heroes He has found the way, as He always does, to reach us in our extremity with His Truth and Love. His reassuring words ring like the bells of Ladakh with their all-pervasive crystalline sound:

> And I will pray the Father and He shall give you another Comforter, that He may abide with you forever;
> Even the Spirit of Truth, whom the world cannot receive because it seeth Him not, neither knoweth Him: but ye know Him, for He dwelleth with you and shall be in you.
> I will not leave you comfortless; I will come to you.
> Yet a little while and the world seeth me no more; but ye see me: because I live, ye shall live also.
> At that day ye shall know that I AM in my Father, and ye in me, and I in you. . . .
> These things have I spoken unto you, being yet present with you. But the Comforter, which is the Holy Ghost, whom the Father will send in my name, He shall teach you all things

and bring all things to your remembrance, whatsoever I have said unto you. . . . [13]

Verily, verily, I say unto you, He that believeth on me, the works that I do shall he do also; and greater works than these shall he do, because I go unto my Father. [14]

The curtain is going up on the final act: Jesus spotlighted stage right (the Father seated, center background, in the twilight of humanity's unawareness) is in the role of initiate on the path of personal Christhood. He emerges vigorous, viable, from the parchments of the lost years, as the personification in the flesh of the same Law 'written in our inward parts' [15] whose outer sign we have been waiting for.

The One sent to save us has come to portray our mission in life. This he has chosen to do against the backdrop of his own soul's victory over Death and Hell. Now we know—for we see him face to face, we are known of him, and we would be like him [16]—that we, too, must pursue the calling of Christ's works, shunning not the goal of self-mastery which our own Teacher's discipleship discloses.

Not forever sinners are we, nor disciples ever learning but never able to come to the knowledge of the Truth. [17] We would espouse the goal of friend of Christ, [18] of brother, sister, and finally, fully, joint-heirs [19] of the same mantle of Sonship he put on (for our learning and example)—though all the while He forever is, was the Son of God: 'from the beginning', The-Before-Abraham-Was-"I AM." [20]

Seeing him standing there, our eyes are transfixed. Before us his figure merges with the ancient scenes and we see as if on film the records of all that transpired in his life—from birth and childhood through his youth and missing years, his ministry and beyond, until the scenes fade into the mists of ensuing centuries.

Having so seen his magnificent performance, we can only confirm the immortal Truth that within us this Son also dwells: within us this Sun of Righteousness shall also rise![21] This is the message of his dramatization of our life as seen through his. That we, too, shall see the Daystar from on high[22] appearing in the beautiful Presence of the I AM THAT I AM[23]— the same, the One whom our Lord addressed saying, "Abba, Father."[24] This is the communication of his heart. He speaks no longer in parable but tells us:

We, too, can try. We can set the goal of Christhood for our life. See before and above us the Light of our God-Reality beaming, beckoning us onward. We can follow our Lord all the way to the Himalayas and Home again—awakened at last to the kingdom (consciousness) within, whose unlimited energy Source and creative Power he tapped, assuring us access in this time of trouble[25] to the sublime Universal One: *"Greater is He that is in you than he that is in the world."*[26]

The house lights are on, the curtain is closed. There are no bows or encores by the cast. We apprehend the message: It is we who are on stage. And the curtain is about to go up on our final embodiment.

Let us ready ourselves to demonstrate the same spiritual Self-knowledge he possessed to a world that has waited too long for the Truth.[27] A Truth so desperately needed to forestall the prophesied calamities of the Day of Vengeance of our God.[28] The Truth of the sacred fire that burns in the breasts of all God's children and of the threefold flame of the Trinity he bore, nation to nation, in his heart's chalice as he went his way in search of "them that were lost."[29]

By God, we must not, in his name we cannot—fail!

_____

May hearts one with his find in these tracings of the life of Jesus the thread of contact with their own immortal destiny to be outplayed on the world stage here and now. For, no otherworldly Master is our Issa. He moves among us, despite the gruel of the false pastors, to tell us one by one—because he loves us—the true gospel of his everlasting kingdom so imminent in the very midst of the chaotic world scene.

Two thousand years hence he is still looking for pragmatic laborers for his harvest[30] who will wield his two-edged sword of the Spirit.[31] The Faithful and True with us summons his armies,[32] conscripted from among us, to pierce illusions, strong delusions, about to drown soul and society in a cataclysm of major proportions. And if it come, such planetary upheaval will be the return current (karma) of our ignorance (ignoring) of the Law, our self-slavery to false gods, our nonappropriation of God's grace that all around us hangs fragrant in the air like sweet wisteria in summer.

We put down our pen and send this book on its way to you, dear seeker, that in the final hours of your own life's drama, you might reach, if you will, for the Star of your Divinity so nobly, so passionately displayed on the world stage by our brother Jesus. And in his name hurl it into the midst of chaos to sound the single note of Christ's victory in another soul . . . and of the Truth that shall make all men free.

_____

Wherefore, in the light of all that has gone before and all that is to come, the author does acknowledge and express her profound appreciation for the cooperation and true spirit of givingness of the following collaborators on this volume—without whose contributions *The Lost Years of Jesus* would not be the bearer to you, the reader, of that fullness of joy which was borne by all the players whose eyewitness accounts unfold the drama of Saint Issa:

Dr. Robert S. Ravicz—professor of anthropology at California State University, Northridge, for his most necessary concluding chapter bringing to the pilgrim who has followed Issa and his chroniclers, through photographic and personal impressions, his feeling for the colorful people of "Little Tibet" today. We are indebted to Dr. Ravicz for his sensitive portraits of those who sit atop the world on one of history's heretofore best-kept secrets and for his captions which lead us through their everyday lives.

Dr. John C. Trever—director of the Dead Sea Scrolls Project of the School of Theology at Claremont, California, for his generous gift of time and knowledge on the history of early Christianity, and for his lifetime scholarship and devotion to the subject, which so enriched our understanding.

Elisabeth Caspari—for the hearty soul she is to have made the trek at all and then for sharing her fascinating story and so many pertinent photographs which no doubt retrieve that which was lost by Notovitch's servant—photographs taken by herself and her late husband Charles, whose brave spirit we also salute. Mrs. Clarence Gasque—in memory, for her inquiring spiritual mind and lifelong support of universal Truth and for organizing and financing the trip, thus preparing the way for the jackpot: "These books say your Jesus was here!"

Edward F. Noack—traveler to the forbidden lands of the East, for his lifelong one-pointedness to the high country of the Himalayas that led him and Mrs. Helen Noack, his companion trailblazer, to *the special spot;* and for his sharing of his photographs and his love.

Jayasri Majumdar, Per Sinclair, and Prasan Kumar De—for their translation of *In Kashmir and Tibet,* freely given to the glory of God, rendered with the goal of the meeting of East and West, and conveyed for the opening of our understanding.

Richard and Janet Bock—for taking five years of their lives to painstakingly illustrate on film *The Lost Years* and for allowing us free use of their achievement, which has inspired many to pursue the quest of the historical Jesus to the incarnation of the avatar; for their generous consideration in allowing us the use of the title *The Lost Years of Jesus* for this volume; and not least, for Janet Bock's effort and joy in writing her popular paperback, *The Jesus Mystery,* which in 1980 reacquainted the West with the discoveries of Notovitch, Roerich, and Abhedananda.

J. Michael Spooner—for his evident delight in executing in the artistic tradition of Nicholas Roerich the cover painting of *Jesus Approaching Ladakh as a Youth,* whose conception was born out of our mutual desire to inspire this generation to pursue the holy mountain of God in the Master's footsteps.

The beloved staff of Summit University Press—including Editorial, Research, Graphic Arts, and Printing—the salt of the earth, more precious than the gold of Ophir,[33] without whom this book would not have been born! And all of the co-workers of our community at Camelot and the Royal Teton Ranch, whose support, service, and unspeakable Love are surely a tribute to the eternal path of Saint Issa, their guiding Light.

Elizabeth Clare Prophet

The Western Shamballa
All Saints Day, 1984

Notes

Chapter One THE LOST YEARS OF JESUS

1. Raymond E. Brown, *The Birth of the Messiah* (Garden City, N.Y.: Doubleday & Co., 1977), pp. 513–16.
2. It was a common practice in Israel to compile genealogical records, especially since succession to high priest and to leadership of tribe, of tribal family, and of father's house depended on lineage. Records are traceable from the beginning of the Hebrew nation (Num. 1:2, 18; I Chron. 5:7, 17).

    Biblical genealogies were seldom concerned with purely biological descent, and generation was only one way of getting a son. A man could adopt a child simply by declaring him to be his son or, posthumously, by the law of the levirate marriage wherein the brother of the deceased was required to marry his childless widow and raise up seed in his name (Deut. 25:5–10).

    Members of a tribe or clan traced their lineage from a common ancestor by fact or legal fiction, i.e., those who were not of natural descent were effectively amalgamated into the group by the adoption of its ancestors. Ancient chroniclers frequently preferred symmetry (often based on a pattern of seven or ten generations) to the unbroken line of father to son; links were freely omitted to preserve the numerical scheme.

    Remarkably different genealogies for Jesus appear in the Gospels of Matthew and Luke. Matthew's genealogy (1:1–17) contains forty-two names listed in descending order from Abraham to Jesus, artificially grouped into three fourteen-generation periods: the pre-monarchical period, Abraham to David (750 years); the monarchical period, David to the Babylonian Exile (400 years); the post-monarchical period, Babylonian Exile to Jesus (575 years).

In order to maintain the stylized fourteen-generation scheme, Matthew had to eliminate four kings between Solomon and Jechonias. There are only thirteen names in his third set of fourteen generations. Since Matthew could count, some believe that one name was dropped from the list by an early copyist, lost forever.

The genealogy of Luke (3:23–38) moves in ascending order from Jesus back to Adam. While Matthew has forty-two names, Luke has seventy-seven (thirty-six of which are completely unknown) organized into eleven sets of seven. In all but the first two groupings, the last name of each of the sets of seven (David, Joshua, Joseph, etc.) marks some sort of a climax, calling to mind a historic panorama covering the departure from Ur, the enslavement in Egypt, the first monarchy, the long period of messianic expectation, the Babylonian Exile, the second monarchy, and the era of the true Messiah. Since the number seven figures so prominently in their genealogical arrangements, Matthew and Luke may have had some kind of numerological pattern in mind.

There are other important differences between the two texts. Matthew intends to demonstrate that Jesus is the Davidic Messiah; Luke to show he is the Son of God. Luke's line contains fifty-six names from Abraham to Jesus; Matthew's, forty-one. The section from Abraham to David is the only place the two lists show any extended agreement. The two lines diverge at David— Matthew's passes through Solomon while Luke's passes through his brother Nathan. They come together briefly at Shealtiel and Zerubbabel, and then diverge again. With the exception of these two names, and Joseph and Jesus, the two lists contain different names, about whom nothing is known since they are not mentioned in either the Old Testament or the interbiblical literature. Despite the discrepancies, most scholars believe the gospelers were working from known genealogical records and traditions.

The early Church accepted both lists as the lineage of Joseph. The first person known to have looked into the question of the divergent genealogies was Julius Africanus (c. A.D. 220). His explanation for the seemingly irreconcilable differences depends upon the law of levirate marriage, which held that if a married man died childless, his brother was required to marry his widow and raise up seed in his name. The firstborn son of that union would be considered the child of the deceased brother rather than of the biological father.

Africanus suggested that Joseph's grandfathers, Matthan (from Matthew's genealogy) and Melchi (from Luke's), married successively the same woman, Estha—first Matthan and, when he died, Melchi. Their sons, Jacob and Heli, were half-brothers of the same mother but different fathers. Heli married but died childless. According to the law of the levirate marriage, Jacob married his brother's wife and begot Joseph. As a result, Matthew could say "Jacob begat Joseph" and Luke, "Joseph, the son of Heli."

Since both Gospel writers are trying to establish by their genealogies a claim to legitimate Davidic ancestry, some have argued that Matthew's table contains the *legal successors* to the throne of David while Luke's contains the *paternal ancestors* of Joseph.

Another solution is that Matthew gives Joseph's genealogy while Luke gives Mary's. (There is also minor support for the reverse.) This solution, usually credited to Annius Viterbo (c. 1490), became more popular after the Reformation, but its roots are traceable to the fifth century and possibly even to the second-century writings of Justin Martyr. Since lineal descent passed through the man, it has been argued that no genealogy of a woman was ever given and that descent through women was considered to be of no account to the Jews. An examination of the scriptures shows that was not always the case. There is a lengthy genealogy of Judith (8:1) and genealogies of heiresses in both Numbers and Chronicles. That Luke wrote the genealogy of Mary finds acceptance with the Eastern Orthodox church, the Coptic church, and some Western scholars, such as the editors of *The Scofield Reference Bible.*

Both genealogies are intimately related to the concept of the virginal conception—i.e., the doctrine that Jesus was conceived by the Holy Ghost without the agency of his father, Joseph, and hence was born of a virgin—usually referred to as the virgin birth.

It is not the purpose of the genealogies to defend the virginal conception of Jesus; that is its presupposition—at least in the case of Matthew. Immediately after the genealogy Matthew includes a short passage which explains how Jesus was conceived (Matt. 1:18–25).

"Now the birth of Jesus Christ was on this wise: When as his mother Mary was espoused to Joseph, before they came together, she was found with child of the Holy Ghost" (Matt. 1:18),* which occurred in fulfillment of that "which was spoken of the Lord by the prophet, saying, Behold, a virgin shall be with child, and shall bring forth a son, and they shall call his name Emmanuel, which being interpreted is, God with us" (Matt. 1:22, 23).

One purpose of this passage is to show that Jesus was incorporated by divine command into the house of David, which occurred when Joseph named his son—an exercise that would have been unnecessary if Joseph had been Jesus' natural father. Joseph's act of naming the child, which is the prerogative of the father, is also an act of adoption and thus inclusion into the Davidic line.

It is likely that the author of this part of Matthew had a "Messianic proof text"—that is, a list of passages lifted from the Old Testament to demonstrate that Jesus was the Messiah, used as a preaching aid by early

---

*All Bible references are King James Version (KJV) unless otherwise noted. RSV: Revised Standard Version; JB: Jerusalem Bible.

Christians—and took from it a mistranslated version of Isaiah 7:14 and incorporated it into the infancy narrative (Matt. 1:22, 23). The passage in Isaiah reads in the King James Version: "Therefore the Lord himself shall give you a sign; Behold, a virgin shall conceive, and bear a son, and shall call his name Immanuel." Any discussion of the virginal conception, particularly with reference to Matthew, must take into consideration Isaiah 7:10–17, particularly verse 14.

Examination of Isaiah 7:14 (and whether it prophesied the birth of the Messiah) and of the use and meaning of the word "virgin"—especially as it forecast the virginal conception as a Messianic sign—has given rise to some of the most famous debates in theological history.

Some versions of the Old Testament use the words "a young woman" (RSV) or "maiden" (JB) rather than "virgin." The text of the Isaiah scroll found at Qumran library has made it clear that the original Hebrew word used to describe the woman was *almâ,* which means "young woman." Since the verse in the original says "*the* young woman," it is likely the young girl was someone known to Isaiah and King Ahaz. The *almâ* is certainly a young girl who has reached puberty and is thus marriageable if not already married and, given the context, may be referring to the wife of the king or the wife of Isaiah. But it is not clear whether she is a virgin and, if not, if she was already pregnant.

When the Hebrew Masoretic text of the Old Testament was translated into Greek in the Septuagint, the word *almâ* was translated (for reasons that are not clear) into the word *parthenos,* which means "virgin," rather than *neanis,* literally "a young woman." Some scholars believe this was done in the last century before the birth of Jesus. But there is no existing Greek manuscript that was taken from the Hebrew prior to Christian times to show that. Consequently, it is impossible to determine who changed the word, and thus the interpretation of Isaiah 7:14, and whether it was done by Jews *prior* to the birth of Jesus or by Christians *after* the time of Jesus tampering with the Septuagint text in order to bring the translation into line with the virgin doctrine. (Later editors of the Septuagint deleted *parthenos* and reverted to *neanis* to bring the Greek text into conformity with the Hebrew original.) In any event, the Greek translation *parthenos* (virgin) still would have meant that a woman who is now a virgin will, by natural means, once she has united with her husband, conceive the child Immanuel.

While scholars do not agree on the identity of the child, *at most* it may refer to a Davidic prince who would deliver Judah from her enemies. What is really at issue in Isaiah 7:14 is not the manner of conception, nor the prophecy of the Messiah—messianism had not yet developed to the point of expecting a single future king—but rather the timing of the birth of the providential child vis-à-vis events in the Fertile Crescent.

Thus, in the final analysis, neither the Hebrew nor Greek of Isaiah 7:14 refers to the virginal conception about which Matthew writes; nor was there anything in the Jewish understanding of the verse which would give rise either to the idea of conception through the Holy Spirit or to the Christian belief in the virginal conception of Jesus. In the opinion of Jesuit scholar Raymond Brown, an expert on the infancy narratives, at most, reflection on Isaiah 7:14 colored the expression of an already existing Christian belief in the virginal conception of Jesus (Brown, *The Birth of the Messiah*, pp. 143–53).

Further analysis of the infancy narratives (Matt. 1–2; Luke 1–2) and of Luke's genealogy (the latter thought to have been inserted into the third chapter of the Gospel when the first two chapters were composed) in relation to the rest of the New Testament casts doubt on the historicity of the virginal conception. The Messiah was anticipated as the fulfillment of Jewish history. Nevertheless, there was no expectation of a virgin birth in Israel, nor was there any indication in the New Testament literature (outside of the infancy narratives) that anyone was aware that Jesus was born without the agency of a human father. The Gospels were preached for years without any mention of the virginal conception, and it is never touched upon in the writings of Paul.

The baptism of Jesus is the starting point of the earliest preaching of the Church as seen in the Pauline Epistles and Acts. Mark begins there and so does John, following a brief introductory passage on the preexistence of the Word. Matthew and Luke deal with Jesus' birth in the infancy narratives, but do not mention his birth again in their Gospels. If the infancy narratives (which were probably composed after the narratives of Jesus' ministry) are taken as a foreword to the Gospels of Matthew and Luke, then these Gospels are seen to also begin with the baptism of Jesus.

Apart from their introductory placement, the events of the infancy narratives seem disconnected from Matthew and Luke and none of the characters in their writings appears to have any knowledge of the miraculous circumstances of Jesus' birth; even his sisters, brothers and mother appear unaware of Jesus' virginal conception. Furthermore, Mark 3:21-31, especially Mark 3:20, 21, suggests that they saw him more like themselves: "He went home again, and once more such a crowd collected that they could not even have a meal. When his relatives heard of this, they set out to take charge of him, convinced he was out of his mind" (JB). If they were aware of his miraculous conception, it seems unlikely they would have thought his behavior out of character with his mission.

There are no statements in the New Testament indicating that Joseph was a foster father or a legal guardian. When giving the Matthew genealogy, the old Sinaitic Syriac version of the New Testament (an important Greek manuscript based on early source material from the late second or early third century) says, ". . . Jacob begat Joseph; Joseph to whom was betrothed Mary the virgin, begat Jesus who is called the

Messiah." In the next section referring to Joseph (Matt.
1:18-25) the Sinaitic Syriac version reads, "She will
bear *you* a son. . . and he took his wife and she bore a
son and he called his name Jesus." Shortly thereafter
the same text reads, "but knew her not until. . .," referring to the Matthew assertion that Joseph and Mary did
not have sexual relations until after she brought forth
her firstborn son.

This has led some scholars to argue that this passage in the Sinaitic Syriac text does indeed speak of a
virginal conception—an assertion which for some theologians is not entirely convincing, especially in light of
Matthew 13:55, 56 (KJV), which discloses Jesus to be
the son of Joseph: "Is not this the carpenter's son? is not
his mother called Mary? and his brethren, James, and
Joses, and Simon, and Judas? And his sisters, are they
not all with us?" *A New Catholic Commentary on Holy
Scripture* notes that regarding "the problem of the historicity of the [infancy] stories in Matt.," which often
have a legendary or 'apocryphal' nature, "it is impossible to be dogmatic" (Reginald C. Fuller, ed. [London:
Thomas Nelson, 1975], p. 907).

If Jesus were conceived by the normal means,
there still remains the question of why Joseph and
Mary would have had sexual relations prior to their
marriage. Assuming the accuracy of the report in Matthew that Mary was with child after she and Joseph
were betrothed but before their marriage, prevailing
customs of the day would not make that such an unusual situation.

Betrothal at the time of Jesus legally effected a
marital relationship as attested to in both the Old Testament and the Talmud. It was sealed when the hus-
band-to-be paid the future bride's father or guardian a
"bride price" as compensation for his loss. Thereafter
she was in his power and considered him her "Baal,"
i.e., lord, master, husband. The betrothal could only be
repudiated by a bill of divorce. If the woman lay with
another man it was considered adultery. If the man

died the woman was considered a widow and subject to the levirate. Thus marriage and betrothal carried similar rights and responsibilities.

"Within a short time after the betrothal covenant was completed the boy had the privilege and obligation of cohabitation with his spouse. In the case of the earliest tradition pertaining to Hebrew marriage customs, there appears to have been only a few days lapse between the betrothal transaction and the cohabitation. The girl remained at the home of her father until the husband was ready to receive her. At that time there was usually a nuptial drinking party to celebrate the bride's transference to the groom's home. Intimate relations by betrothed couples were not prohibited in Jewish Scriptures. The Mishnah and the Talmud indicate that Palestinian Judaism showed considerable tolerance towards prenuptial unions in the era of the New Testament, and children conceived as a result were not stigmatized as illegitimate" (William E. Phipps, *Was Jesus Married?* [New York: Harper & Row, 1970], pp. 39–40).

A review of Hebrew attitudes toward procreation may help to clarify the controversy over the virginal conception. For some time prior to the birth of Jesus, the Hebrews assumed that God was active in the generation of each individual—that Yahweh creates when parents procreate—something that biblical scholar William E. Phipps says might be called a theory of dual paternity: "This double sonship outlook became established in Jewish tradition. One ancient rabbi said that human creation occurs in this manner: 'Neither man without woman nor woman without man, and neither of them without the Divine Spirit.'

"In the first birth account of the Bible, Eve exclaims: 'I have brought a child into being with the help of YHWH.' ["I have gotten a man from the LORD."] This was interpreted by a rabbi: 'There are three partners in the production of a man: the Holy One, blessed be he, the father, and the mother.' In that talmudic assertion 'the rabbinic theory of marital inter-course is summed up.'"

The concept of dual paternity, Phipps points out, was not a uniquely Jewish idea. Confucius wrote: "The female alone cannot procreate; the man alone cannot propagate; and Heaven alone cannot produce a man. The three collaborating, man is born. Hence anyone may be called the son of his mother or the son of Heaven."

Phipps argues that the doctrine of the virginal con-ception, at least in Luke, depends upon two Greek words in Luke 3 and four words in Luke 1 that were probably added by a scribe who misunderstood the Hebrew doctrine of dual paternity. Luke 3:23 contains an obvious scribal insertion: "And Jesus himself began to be about thirty years of age, being (as was supposed) the son of Joseph, which was the son of Heli." Phipps declares that the words "as was supposed" render irrel-evant the aim that the genealogical compiler had in mind, which was to trace Jesus' descent through Joseph.

Luke 1:34 contains a less obvious scribal insertion. "Then said Mary unto the angel, How shall this be, seeing I know not a man?" The statement is incon-gruous when the words "seeing I know not a man" remain in the text. Phipps points out that an intelligent bride would hardly be puzzled by the means by which she would become pregnant. But if "seeing I know not a man" is deleted, then Mary's puzzlement refers to the magnificent destiny for a carpenter's son prophesied by Gabriel in the preceding verses, not the method of fertil-ization. Some scholars suggest that an old Latin version of this passage, without reference to the virginal concep-tion, may be the way Luke wrote it (Ibid., pp. 40–42).

Considering this and other scribal insertions, Dr. John C. Trever, head of the Dead Sea Scrolls Project at Claremont, believes that it is not necessary to assume that the author of the Gospel of Luke ever referred to the virginal conception; it seems that Luke was doc-tored to harmonize with Matthew. Trever concludes:

"We might say with considerable support that the Gospel of Matthew may be the origin of the doctrine of virgin birth."

Phipps notes that there is no way to prove or disprove that the original texts of Matthew and Luke were tampered with, because the earliest existing manuscripts are several centuries later than the lost originals. However, it was in the second and third centuries that the virginal conception became exalted among Gentile Christians as the only fitting way for the Divine Logos to have become enfleshed (Ibid., p. 43). Today it is the position of the Roman Catholic church, the Eastern Orthodox church, and the Coptic church that Jesus was the product of a virginal conception.

It is important to draw a distinction between the virginal conception and the virgin birth, which deals with the way Jesus actually passed out of Mary's womb. Christian traditions of the second century hold that Jesus was born miraculously, without pain to his mother and leaving her physically intact.

As Raymond Brown points out, Matthew is concerned only with showing Mary's virginity before Jesus' birth so that the Isaiahan prophecy will be fulfilled. As time passed, however, the notion of the virginal conception grew, and by the second century traditions of the virgin birth developed, followed by the idea that Joseph and Mary never had normal sexual relations, finally concluding that Joseph, too, was a virgin!

Jesus' brothers and sisters are sometimes held to be children of Joseph by a previous marriage. "In antiquity there were debates whether these were half-brothers of Jesus (sons of Joseph by a previous marriage—*Protevangelium of James;* Epiphanius), or cousins (sons of either Joseph's brother or of Mary's sister—Jerome), or blood brothers (children of Joseph and Mary—Helvidius)" (Brown, *The Birth of the Messiah,* p. 132).

This author does not believe that the conception of Jesus by his father Joseph, as the agent of the Holy

Spirit, in any way detracts from the divinity of his soul or the magnitude of the incarnate Word within him; rather does it enhance the availability of the fullness of God through his chosen and anointed human instruments. Sources: John D. Davis, *A Dictionary of the Bible,* 4th rev. ed. (Grand Rapids, Mich.: Baker Book House, 1954); Matthew Black and H. H. Rowley, eds., *Peake's Commentary on the Bible* (Walton-on-Thames, Surrey: Nelson, 1962); *New Catholic Encyclopedia,* s.v. "Genealogy," and "Luke, Gospel According to St."; Isaac Asimov, *Asimov's Guide to the Bible—Volume Two: The New Testament* (New York: Avon, 1969); D. Guthrie and J. A. Motyer, eds., *The New Bible Commentary Revised,* 3rd ed. (Grand Rapids, Mich.: Wm. B. Eerdmans Publishing Co., 1970); Phipps, *Was Jesus Married?; The Anchor Bible: Matthew* (Garden City, N.Y.: Doubleday & Co., 1971); Fuller, *A New Catholic Commentary on Holy Scripture;* Brown, *The Birth of the Messiah;* and *The Anchor Bible: The Gospel According to Luke (I–IX)* (Garden City, N.Y.: Doubleday & Co., 1981); Telephone interview with Dr. John Trever, 9 November 1984.

3. For other views on the resurrection, see John Dart, *The Laughing Savior* (New York: Harper & Row, 1976), pp. 104–6; Elaine Pagels, *The Gnostic Gospels* (New York: Random House, 1979), pp. 3–27; The Secret Book of John, in Willis Barnstone, ed., *The Other Bible* (New York: Harper & Row, 1984), p. 53 (hereafter cited as TOB); Basilides, in TOB, pp. 628, 634; The Sethian-Ophites, in TOB, p. 664; and "Mani and Manichaeism," in TOB, p. 674.

4. There was a tradition during the sub-apostolic age and the second century of a long interval between the resurrection and the ascension. Evidence of it appears in Pistis Sophia, a Gnostic manuscript of the second century, and the writings of the eminent Church Father Irenaeus, who held that Jesus suffered in his thirtieth year but taught until he was forty or fifty years old.

A number of other Gnostic works besides Pistis Sophia deal with an extended post-resurrection stay on earth. The Apocryphon of James (c. second century) states that after the resurrection Jesus appears to the twelve disciples and they converse with him for 550 days. Later Jesus ascends. (See The Apocryphon of James, in TOB, pp. 343-49.)

The Ascension of Isaiah, an apocryphal Christian apocalypse (composed in stages during the first and second centuries), "predicts" after the fact, as was often the case in pseudepigraphical works, that Jesus "will arise on the third day and will remain in that world 545 days; and then many of the righteous will ascend with him, whose spirits do not receive their garments till the Lord Christ ascends and they ascend with him." Later in this work Isaiah reports, "In Jerusalem indeed I saw how he was crucified on the tree, and how he was raised after three days and remained still many days" (TOB, pp. 527, 530). A Sethian-Ophite legend and Valentinian writings mention that Jesus remained on earth for eighteen months following the resurrection (see The Sethian-Ophites, in TOB, p. 664; "Valentinius and the Valentinian System of Ptolemaeus," TOB, p. 613). The discrepancy in these dates may be an indication of the varying length of time the writers or their sources actually saw Jesus after his resurrection. Or the numbers may be an attempt at their sense of a divine numerology; Francis Legge, *Forerunners and Rivals of Christianity,* 2 vols. (New Hyde Park, N.Y.: University Books, 1964), 2:61.

5. Irenaeus, *Against Heresies* 2.22.5, in Alexander Roberts and James Donaldson, eds., *The Ante-Nicene Fathers,* American reprint of the Edinburgh ed., 9 vols. (Grand Rapids, Mich.: Wm. B. Eerdmans Publishing Co., 1981), vol. 1, *The Apostolic Fathers with Justin Martyr and Irenaeus,* pp. 391-92.

6. G. R. S. Mead, trans., *Pistis Sophia,* rev. ed. (London: John M. Watkins, 1921), p. 1.

7. David B. Barrett, ed., *World Christian Encyclopedia* (Oxford and New York: Oxford University Press, 1982), p. 3.

8. W. D. Davies, *Invitation to the New Testament* (Garden City, N.Y.: Doubleday & Co., 1966), pp. 78-79.

9. The New Testament provides no information about the sojourn of the Holy Family in Egypt outside of Matthew 2:13-15, which says that Joseph "took the young child and his mother by night, and departed into Egypt: And was there until the death of Herod." Apocryphal writings and Coptic Christian tradition, which are largely parallel, point to numerous places where Jesus and his parents went during their stay in Egypt. "Tradition records some sites in Lower and Upper Egypt upon which churches were built to commemorate this visit; some of these are the monasteries of Wadi El Natrun, Mataria and the monastery of Al Moharrak. But the most famous of these sites is Babylon, the Roman fortress of Old Cairo. It embraces within its walls the ancient church of 'Abu Sarga' (St. Sergius), built on a crypt, in which our Lord dwelt during His sojourn in the ancient Jewish quarter in Babylon. Tradition also says that the earlier church of the crypt was built in the Apostolic age. To quote Butcher, 'It was the Jewish quarter of Babylon, and there is no reason to doubt the tradition which brings Joseph and Mary to settle there during the greater part of their stay in Egypt—a period, the length of which is variously estimated by Western and Eastern controversialists. Some reduce it to six months, others extend it from two to four or even six years'" (Hakim Ameen, "Saint Mark in Africa," in *St. Mark and the Coptic Church* [Cairo: Coptic Orthodox Patriarchate, 1968], p. 8).

A brochure distributed by the Egyptian Ministry of Tourism, entitled "The Holy Family in Egypt," contains a fuller list of churches that have been built on the sites where the Holy Family are reported to have visited. The Gospel of the Infancy of Jesus Christ, an apocryphal work from about the second century, contains many of the same elements embodied in the Coptic tradition. See Gospel of the Infancy of Jesus Christ, in *The Lost Books of the Bible* (Cleveland: Collins

World, 1977) and E. L. Butcher, *The Story of the Church of Egypt* 2 vols. (London: Smith, Elder, & Co., 1847).

10. There are at least four separate and independent British traditions that say Jesus traveled to Britain as a youth with Joseph of Arimathea, who may have been his great-uncle. By tradition, Joseph was in the tin trade and he brought Jesus with him to Glastonbury and other nearby towns while on business. At that time, there were forty Druidic universities in Britain whose 60,000 students included British nobility as well as sons of important men from all over Europe. Glastonbury was a prominent center of Druidism. According to Reverend C. C. Dobson, an expert on the Glastonbury traditions, Druid beliefs embodied such concepts as the Trinity and foreshadowed the coming of Christ.

Reverend Dobson does not think it unlikely that Jesus studied Druidism. He writes: "May it not have been that Our Lord, bringing with Him the Mosaic law, and studying it in conjunction with the oral secrets of Druidism, prepared to give forth His message, which occasioned so much wonderment among the Jewish elders?

"In Britain He would be free from the tyranny of Roman oppression, the superstition of Rabbinical misinterpretation, and the grossness of pagan idolatry, and its bestial, immoral customs. In Druid Britain He would live among people dominated by the highest and purest ideals, the very ideals He had come to proclaim."

For the legends on Jesus at Glastonbury, see "Following the Grail" and "Did Jesus Go to High School in Britain?" *Heart: For the Coming Revolution,* Winter 1985, pp. 4–22, 112–15; C. C. Dobson, *Did Our Lord Visit Britain as They Say in Cornwall and Somerset?* (London: Covenant Publishing Co., 1974); Lionel Smithett Lewis, *St. Joseph of Arimathea at Glastonbury* (Cambridge: James Clarke & Co., 1955); George F. Jowett, *The Drama of the Lost Disciples* (London: Covenant Publishing Co., 1980); and E. Raymond Capt, *The Traditions of Glastonbury* (Thousand Oaks, Calif.: Artisan Sales, 1983).

11. Ibid.; Dobson believes that Jesus may have come back to Glastonbury when he was about 28 or 29 years of age, just prior to his Palestinian mission. Since his age is not specified in the Glastonbury traditions, Jesus may also have gone to Britain with Joseph of Arimathea during the lost years; The Arabic Gospel of the Infancy of the Saviour, in *The Ante-Nicene Fathers,* vol. 8, *Fathers of the Third and Fourth Centuries: The Twelve Patriarchs, Excerpts and Epistles, the Clementina, Apocrypha, Decretals, Memoirs of Edessa and Syriac Documents, Remains of the First Ages,* p. 415.

12. James M. Robinson, *A New Quest of the Historical Jesus* (Philadelphia: Fortress Press, 1983), p. 172.

13. Harvey K. McArthur, ed., *In Search of the Historical Jesus* (New York: Charles Scribner's Sons, 1969), p. vii.

14. The first of these references appears in *The Antiquities of the Jews,* written by the Jewish historian Flavius Josephus in A.D. 93 or 94. Josephus records the death of "the brother of Jesus, who was called Christ, whose name was James" (Josephus, *The Antiquities of the Jews* 20.9.1), at the hands of the high priest Annas—son of the better-known Annas, also a high priest and father-in-law of Caiaphas, whose deeds are recorded in John 18:13–24.

Another reference to Jesus in *The Antiquities of the Jews* (18.3.3) is thought to be an embellishment of later Christian writers in that it amounts to a confession of faith—an unlikely occurrence from the pen of a Jew anxious to please either the Romans or Jews, who were both in conflict with Christianity at the time. But even though the passage has almost certainly been altered, it bears witness to Jesus' historicity.

Tacitus, the aristocratic Roman historian, describes Nero's persecution of Christians following the great fire of Rome (A.D. 64) in his *Annals* published about A.D. 116. A rumor was circulating that Nero had ordered the fire started. "Hence, to suppress the rumor, he falsely charged with the guilt, and punished with the most exquisite tortures, the persons commonly called Christians, who were hated for their enormities. Christus, the founder of that name, was put to death as a criminal by Pontius Pilate, procurator of Judea, in the reign of Tiberius. . ." (Tacitus, *Annals* 15.44).

In A.D. 111, Pliny the Younger, a Roman states-man, sent a now-famous letter to the Emperor Trajan asking how he should deal with Christians who sing "hymns to Christ, as to a god" (Pliny the Younger, *Letters* 10.97). Suetonius, another Roman historian, recorded Claudius' expulsion of the Jews from Rome after disturbances instigated by "Chrestus"—thought to be an obvious corruption of Christus (Suetonius, *Vita Claudii* 25.4).

15. Telephone interview with James A. Sanders, Professor of Intertestamental and Biblical Studies, School of Theology at Claremont, California, 7 September 1984.

16. Ibid.; James M. Robinson, ed., *The Nag Hammadi Library in English* (New York: Harper & Row, 1977), pp. ix, 1–25; Morton Smith, *The Secret Gospel* (New York: Harper & Row, 1973); Elaine Pagels, *The Gnostic Gospels* (New York: Random House, 1979), pp. xiii–xxxvi. Some of the Gnostic gospels may be based on traditions that predate the Gospels. The Gospel of Thomas, for example, contains sayings of Jesus used in the Gospels but in an older form. The fragment of the Secret Gospel of Mark is included in a letter attributed to Clement of Alexandria. The letter states that after the martyrdom of Peter, Mark went to Alexandria where "he composed a more spiritual Gospel for the use of those who were being perfected" (Smith, *The Secret Gospel,* pp. 14–15). While Professor Smith's discovery is highly controversial and originally met with a good deal of skepticism, Birger A. Pearson, Professor of Religious Studies at the University of California at Santa Barbara, notes that "many scholars, maybe even most, would now accept the authenticity of the Clement fragment, including what it said about the Secret Gospel of Mark" (Telephone interview, 4 September 1984).

17. Davies, *Invitation to the New Testament,* pp. 78–79.

18. Telephone interview with James M. Robinson, Professor of Religion and Director of the Institute for

Antiquity and Christianity at the Claremont Graduate School, Claremont, California, spring 1983.

19. Brown, *The Birth of the Messiah,* p. 538, n. 15.
20. Gospel of the Infancy of Jesus Christ 18:14, 16–17, in *The Lost Books of the Bible,* p. 55; see Edgar Hennecke, *New Testament Apocrypha,* 2 vols., ed. Wilhelm Schnee-melcher (Philadelphia: Westminster Press, 1963).
21. Matt. 1, 2; Luke 1, 2.
22. Luke 2:46–49.
23. Luke 2:51.
24. Luke 2:52.
25. Kenneth Scott Latourette, *A History of Christianity— Volume I: to* A.D. *1500* (New York: Harper & Row, 1975), p. 34.
26. Personal interview with Dr. John C. Trever, spring 1983.
27. Philip P. Wiener, ed., *Dictionary of the History of Ideas* (New York: Charles Scribner's Sons, 1973), 2:470.
28. Robinson, telephone interview.
29. *Catalogue Général de la Librairie Française (Période de 1906 à 1909),* s.v. "Notowitch (Nicolas)."
30. Edgar J. Goodspeed, *Strange New Gospels* (Chicago: University of Chicago Press, 1931), p. 10.
31. *Encyclopaedia Judaica,* s.v. "Notovich, Osip Konstanti-novich"; *Catalogue Général de la Librairie Française (Période de 1891 à 1899),* s.v. "Notowitch (O.K.)."
32. L. Austine Waddell, *The Buddhism of Tibet* (Cambridge: W. Heffer & Sons, 1967), pp. 255–56.
33. Nicholas Notovitch, *The Unknown Life of Jesus Christ,* trans. Virchand R. Gandhi (Chicago: Progressive Thinker Publishing House, 1907), p. xv; Waddell, *The Buddhism of Tibet,* p. 257.
34. Waddell, *The Buddhism of Tibet,* p. 282.
35. David L. Snellgrove and Tadeusz Skorupski, *The Cultural Heritage of Ladakh* (Boulder, Colo.: Prajña Press, 1977), p. 127.
36. Nicolas Notovitch, "Résumé," in *The Unknown Life of Jesus Christ,* trans. Violet Crispe (London: Hutchinson and Co., 1895), pp. 206, 208.

37. Goodspeed, *Strange New Gospels*, p. 11n; *The National Union Catalog*, s.v. "Notovich, Nikolai."
38. "New Publications: The Life of Christ from Tibet," *New York Times*, 19 May 1894, p. 3.
39. "Literary Notes," *New York Times*, 4 June 1894, p. 3.
40. Edward Everett Hale, "The Unknown Life of Christ," *North American Review* 158 (1894):594–601.
41. F. Max Müller, "The Alleged Sojourn of Christ in India," *Nineteenth Century*, October 1894, pp. 515–21.
42. Notovitch's rebuttal quoted and summarized on pages 24–28 is taken from his preface and note "To the Publishers" originally published in *The Unknown Life of Jesus Christ* and reprinted in this volume, pp. 89–107.
43. Müller, "Alleged Sojourn of Christ in India," p. 521.
44. Leslie Brown, *The Indian Christians of St. Thomas* (Cambridge: Cambridge University Press, 1982), p. 47.
45. *The Catholic Encyclopedia*, s.v. "Thomas, Saint."
46. Ibid.
47. Acts of the Holy Apostle Thomas, in *The Ante-Nicene Fathers*, vol. 8, *Fathers of the Third and Fourth Centuries*, pp. 535–49.
48. Consummation of Thomas the Apostle, in *The Ante-Nicene Fathers*, vol. 8, *Fathers of the Third and Fourth Centuries*, pp. 550–52.
49. *The Catholic Encyclopedia*, s.v. "Thomas, Saint."
50. "Hamis Knows Not 'Issa,'" *New York Times*, 19 April 1896, p. 28.
51. J. Archibald Douglas, "The Chief Lama of Himis on the Alleged 'Unknown Life of Christ,'" *Nineteenth Century*, April 1896, pp. 667–77.
52. Ibid., pp. 677–78.
53. See Bruce M. Metzger, "Literary Forgeries and Canonical Pseudepigrapha," *Journal of Biblical Literature* 91, no. 1 (March 1972):3–24.
54. Hale, "The Unknown Life of Christ," p. 594.
55. Müller, "Alleged Sojourn of Christ in India," p. 516.
56. Snellgrove and Skorupski, *The Cultural Heritage of Ladakh*, p. 127.

57. For biographical information on Swami Abhedananda, see Sister Shivani, *An Apostle of Monism* (Calcutta: Ramakrishna Vedanta Math, 1947); Ashutosh Ghosh, *Swami Abhedananda: The Patriot-Saint* (Calcutta: Ramakrishna Vedanta Math, 1967); Moni Bagchi, *Swami Abhedananda: A Spiritual Biography* (Calcutta: Ramakrishna Vedanta Math, 1968); and Swami Gambhirananda, comp. and ed., *The Apostles of Shri Ramakrishna* (Calcutta: Advaita Ashrama, 1982).

58. Swami Abhedananda's travel diary, *In Kashmir and Tibet*, states that Abhedananda read Notovitch's *Unknown Life of Jesus Christ* while in America, but it does not indicate whether or not he had ever read it previously (see p. 230 of this volume).

59. Shivani, *An Apostle of Monism*, p. 199.

60. Ibid.

61. Ibid., p. 198; Bagchi, *Swami Abhedananda*, p. 409.

62. Gambhirananda, *The Apostles of Shri Ramakrishna*, p. 261.

63. Bagchi, *Swami Abhedananda*, p. 408.

64. Shivani, *An Apostle of Monism*, p. 198. Himis actually lies 25 miles south of Leh, Ladakh.

65. Abhedananda, *Kashmir O Tibbate*, p. 230 of this volume.

66. Bagchi, *Swami Abhedananda*, pp. 400–401.

67. Abhedananda, *Kashmir O Tibbate*, p. 230 of this volume.

68. Bagchi, *Swami Abhedananda*, p. 401.

69. Ibid., p. 409; Shivani, *An Apostle of Monism*, p. 198.

70. Ghosh, *Swami Abhedananda*, p. 41.

71. Abhedananda, *Kashmir O Tibbate*, p. 236n of this volume.

72. J. Samuel Walker, *Henry A. Wallace and American Foreign Policy*, Contributions in American History, no. 50 (Westport, Conn. and London: Greenwood Press, 1976), p. 53.

73. Garabed Paelian, *Nicholas Roerich* (Agoura, Calif.: Aquarian Educational Group, 1974), pp. 38–39.

74. George N. Roerich, *Trails to Inmost Asia* (New Haven, Conn.: Yale University Press, 1931), pp. ix, x.

75. Ibid., p. xii.
76. Nicholas Roerich, *Altai-Himalaya* (New York: Frederick A. Stokes Co., 1929), p. 122.
77. Paelian, *Nicholas Roerich,* p. 40.
78. Ibid., pp. 40–41.
79. Ibid. For another myth about underground dwellers, see Edward Bulwer Lytton, *Vril: The Power of the Coming Race* (Blauvelt, N.Y.: Rudolf Steiner Publications, 1972).
80. "Book Reviews," *American Magazine of Art* 20, no. 12 (December 1929):719.
81. Roerich, *Altai-Himalaya,* p. xiii.
82. Nicholas Roerich, *Heart of Asia* (New York: Roerich Museum Press, 1929), p. 22.
83. Roerich, *Altai-Himalaya,* p. 125.
84. Roerich, *Heart of Asia,* p. 30.
85. Frances R. Grant et al., *Himalaya* (New York: Brentano's, 1926), p. 148.
86. Ibid.
87. Roerich, *Altai-Himalaya,* pp. 118–19.
88. Grant et al., *Himalaya,* p. 172.
89. Roerich, *Altai-Himalaya,* p. 89.
90. Ibid., p. 120.
91. Grant et al., *Himalaya,* p. 153.
92. "Roerich's Far Quest for Beauty," *Literary Digest* 98, no. 9 (1 September 1928):24.
93. Penelope Chetwode, *Kulu* (London: John Murray, 1972), p. 154.
94. Goodspeed, *Strange New Gospels,* pp. 10–24.
95. Janet Bock, *The Jesus Mystery* (Los Angeles: Aura Books, 1980), p. 22.
96. For eyewitness accounts of the Chinese Communist takeover of Tibet, see *Tibet under Chinese Communist Rule* (Dharamsala: Information & Publicity Office of His Holiness the Dalai Lama, 1976).
97. William O. Douglas, *Beyond the High Himalayas* (Garden City, N.Y.: Doubleday & Co., 1952), p. 152.
98. Personal interview with Dr. Robert S. Ravicz, spring 1983.
99. Personal interview with Edward F. Noack, fall 1984.

Chapter *Four* LEGENDS OF THE EAST

1. For biographical information on Nicholas Roerich, see Christian Brinton, *The Nicolas Roerich Exhibition* (New York: Redfield-Kendrick-Odell Co., 1920); Frances R. Grant et al., *Himalaya* (New York: Brentano's, 1926); Nicholas Roerich, *Altai-Himalaya* (New York: Frederick A. Stokes Company, 1929); Nicholas Roerich, *Heart of Asia* (New York: Roerich Museum Press, 1929); George N. Roerich, *Trails to Inmost Asia* (New Haven, Conn.: Yale University Press, 1931); *Nicholas Roerich* (New York: Nicholas Roerich Museum, 1964); Penelope Chetwode, *Kulu* (London: John Murray, 1972); *Nicholas Roerich* (New York: Nicholas Roerich Museum, 1974); Garabed Paelian, *Nicholas Roerich* (Agoura, Calif.: Aquarian Educational Group, 1974).

2. Helena Roerich, *Foundations of Buddhism* (New York: Agni Yoga Society, 1971), Preface.

3. J. Samuel Walker, *Henry A. Wallace and American Foreign Policy*, Contributions in American History, no. 50 (Westport, Conn. and London: Greenwood Press, 1976), p. 62, n. 25.

4. Grant et al., *Himalaya*, p. 48.

5. Chetwode, *Kulu*, p. 151.

6. "Nicholas K. Roerich," *American Magazine of Art* 12, no. 6 (June 1921):200.

7. *Nicholas Roerich* (New York: Nicholas Roerich Museum, 1974), pp. 7, 8.

8. Roerich, *Altai-Himalaya*, p. xv.

9. Walker, *Henry A. Wallace*, p. 54.

10. Leonid Andreyev, "The Realm of Roerich," *New Republic* 29, no. 368 (21 December 1921):97.

11. Grant et al., *Himalaya*, pp. 66, 68.

12. Nikolai Rerikh, *Zazhigaite serdtsa.* [Set hearts aflame] comp. I. M. Bogdanova-Rerikh (Moscow: Izdatel'stvo "Molodaia gvardia," 1978), p. 22.

13. Paelian, *Nicholas Roerich*, p. 36; Robert C. Williams, *Russian Art and American Money* (Cambridge, Mass. and London: Harvard University Press, 1980), p. 117.

14. Williams, *Russian Art and American Money*, p. 119.

15. See *The Roerich Pact and The Banner of Peace* (New York: The Roerich Pact and Banner of Peace Committee, 1947).
16. Walker, *Henry A. Wallace,* pp. 53–57.
17. Paelian, *Nicholas Roerich,* pp. 39–40.
18. Ibid., p. 28.
19. Ibid., p. 29.
20. Nicholas Roerich, *Shambhala* (New York: Nicholas Roerich Museum, 1978), pp. 304, 307.
21. Roerich, *Heart of Asia,* pp. 7–8.
22. Roerich, *Altai-Himalaya,* pp. vii–viii.
23. Ibid., pp. vi, vii.
24. Roerich, *Trails to Inmost Asia,* p. xii.
25. Ibid., p. 5.
26. Roerich, *Altai-Himalaya,* p. 100.
27. Roerich, *Heart of Asia,* pp. 23, 24, 26–28.
28. Roerich, *Trails to Inmost Asia,* p. 20.
29. Grant et al., *Himalaya,* pp. 170–72.
30. Roerich, *Altai-Himalaya,* p. 114.
31. Roerich, *Heart of Asia,* pp. 30, 28–29.
32. Ibid., pp. 29–30.
33. Roerich, *Altai-Himalaya,* pp. 118–19, 120.
34. Ibid., pp. 120–21, 122–23, 124.
35. Ibid., pp. 125–26.
36. Ibid., pp. 131, 134.
37. Grant et al., *Himalaya,* p. 148.
38. Roerich, *Altai-Himalaya,* pp. 89–90.
39. Ibid., p. 90; Grant et al., *Himalaya,* p. 148.
40. Grant et al., *Himalaya,* pp. 148–53.
41. Roerich, *Altai-Himalaya,* p. 93.
42. Grant et al., *Himalaya,* pp. 153–56.
43. Roerich, *Altai-Himalaya,* pp. 94–96, 97–98.

Chapter Seven EPILOGUE

1. The Notovitch version of the Issa manuscript contains passages (*The Life of Saint Issa* V:12–21, 26, pp. 198–200 of this volume) which indicate that Jesus rejected the Vedas and the Hindu 'idols'. Inasmuch as Jesus'

closest disciple, John, begins his Gospel with a quote from the Vedas, the authenticity of these passages may be questioned. As Sir John Woodroofe notes: "The fourth Gospel opens grandly, 'In the beginning was the Word, and the Word was with God, and the Word was God.' These are the very words of Veda. *Prajapatir vai idam asit:* In the beginning was Brahman. *Tasya vag dvitiya asit;* with whom was Vak or the Word... *Vag vai paramam Brahma;* and the word is Brahman" (*The Garland of Letters,* 7th ed. [Pondicherry: Ganesh & Co., 1979], p. 4).

Notovitch embraced the Russian Orthodox religion. In the conclusion to his book (not published in this volume) he says of Jesus, "In his sermons not only did he deprecate the deprival of a man's rights to be considered as such, while apes or pieces of marble or metal were worshipped, but he attacked the very principle of Brahmanism, its system of gods, its doctrine, and its *Trimurti* (Trinity), the stumbling block of this religion." In a similar vein he declares, "Jesus denied the existence of all these absurd hierarchical gods, who obscure the great principle of monotheism" (Nicolas Notovitch, "Résumé," in *The Unknown Life of Jesus Christ,* trans. Violet Crispe [London: Hutchinson and Co., 1895], pp. 227, 230).

Both observations are incongruous with a passage of *The Life of Saint Issa* (V:4, 5) in which Jesus diligently studies and then teaches the Vedas. Therefore, the reader ought to consider the possibility that the verses which denounce the Vedas may have been inserted by Notovitch himself—taking into account the fact that according to his own testimony he collected the verses that make up *The Life of Saint Issa* from more than one volume and then arranged them in chronological order (see pp. 94–95 of this work)—so that Christians might not be tempted to seek sources of spiritual comfort and enlightenment outside their own doctrine and scripture.

We have no proof whatsoever for this conjecture, only the appreciation of Jesus' vast mind and his ability to comprehend *Trimurti* (Brahma, Vishnu, and Shiva) and the many manifestations of the one God as consistent with and originating in the Law of the One— "Hear, O Israel: The LORD our God is one LORD" (Deut. 6:4)—and with his teaching of the Trinity, his identification of the Father and the Holy Spirit as Persons, and himself exemplifying the Son as a Person— thereby completing our own comprehension of the Great Three-in-One. (Note that the Abhedananda version of the Himis manuscript does not include the denunciation of the Vedas.)

2. Charles Francis Potter, *The Lost Years of Jesus Revealed,* rev. ed. (Greenwich, Conn.: A Fawcett Gold Medal Book, 1962), p. 10. There is some disagreement about the accuracy of Potter's use of the word *zeugos*— especially since scholars do not know of a current Greek word for yoga, much less one in use two millennia ago. Since both yoga and yoke are derived from the same Proto-Indo-European root word *yeug* (which connects the Sanskrit *yuga*/yoke with the Greek *zugon*/ yoke, and the Sanskrit *yoga*/union with the Greek *zeugma*/bond), his use of the word seems reasonable.

Since most people in Palestine spoke Greek as well as Aramaic, biblical scholars now generally agree that Jesus spoke Greek. There are no records available to tell us in what language Jesus originally spoke this phrase. But if he spoke it in Greek, it would be most illumining to find out what word he actually used.

The meaning of *yoga* (Sanskrit, literally "yoking," "union," "disciplined activity") implies the necessity of a path of chelaship—i.e., a path of *youg* (i.e., union with God)—in order to fulfill the responsibility of discipleship and Christhood. As it is used here, yoga means "my way," "my path," or "my dharma." Thus, in this context, yoke/yoga means the mantle and authority of the Teacher and his "teaching." "Burden" entertains the principle of "karma"—"For every man shall bear his own burden" (Gal. 6:5). The dharma of the Lord is his teaching. The karmic burden of the Lord is the world karma or sin he bore for our sakes; for he himself is a karma-free being. Thus, Jesus was beckoning his disciples, or would-be disciples, to "follow my path," i.e., "my disciplined activity." When he declares, "My yoga is easy," he is saying: My path is the best or simplest, most direct way. Out of all paths of the avatars, I have synthesized for you the one true way that will lead to your union with God. (See "the burden of the LORD" [Jer. 23:33–40].)

3. Matt. 14:22–33; Mark 6:45–51; John 6:15–21; Luke 4:28–30; John 8:59; Matt. 28:9, 10, 16–18; Mark 16:9–14, 19; Luke 24:13–53; John 20:11–29; 21:1–14; Acts 1:3, 9–11; The Acts of Barnabas, in Alexander Roberts and James Donaldson, eds., *The Ante-Nicene Fathers,* American reprint of the Edinburgh ed., 9 vols. (Grand Rapids, Mich.: Wm. B. Eerdmans Publishing Co., 1981), vol. 8, *Fathers of the Third and Fourth Centuries: The Twelve Patriarchs, Excerpts and Epistles, the Clementina, Apocrypha, Decretals, Memoirs of Edessa and Syriac Documents, Remains of the First Ages,* p. 493 (hereafter cited as ANF); The Acts of Philip, in ANF, pp. 499, 501, 505–6, 509; Acts of Andrew and Matthias, in ANF, pp. 517–25; Acts of Peter and Andrew, in ANF, pp. 526, 527; Acts and Martyrdom of St. Matthew the Apostle, in ANF, pp. 528–29; Acts of the Holy Apostle Thomas, in ANF, pp. 535, 537, 542; The Secret Book of John, in Willis Barnstone, ed., *The Other Bible* (San Francisco: Harper & Row, 1984), pp. 53, 61 (hereafter cited as TOB); The Gospel of the Hebrews, in TOB, p. 335; The Apocryphon of James, in TOB, pp. 345, 349; The Gospel of Bartholomew, in TOB, pp. 351–55, 357–58; The Acts of John, in TOB, pp. 418–19, 420; The Acts of Peter, in TOB, p. 433; G. R. S. Mead, trans., *Pistis Sophia,* rev. ed. (London: John M. Watkins, 1921), pp. 4, 5. See also note 7.

4. John 2:1–11.

5. John 14:26; 15:26; 16:7–16.
6. John 7:14–16.
7. Acts 9:1–20; 22:6–21; 26:12–18; 18:9, 10; 10:9–16; 23:11; II Tim. 4:17; Acts of the Holy Apostles Peter and Paul, in ANF, pp. 484–85.
8. Matt. 24:28.

CREDITS

1. Heb. 5:12–14.
2. Matt. 10:26; Mark 4:22; Luke 12:2; I Cor. 2:7–10.
3. II Cor. 6:2.
4. Phil. 2:5–8.
5. Matt. 20:25–28; 23:11; Mark 9:35; Luke 22:26, 27.
6. II Tim. 2:15.
7. John 1:14; 17:24.
8. John 10:16.
9. Luke 2:46, 47.
10. *The Life of Saint Issa* V:6–27; VI:15, 16; VII:1–12; VIII:1–22.
11. Matt. 21:12.
12. The long-lost continent of Lemuria which sank beneath the Pacific more than 12,000 years ago in a cataclysm of fire. The Motherland is said to be the origin of the doctrines and scriptures of ancient Hinduism. See James Churchward's books: *The Children of Mu, The Cosmic Forces of Mu, The Lost Continent of Mu, The Sacred Symbols of Mu,* and *The Second Book of the Cosmic Forces of Mu,* all published in New York by Paperback Library, 1968.
13. John 14:16–20, 25, 26.
14. John 14:12.
15. Jer. 31:33; Heb. 8:10.
16. I Cor. 13:12; I John 3:2.
17. II Tim. 3:7.
18. John 15:15.
19. Rom. 8:17; Gal. 4:7.
20. John 1:1–3; I John 1:1; 2:13; John 8:58.
21. Mal. 4:2.

22. II Pet. 1:19.
23. Exod. 3:14.
24. Mark 14:36.
25. Dan. 12:1.
26. I John 4:4.
27. John 18:38.
28. Isa. 61:2; 63:4.
29. Matt. 10:6; 15:24; 18:11; Luke 19:10.
30. Matt. 9:37, 38; Luke 10:2; John 4:35.
31. Heb. 4:12; Eph. 6:17; Rev. 1:16.
32. Rev. 19:11–21.
33. Matt. 5:13; Isa. 13:12.

Bibliography

Abercrombie, Thomas J. "Ladakh—The Last Shangri-la." *National Geographic* 153 (1978):332–59.

Ahluwalia, H. P. S. *Hermit Kingdom: Ladakh.* New Delhi: Vikas Publishing House, 1980.

Andreyev, Leonid. "The Realm of Roerich." *New Republic,* 21 December 1921, pp. 97–99.

Bagchi, Moni. *Swami Abhedananda: A Spiritual Biography.* Calcutta: Ramakrishna Vedanta Math, 1968.

Barnstone, Willis. *The Other Bible.* New York: Harper & Row, 1984.

Bhavnani, Enakshi. "A Journey to 'Little Tibet.'" *National Geographic* 99 (1951):603–34.

Bock, Janet. *The Jesus Mystery: Of Lost Years and Unknown Travels.* Los Angeles: Aura Books, 1980.

Brinton, Christian. *The Nicholas Roerich Exhibition: With Introduction and Catalogue of the Paintings by Christian Brinton.* New York: Redfield-Kendrick-Odell Co., 1920.

Brown, Leslie. *The Indian Christians of St. Thomas: An Account of the Ancient Syrian Church of Malabar.* Cambridge: Cambridge University Press, 1982.

Brown, Raymond E. *The Birth of the Messiah: A Commentary on the Infancy Narratives in Matthew and Luke.* Garden City, N.Y.: Doubleday & Co., 1977.

Chetwode, Penelope. *Kulu: The End of the Habitable World.* London: John Murray, 1972.

Douglas, J. Archibald. "The Chief Lama of Himis on the Alleged 'Unknown Life of Christ.'" *Nineteenth Century,* April 1896, pp. 667–78.

Douglas, William O. *Beyond the High Himalayas.* Garden City, N.Y.: Doubleday & Co., 1952.

Gambhirananda, Swami, comp. and ed. *The Apostles of Shri Ramakrishna.* Calcutta: Advaita Ashrama, 1982.

Ghosh, Ashutosh. *Swami Abhedananda: The Patriot-Saint.* Calcutta: Ramakrishna Vedanta Math, 1967.

Goodspeed, Edgar J. *Strange New Gospels.* Chicago: University of Chicago Press, 1931.

Grant, Frances R.; Siegrist, Mary; Grebenstchikoff, George; Narodny, Ivan; and Roerich, Nicholas. *Himalaya: A Monograph.* New York: Brentano's, 1926.

Hale, Edward Everett. "The Unknown Life of Christ." *North American Review* 158 (1894):594–601.

"Hamis Knows Not 'Issa': Clear Proof That Notovitch Is a Romancer." *New York Times,* 19 April 1896, p. 28.

Hassnain, F. M.; Oki, Masato; and Sumi, Tokan D. *Ladakh: The Moonland.* 2d rev. ed. New Delhi: Light & Life Publishers, 1977.

Hennecke, Edgar. *New Testament Apocrypha.* 2 vols. Edited by Wilhelm Schneemelcher. Philadelphia: Westminster Press, 1963.

Lauf, Detlef Ingo. *Tibetan Sacred Art: The Heritage of Tantra.* Berkeley & London: Shambhala, 1976.

"Literary Notes." *New York Times,* 4 June 1894, p. 3.

Müller, F. Max. "The Alleged Sojourn of Christ in India." *Nineteenth Century,* October 1894, pp. 515–21.

"New Publications: The Life of Christ from Tibet." *New York Times,* 19 May 1894, p. 3.

"Nicholas K. Roerich." *American Magazine of Art* 12 (1921):198–200.

Nicholas Roerich. New York: Nicholas Roerich Museum, 1964.

Nicholas Roerich. New York: Nicholas Roerich Museum, 1974.

Paelian, Garabed. *Nicholas Roerich.* Agoura, Calif.: Aquarian Educational Group, 1974.

Pagels, Elaine. *The Gnostic Gospels.* New York: Random House, 1979.

Phipps, William E. *Was Jesus Married? The Distortion of Sexuality in the Christian Tradition.* New York: Harper & Row, 1970.

Robinson, James M. *The Nag Hammadi Library in English.* New York: Harper & Row, 1977.

Roerich, George N. *Trails to Inmost Asia: Five Years of Exploration with the Roerich Central Asian Expedition.* New Haven, Conn.: Yale University Press, 1931.

Roerich, Nicholas. *Altai-Himalaya: A Travel Diary.* New York: Frederick A. Stokes Co., 1929.

————. *Heart of Asia.* New York: Roerich Museum Press, 1929.

————. *Shambhala.* New York: Nicholas Roerich Museum, 1978.

The Roerich Pact and The Banner of Peace. New York: The Roerich Pact and Banner of Peace Committee, 1947.

"Roerich's Far Quest for Beauty." *Literary Digest,* 1 September 1928, pp. 24–25.

Shivani, Sister (Mrs. Mary LePage). *An Apostle of Monism: An Authentic Account of the Activities of Swami Abhedananda in America.* Calcutta: Ramakrishna Vedanta Math, 1947.

Smith, Morton. *The Secret Gospel: The Discovery and Interpretation of the Secret Gospel According to Mark.* New York: Harper & Row, 1973.

————. *Clement of Alexandria and a Secret Gospel of Mark.* Cambridge, Mass.: Harvard University Press, 1973.

Snellgrove, David L., and Skorupski, Tadeusz. *The Cultural Heritage of Ladakh—Volume One: Central Ladakh.* Boulder, Colo.: Prajña Press, 1977.

Tibet under Chinese Communist Rule: A Compilation of Refugee Statements 1958-1975. Dharamsala: Information & Publicity Office of His Holiness the Dalai Lama, 1976.

Waddell, L. Austine. *The Buddhism of Tibet or Lamaism: With Its Mystic Cults, Symbolism and Mythology, and in Its Relation to Indian Buddhism.* Cambridge: W. Heffer & Sons, 1967.

Walker, J. Samuel. *Henry A. Wallace and American Foreign Policy.* Contributions in American History, no. 50. Westport, Conn. and London: Greenwood Press, 1976.

Williams, Robert C. *Russian Art and American Money: 1900-1940.* Cambridge, Mass. and London: Harvard University Press, 1980.

A Place to Retreat. . .
to Study the Path of Christ as It Applies to Today's Challenges.

Near as heartbeat, yet far as distant nebulae, happiness is. Even as Jesus withdrew to the wilderness to pray, men and women sometimes feel compelled to withdraw from the turmoil of the world to commune with God and his saints and to reestablish a spiritual equilibrium.

The teachings of Christ are for all times and generations. They provide soul nourishment to those seeking a higher way in a world growing ever more complex. They can help you to evolve practical solutions to problems as personal as how to find your soul mate, and as global as nuclear war.

The Inner Retreat is a spiritual fortress consecrated for the study of the path of Christ as taught by the Ascended Masters. Located on the 30,000-acre Royal Teton Ranch, running through the Paradise Valley south of Livingston, Montana, to the border of Yellowstone National Park, it is a land set aside for those seeking the joy of living, born of self-fulfillment in Him.

Here, midst the grandeur of nature, you can learn to make greater contact with the sacred fires of the heart and to cultivate spiritual techniques that can truly make the difference between creative living and a deadening rote existence. In meditation beside a rushing mountain stream discover how to harness the most powerful force in the universe to solve personal and planetary problems.

You can find out how to strengthen your aura and master the circumstances of your life by charting the cycles of your psychology on the cosmic clock. Through self-awareness and Nature's pharmacopoeia, practice ancient methods for the self-healing of body, mind, and soul.

The Inner Retreat is a self-sufficient spiritual community-in-the-making, the cradle of a new age, a bold adventure in living for families and solitary climbers of the highest mountain.

You can know the delight of self-mastery. Dare to apply the teachings of Christ to today's challenges—and realize your fiery destiny in Him.

Write for information about the teachings of the Ascended Masters as taught by Mark L. Prophet and Elizabeth Clare Prophet. And subscribe to *Heart: For the Coming Revolution*, the magazine for Higher Consciousness, $10.00/yr. ppd. (4 issues); international, $12.50/yr. ppd., Summit University Press, Dept. 182, Box A, Malibu, California 90265 U.S.A., phone: (805) 583-0004.